The Qur'an

What is the Qur'an? Where did it come from? How have Muslims interacted with the Qur'an in the past, and how do they view it today? How does the Qur'an interact with the scriptures of the other major Abrahamic religions – Judaism and Christianity?

This book is an essential introduction for all students who wish to learn more about Islam and the Qur'an. Abdullah Saeed introduces students to the Qur'an in three aspects: its history, understanding and interpretation, in both the pre-modern and modern periods. He traces the history of the Qur'an to its conception as revelation and scripture by Muslims, its compilation, and its reception through history through to the present day. He explores the major themes of the Qur'an, such as God, creation and the prophets, paying particular attention to the complex subject of interpretation and the influence of Western scholarship.

Designed to be suitable both for Muslims and non-Muslim students, with a full glossary, helpful chapter summaries and suggestions for further reading, *The Qur'an: An Introduction* is a student-friendly guide to one of the most influential and important religious scriptures of the contemporary world.

Abdullah Saeed is Sultan of Oman Professor of Arab & Islamic Studies and Director, National Centre of Excellence for Islamic Studies at the University of Melbourne, Australia. His previous works include *Islamic Thought* (2006) and *Interpreting the Qur'an* (2006) both published by Routledge.

The Qur'an

An Introduction

Abdullah Saeed

Routledge
Taylor & Francis Group

LONDON AND NEW YORK

First published 2008
by Routledge
2 Park Square, Milton Park, Abingdon, Oxon OX14 4RN

Simultaneously published in the USA and Canada
by Routledge
270 Madison Ave., New York, NY 10016

Routledge is an imprint of the Taylor & Francis Group, an informa business

© 2008 Abdullah Saeed

Typeset in Sabon by
Keystroke, High Street, Tettenhall, Wolverhampton
Printed and bound in Great Britain by
TJ International Ltd, Padstow, Cornwall

British Library Cataloguing in Publication Data
A catalogue record for this book is available from the British Library

Library of Congress Cataloging in Publication Data
A catalog record for this book has been requested

ISBN10: 0–415–42124–1 (hbk)
ISBN10: 0–415–42125–X (pbk)
ISBN10: 0–208–93845–3 (ebk)

ISBN13: 978–0–415–42124–9 (hbk)
ISBN13: 978–0–415–42125–6 (pbk)
ISBN13: 978–0–203–93845–4 (ebk)

Dedicated to
my late father Muhammad Saeed

Contents

Acknowledgements

I would like to thank a number of colleagues, friends and others for contributing significantly to the development and writing of this book. In particular I would like to thank Rowan Gould, Brynna Rafferty-Brown, Muhammad Eeqbal Hassim, Andy Fuller, Helen McCue, Donna Williams and Redha Ameur for assisting me in the research for the book as well as the polishing of the draft manuscript. Any errors, omissions and problems in the book are of course mine.

I thank Lesley Riddle of Routledge for her encouragement to write the book, Andrew Rippin for reviewing the manuscript thoroughly and making many suggestions for improvement, Julene Knox for copy-editing and Gemma Dunn for editorial support. I thank my wife, Rasheeda, and my son, Isaam, for their wonderful support, as always, throughout the project.

The extracts from the Qu'ran in this book appear by permission of Oxford University Press, from *The Qu'ran: A New Translation* (2004), edited by Muhammad Abdel Haleem (trans).

*I*ntroduction

The Qur'an provides guidance to over one-fifth of the world's population. As the holy scripture of Islam, it is the primary text from which Islamic ethics, law and practice are derived. Muslims believe it is the direct Word of God. It represents not only doctrines and religious teachings but also a way of life for millions of people.

As the primary foundation text of Islam, the Qur'an is highly complex, and its interpretations are likewise diverse. From the time of the Prophet Muhammad (d.11/632) to the present day, the meanings and interpretations of the Qur'an have been debated by scholars and lay people alike. Different interpretations have developed over time into various streams of theology, philosophy, mysticism, ethics and law. Underlying the development of these understandings is the complex and poetic language of the Qur'an itself. In addition, Muslims have relied on historical knowledge of the time of the revelation of the Qur'an as well as the person of the Prophet Muhammad to understand the context in which the Qur'an was revealed. They have also relied on historical accounts of the Prophet's interpretation of the Qur'an, as well as those of the early Muslims and other scholars through the history of Islam. Thus, in the twenty-first century, we have a rich array of sources from which to draw in attempting to understand the meanings of the Qur'an and the religion of Islam.

Despite this complexity, we live in a world where not only are many basic aspects of Islam poorly understood, but core aspects of its teachings, practices and history are often over-simplified and at times misrepresented, by both Muslims and non-Muslims. In the light of recent world events and the constant reference to Islam and Muslims in global debates, there has perhaps never been a greater need for people of all backgrounds to gain a more balanced and fuller understanding of Islam. In this context, a basic understanding of the Qur'an is all the more necessary.

Many valuable works have already been written about the Qur'an; some of these deal mainly with classical Islamic principles of interpretation and understanding; others are written by Muslim scholars for a Muslim audience, and some are written by Western scholars for a Western audience. This textbook aims to bring together aspects of these perspectives by providing a holistic overview of the Qur'an, its place in history and its role in the life of Muslims today. In writing this book, I relied heavily on my earlier published writings on the topic as readers will notice.

Overview

This book will explore in the first three chapters the historical context in which the Qur'an was revealed, and the ways in which the Qur'an has been understood as both revelation and scripture. This will give the reader some insight into how the Qur'an was perceived during the life of the Prophet, and the various ways in which it has been understood by later Muslim and non-Muslim scholars. The book also explores the important issue of the Qur'an's compilation, and contrasts the traditional Muslim view with more recent scholarship on the subject.

The Qur'an is not a series of clear, logical discussions of discrete topics. For example, its style at times juxtaposes passages of poetic beauty with detailed prescriptions on seemingly mundane matters of family life, and can thus be difficult to follow. For this reason, Chapter 4 discusses a number of the major themes of the Qur'an, particularly the recurring references to God. The next chapter describes some of the ways in which ordinary Muslims, historically and in the modern world, interact with the Qur'an in their day-to-day lives. As Islam's sacred text, both the linguistic content and the written text of the Qur'an are infused in much of the art, languages, customs and daily rituals of Muslim cultures around the world.

Muslim and Western scholarship on the Qur'an have, for much of history, developed separately. Since the time of Muslim Spain, many Christians in particular coming into contact with the new religion of Islam sought to understand it and its holy book, mainly for polemical purposes. With the Enlightenment came greater academic rigour, and the age of the 'Orientalists'. The history provides valuable insights into the origin of many of the modern Western understandings and ideas about Islam. Today, studies of Islam and the Qur'an are increasingly being undertaken collaboratively, by Muslim and non-Muslim scholars around the world. The history of Western scholarship on the Qur'an and contemporary developments in the field are discussed in Chapter 6.

A related topic is the translation of the Qur'an, which is covered in Chapter 7. Over time, Muslims have questioned whether the Qur'an can indeed be translated without losing any of its meaning. Many Muslims argue that a translation of the Qur'an is no longer really the Qur'an. Nevertheless, the Qur'an, or parts of it, has been translated since the earliest period of Islam. Another topic of particular importance to us today is the Qur'an's view of the scriptures of other religions. This topic is discussed in Chapter 8, which looks in particular at the contrast between popular Muslim views of the Qur'an's stance on Jewish and Christian scriptures, and those of several classical Muslim scholars.

The final chapters address the complex subject of interpretation. Beginning with a topic of particular interest to Muslims today, Chapter 9 describes the different types of ethico-legal teachings found in the Qur'an and explores the way in which these ethical and legal texts are understood and put into practice in today's world. Chapters 10 and 11 deal with the field of Qur'anic exegesis or *tafsir* more generally and offer an overview of the development of this discipline, highlighting some of the major trends in this field both from the classical period and in modern times. The differences between approaches that prefer tradition to reason and vice versa are examined, and their implications are discussed. The final chapter looks beyond classical scholarship, and explores the contributions of some contemporary scholars who are developing innovative ways to interpret the Qur'an's message for the modern world.

It is hoped that this text will provide a broad and engaging introduction to the study of the Qur'an. Thus, I have tried to make it as accessible and as relevant as possible. I have included numerous examples to illustrate the issues and points raised. Many examples I have chosen to use are connected to issues related to women. In addition, although much of the book focuses on the Islamic tradition, I have, where possible, added brief examples of new ideas that are beginning to develop in contemporary Muslim scholarship. Many of these ideas combine aspects of traditional Muslim approaches with some more modern theories and ideas.

I have tried to avoid academic and Islamic studies jargon as much as possible. However, where relevant I have used certain Arabic terms (with English translation) that I believe to be necessary for an understanding of the Qur'an. A glossary is also provided for quick reference. In each chapter, I have recommended several texts for readers who wish to enhance their knowledge of topics covered in this book.

Translation and transliteration

I have used M.A.S. Abdel Haleem's translation for all Qur'anic verses quoted in the text.

For transliteration of Arabic terms, I have used a simple system. I have avoided the use of macrons (for example ū, ī or ā) or dots below certain letters. I have also avoided the use of the symbol ' for *'ayn* at the beginning of a word, but I use it where it occurs in the middle (for instance, *shari'a*) or at the end. Similarly, where the *hamza* occurs at the beginning of a word, I have avoided using the symbol ', but where it occurs in the middle or end, I have generally used it (for instance, Qur'an). In words which end with a *ta' marbuta* the *h* indicating this is also omitted.

Dates

Where the text refers to dates, in general, I have provided two dates as follows: 1/622. The first date refers to the year in the Islamic calendar and the second refers to the year in the Common Era (CE). For the modern period and when referring to Western scholars and their scholarship I have given the CE dates only. I have also provided the year of death for the key figures mentioned in the book.

1 The Qur'an in its context

THE REVELATION OF THE QUR'AN HAPPENED WITHIN the broad political, social, intellectual and religious context of Arabia in the seventh century CE, and in particular the context of the Hijaz region, where Mecca and Medina are situated. Understanding the key aspects of this context helps us to make connections between the Qur'anic text and the environment in which the text emerged. This includes the spiritual, social, economic, political and legal climate and the associated norms, customs, institutions and values of the region. Social norms, for instance, included those relating to family structure, social hierarchy, taboos and rites of passage, as well as issues of housing, gender relations, diet and distribution of wealth. The importance of all these aspects is supported by the frequency with which the Qur'an refers to them.

Understanding the context of the Qur'an also requires a detailed knowledge of the events of the Prophet's life, both in Mecca and Medina. Many of the major events in the Prophet's life, such as his Night Journey from Mecca to Jerusalem (which some Muslims consider to be a 'spiritual' journey), migration to Medina (*hijra*) in 622 CE, and the battles and skirmishes between the Muslims and their opponents, are mentioned in the Qur'an, but not in detail. Hence, an understanding of the background of the Prophet's life and the developments taking place at the time are essential for understanding the significance of many verses. In the following, we will refer to this context as a 'socio-historical' one.

By the fourth/tenth century, the socio-historical context of the Qur'an played a less significant role in Islamic scholarship with the establishment of the discipline of Islamic law. Before then, the non-linguistic, historical context of revelation had been emphasized to a degree through the reports of *asbab al-nuzul* (occasions of revelation), which narrated the context surrounding the revelation of particular verses. While these reports purport to explain the immediate contexts of certain verses, we could argue that their ability to provide an understanding of the actual socio-historical context is limited. Many reports are contradictory and others are historically suspect, so they are often difficult to piece together into a coherent illustration of the context of a specific revelation.

Despite the importance of the socio-historical context for understanding the Qur'an, many Muslims today continue to be suspicious of this concept. For some Muslims, any discussion of the socio-historical context of revelation is perceived as a threat to their fundamental beliefs about the divine origins of the Qur'an. However, as far as a significant number of verses of the Qur'an are concerned, it is difficult to understand their meaning properly without having a basic understanding of the context in which they were revealed. Moreover, the more we know about the communities of Hijaz and

Arabia in a cultural and historical sense, the clearer our understanding of the message of the Qur'an will be.

In this chapter we will discuss:

- the social, environmental and political context of Arabia during the time of the Prophet;
- how the message of the Qur'an was received within, and reflects, that context;
- how the Qur'an deals with the cultural practices and norms of seventh-century Arabia;
- the type of language used by the Qur'an to express ethical messages, and the way the interpretation of such messages is influenced by prevailing culture; and
- the early development of various currents of thought that influenced Muslim engagement with the Qur'an.

The world of the Prophet Muhammad

The Qur'an makes many references to the cultural and material world of Hijaz where Mecca and Medina are located, and Arabia in general. For instance, it refers to several important events that occurred there as well as prevailing attitudes and how the people of Arabia responded to the message of the Prophet Muhammad. It mentions several of the community's institutions, norms and values.

Hijaz itself encapsulated the cultures that existed in much of Arabia and surrounding areas. These ranged from Mediterranean cultures, including Jewish and Christian, to southern Arabic, Ethiopian and Egyptian; all these influenced Hijaz and its people to varying degrees. Consequently, the socio-cultural life of Hijaz at the time of the Qur'an was highly diverse. Understanding this will help today's reader of the Qur'an to make connections between the Qur'anic text and the environment that gave rise to the revelation.

Hijaz and Bedouin life

Much of the Hijaz and the surrounding region had a harsh climate, with little rainfall. There were a few agricultural settlements, such as the oasis of Yathrib, later known as Medina, and that of Ta'if, near Mecca. However, many of the region's inhabitants were Bedouin nomads, rather than town dwellers. Both the Bedouin and the town dwellers adhered to ancient tribal codes of conduct that upheld values such as courage, patience in the face of adversity, generosity, hospitality, defending the honour of the clan or tribe, and avenging wrongs. On the negative side, there was no concept of universal care for other human beings. Instead, courage and selflessness were valued only in the service of one's tribe.[1] It was always noble to help your kinsman, whether he was in the right or in the wrong. It was not considered courageous or manly to wait until one was attacked to retaliate, for example; the brave Bedouin would attack others before he himself was attacked.[2]

The tribal raid was a common feature of life in the region. These raids were essential to the economy of the region, as resources were extremely scarce. Most Bedouin lived in extreme conditions, with a small amount of food and income coming from herding sheep and goats. In difficult times, there was often no choice but to raid settlements for livestock or slaves. Care was taken not to kill anyone, because this would lead to a blood feud that would last for generations and be extremely costly to the tribe. Such raids and skirmishes were an accepted part of the harsh environment in the sixth century CE. In the religious sphere, each tribe often had its own deity. Each year, at the end of the cycle of markets around the peninsula, merchants and pilgrims would gather in Mecca to perform the ancient rites of pilgrimage.

Cities of the Prophet: Mecca and Medina

Mecca itself was a relatively small town in the early seventh century CE. As it was situated on rocky land, it was almost entirely dependent on the nearby oasis of Ta'if for its food supply. However, it also had an apparently miraculous source of water, the well of Zamzam, which made settlement possible.

The people of Mecca mostly belonged to several clans which made up the larger tribe of Quraysh. Some clans were rich and powerful and dominated societal affairs, while others were less wealthy and were becoming increasingly marginalized. Mecca also had the Ka'ba, which was believed to have been built by Abraham and his son Ishmael. As it attracted pilgrims every year, Mecca had become a significant trading town, strategically situated on several of the major caravan trade routes by the sixth century. Thus, many Meccans had become involved in the caravan trade.

Meccan affairs were managed by a collective of influential elders and leaders of the rich clans, through an informal consultative process. There was no ruler or formal state; instead, as in the desert, the clans provided safety and security for their members. Custom dictated that when a person from a tribe or a clan was threatened, it was the duty of the entire tribe or clan to defend that person, if necessary by force.[3]

Although Mecca was a settled town, many nomads, mostly herders of camels and sheep, lived around Mecca. The nomads and their herds were often raided by competing nomadic clans, and trade caravans also came under attack. This meant that settled communities had to enter into understandings and agreements with nomadic tribes to protect their caravan trade from raids. As a result of this harsh and uncertain environment, many Meccans held a fatalistic outlook on life.

Settled life had also diluted many of the traditional values of the desert. The Meccans still held courage and self-sufficiency in high regard, but many were becoming increasingly elitist and arrogant. With growing wealth through trade and power, many apparently had lost some of the positive qualities, such as care for the weak and needy.

The oasis of Yathrib, later known as Madinat al-Nabiy ('City of the Prophet') or simply Medina, was different to Mecca in many ways. Yathrib was populated by a number of different tribes that were making a transition from nomadic life to settled agriculture. Each tribe lived in its own part of the oasis in heavily fortified strongholds. The old values of desert life were stronger than they were at Mecca, but this also meant that most of the tribes were intensely hostile to one another.[4] Although the oasis was fertile, land for crop-yielding fields was scarce.

The two largest 'Arab' groups in Medina were the tribes of Aws and Khazraj. By the early seventh century, these two tribes were caught up in a cycle of hostile competition over resources, which had degenerated into open warfare. Medina was also home to a number of Jewish tribes. Although they shared a Jewish religious identity, they too were divided and often fought each other. Many Jewish tribes were also allied with either the Aws or Khazraj tribes or one of their sub-clans, and had become caught up in the conflict.[5]

Religious context of the Hijaz

At the time of the Prophet, there were already several different religious traditions existing in Arabia. Christian and Jewish communities were scattered throughout the region. Mecca itself, however, was largely 'pagan', its people worshipping the many tribal deities housed in and around the Ka'ba. Even in Medina the non-Jewish tribes were largely pagan. However, this tribal religion was not highly developed and most of the pagan Arabs were not greatly spiritual. Belief in an afterlife was not common, and the deities they worshipped were not given great respect. Religion seems to have been used mainly for striking bargains with a deity, that is, making offerings in return for favours. Although many believed in a supreme deity, 'Allah' or 'the God', and a very few, known as *hanifs*, sought to serve Him only, His presence added little to the tribe-oriented life of the pagan Arabs.[6]

Allah

Allah is the Arabic word for the Supreme Being, God; it simply means *'the* God'. It was used during the time of the Prophet Muhammad by pre-Islamic Arabs in Mecca to refer to a high God, above the idols that many Arabs worshipped. In Islam, this name came to be used for the one and only God. Muslims believe this God is the God of Abraham, Moses, Jesus and Muhammad.

Many Christian communities existed in the north of Arabia and in parts of southern Arabia, though Christianity was less significant in the Hijaz. However, Judaism had a strong presence in Medina and Yemen. The Jewish influence in Medina had been strengthened through intermarriage, adoption and conversion. Although the concept of monotheism was slowly becoming better known, it was still viewed by many as foreign to and incompatible with Bedouin tribal society.

By the late sixth century CE, there was substantial interaction between the people of Hijaz and those in other parts of Arabia. This generally occurred through trade, especially with the towns and cities of the Byzantine and Persian empires, and through visits to Mecca by other Arabs wishing to pay their respects at the Ka'ba. This interaction gave rise to a rich resource of legends, myths, ideas, figures, images and rituals that the Qur'an would later use to relate its narratives, norms and values to the context of Hijaz. The stories it would choose to narrate were those that were relevant to the region, whether they referred to people and narratives in biblical sources or local, Arabian legends.

Prophet Muhammad's life as part of the context

Muslims believe that Muhammad was the final prophet of God. His life story is essential for understanding the development of Islamic ideals as well as the context of the Qur'anic revelation.

Muslim tradition holds that Muhammad was orphaned at a very young age and was cared for by his relatives. As a young man, he began a career as a merchant, as was the norm in Mecca. At the age of 25, he accepted a proposal of marriage from Khadija, his employer, a wealthy Meccan woman who was somewhat older than Muhammad. He was devoted to her until her death. Together, they had four daughters and two sons, although their sons died in infancy. Muhammad was known as an honest man, who spent time in meditation and solitude; he lived an otherwise unremarkable life until he reached middle age.

When Muhammad was 40 years old, he received a 'revelation' while meditating in a cave near Mecca. At the time, he was unable to comprehend fully what was happening to him and what the implications of the revelation actually were. It was some time before he was fully convinced that he was a prophet of God, entrusted with communicating God's Word to his people. Once he had accepted this responsibility, Muhammad's first step was to communicate the message to his own family, close relatives and very close friends. Slowly, he began to attract converts to his teachings; the first of these came from among family and friends, but, later, a small number of individuals from the more disadvantaged sections of Meccan society began to respect and follow his teachings.

Muhammad's message emphasized the Oneness of God, as opposed to the multiple deities of the Meccans, and the need to worship God exclusively and be mindful of a Day of Reckoning when all would be judged according to their actions. One of the earliest Qur'anic texts says:

> When the sky is torn apart, when the stars are scattered, when the seas burst forth, when graves turn inside out; each soul will know what it has done and what it has left undone. Mankind, what has lured you away from God, your generous Lord who created you, shaped you, proportioned you, in whatever form He chose? Yet you still take the Judgment to be a lie![7]

The Qur'an's early revelations called upon people to reflect on the splendour of creation and the majesty of its Creator:

> Exalted is He who holds all control in His hands; who has power over all things; who created death and life to test you [people] and reveal which of you performs best – He is the Mighty, the Forgiving; who created the seven heavens, one above the other. You will not see any flaw in what the Lord of Mercy creates. Look around you! Can you see any flaw?[8]

Muhammad preached a new social order that transcended that of the tribe, encouraged humility rather than arrogance, and urged the rich and powerful to take care of the weak and needy:

> Yet he [human being] has not attempted the steep path. What will explain to you what the steep path is? It is to free a slave, or to feed at a time of hunger – an orphaned relative or a poor person in distress – and to be one of those who believe and urge one another to steadfastness and compassion.[9]

Thus, he quickly began to be seen as a threat to the underlying framework of Meccan society. The greater the number of his followers, the more restive the Meccan leaders became.

This tension between Muhammad and the powerful elders of Mecca continued to increase, and within a few years of the initial revelation, the persecution that he and his followers faced was so intense that Muhammad was forced to ask many of his followers to flee Mecca and seek protection with the Christian ruler of Abyssinia. Meanwhile, he and others in Mecca continued to suffer persecution. The emerging Muslim community endured these trials patiently. In the years preceding the death of Abu Talib, the Prophet's uncle and a respected community leader, Muhammad was granted a certain degree of protection from those who wished to persecute them. Following Abu Talib's death, however, this protection ceased and the situation in Mecca became unbearable. It was also at this time that the Prophet experienced his miraculous Night Journey (*Isra'*) from Mecca to Jerusalem, followed by the Ascent, or *Mi'raj*, through the seven heavens. The following verses are believed to describe part of the Prophet's experience:

> Glory to Him who made His servant [Muhammad] travel by night from the sacred place of worship [in Mecca] to the furthest place of worship [in Jerusalem], whose surroundings We have blessed, to show him some of Our signs; He alone is the All Hearing, the All Seeing.[10]

And:

> A second time he [Muhammad] saw him [Gabriel]: by the lote tree beyond which none may pass, near the Garden of Return, when the tree was covered in nameless splendour. His sight never wavered, nor was it too bold, and he saw some of the greatest signs of his Lord.[11]

Around this time, Muhammad met a group of *hajj* pilgrims from Medina, which was then engulfed in the conflict between its warring factions. They were so impressed by Muhammad's message and his character that they converted to Islam. It is likely that they also probably saw the potential for Muhammad to be a neutral arbiter in the tribal conflict in Medina. The following year they returned and made what became known as the Pledge of Aqaba, promising to obey Muhammad's instructions regarding right action, and to worship only God. They returned to Medina with one of the Prophet's Meccan followers, and the new faith began to spread quickly among the Arabs in Medina, where it was much less of a threat to the establishment than in Mecca.

Meanwhile the situation for Muslims in Mecca worsened. The Prophet arranged to hold a secret meeting with a Medinan delegation, during which a stronger pledge was made, one which promised the Prophet support and protection as if he were a member of their tribes, if he went to settle in Medina. In return Muhammad would arbitrate in the conflict between the tribes.

Soon afterwards, and approximately 12 years after he had started preaching, the Prophet took an important step: he instructed most of his followers to leave their kin and relatives in Mecca and to flee to Medina in the north. Such was the significance of this *hijra* or 'migration' that the Muslims later decided to begin their calendar from the time of this event. This remains the base date for the Islamic calendar – the *hijri* calendar – used by Muslims today.

The Islamic calendar

The Islamic calendar is a lunar calendar and contains 12 months (which have either 29 or 30 days) that are based on the cycles of the moon. This book often gives dates as 1/622. This means Year 1 of the Islamic calendar, which is equivalent to Year 622 in the Gregorian calendar (which is based on the solar cycle). The Islamic year is shorter than the Gregorian year by about 11 days, and so Islamic months and festivals occur at different dates in the Gregorian calendar each year. Today, Muslims still use the Islamic calendar for religious purposes but in other spheres of life the Gregorian calendar is often used. In some cases both calendars are used. Some books use AH (Anno Hegirae) after Islamic dates to indicate that they are referring to the period after the *hijra* (migration).

It was in Medina that the Prophet Muhammad established the first Muslim community, and he was to live there until his death in 11/632. In Medina, most of the Arabs had converted; however, some who opposed Muhammad's presence remained, despite having nominally converted to Islam. Many of these were tribal chiefs who had been aspiring to control all of Medina, and were resentful of what they saw as Muhammad's usurpation of their power.

The few remaining pagan Arabs offered little opposition to Muhammad. However, the Jewish tribes of Medina chose not to convert, and Muhammad initially seems to have seen no reason for them to do so, as they had scriptures of their own from the One God.[12] The Qur'an had instructed him:

> Say, 'People of the Book, let us arrive at a statement that is common to all: we worship God alone, we ascribe no partner to Him, and none of us takes others beside God as lords.' If they turn away, say, 'Witness our devotion to Him.'[13]

Tension and difficulties between the Jewish community and Muslims increased, gradually leading to an end to the Jewish presence in Medina. Five years after the Prophet's arrival, most of the Jews had either left or been expelled from the city. There are many sections in the Qur'an which comment on these tensions and related conflicts.

As for the Muslim community, Muhammad's role was as the spiritual leader of the new faith, as well as, increasingly, the political leader of the *umma* or religious and political community that had supplanted the tribe as the key political and social focus of allegiance for Muslims. Gradually, Muhammad introduced a number of religious practices, including regular Friday prayers. He also introduced social reforms that gave women additional rights, including rights related to inheritance, marriage and divorce.

The Prophet also received a new revelation permitting him to engage in warfare against his pagan opponents, particularly from Mecca. Although raids were commonplace among the Arabs, the Muslims had not been permitted until then to engage in any sort of fighting. One of the texts that give permission to Muslims to engage in warfare in defence of their religion says:

> Those who have been attacked [Muslims] are permitted to take up arms because they have been wronged – God has the power to help them – those who have been driven unjustly from their homes only for saying, 'Our Lord is God.' If God did not repel some people by means of others, many monasteries, churches, synagogues, and mosques, where God's name is much invoked, would have been destroyed.[14]

Over time, Muslims would engage with their pagan opponents in a series of raids and battles. Among the most important and one of the first such battles is the Battle of Badr (2/624). In this battle the Muslims from Mecca and Medina confronted the more powerful pagan Meccans, with relatives fighting each other: brother against brother, father against son, uncle against nephew. Despite overwhelming odds, the Muslims held their ground and the Meccans were defeated; some of the leading figures of the Meccan opposition to Muhammad were killed. This was a major victory for the Muslims, who were convinced that God was on their side against their pagan opponents.

The defeat of the Meccans at Badr did not mean their opposition to Muhammad ended. In the following year, they came back to Medina with a larger force to avenge their defeat. This second battle, fought near Mount Uhud, was a defeat for the Muslims, although the Meccans were unable to enter Medina and retreated. Two years later in 5/627, the Meccans, now in alliance with a large number of tribes, returned with a 10,000-strong force to finally destroy the Muslims. The Muslims were clearly no match for them. However, the Prophet had built defences to prevent them from entering Medina. After a long siege, the Meccans were forced to return home, without achieving any of their objectives. This would be the final major military confrontation between the Meccan-pagan opposition and the Muslims.

Muhammad increasingly came to be seen in Arabia as a strong and powerful figure. Slowly, his influence grew in Hijaz and in large parts of Arabia, and his teachings spread widely. In a bloodless conquest, Mecca itself finally came under the control of the Muslims (in 8/630) eight years after the flight of the Prophet to Medina. Upon entry to Mecca, Muhammad granted a general amnesty, and most Meccans embraced the new religion. The Prophet cleansed the sanctuary, the Ka'ba, of all idols placed there, declaring that it would be free from any pagan worship and that it would be devoted entirely to the worship of the One God. Two years later, Muhammad died (in 11/632) at his home in Medina. By the time of his death, tradition holds that much of Arabia was either allied with him or had converted to Islam.

This is the traditional Muslim account of Muhammad's life. Although some Western scholars have questioned aspects of this account, Muslims in general accept it, and relate it to various events that are mentioned repeatedly in the Qur'an. The struggles of Muhammad in Mecca and Medina, the battles he fought against his opponents, the stories of Jewish–Muslim tension in Medina, and the regulations that were introduced to govern the Muslim community in Medina, can all be related to this broad overview.

Socio-historical context and cultural language

In framing the terms of the new religion taking shape in Mecca and Medina, the cultural context of Hijaz was a point of departure for both the Qur'an and the Prophet. The Prophet never claimed that he came to eradicate all the cultural elements from Hijaz. His essential task was to teach certain new ideas that related primarily to God, God's relationship to people and His creation, ethical-moral values and life after death. Largely, the way of life of the people of Hijaz and elements of their worldview were retained. The innovations introduced by the Prophet were primarily in theological, spiritual, legal and ethical-moral areas.

The Qur'an contains its own culturally specific language appropriate to the worldview of its first recipients, which includes the symbols, metaphors, terms and expressions that were used in Hijaz. Even in describing the Islamic concept of Paradise, the Qur'an uses language that is closely associated with the local culture and popular imagination: flowing rivers, fruit, trees and gardens. For people who were used to arid, dry, and mountainous topography with little water, trees or fruit, this description of Paradise was an attractive depiction of the afterlife that awaits a believer. Similarly, the descriptions of Hell also rely on images borrowed from the prevailing culture, and would have resonated strongly with the people of Hijaz.

The Qur'an also appropriated a number of pre-existing practices such as fasting; it also came to accept other pre-Islamic practices, with some modifications. For instance, the *hajj* (pilgrimage) had existed in pre-Islamic times and was made part of the new religion. It was 'purified' and stripped of its polytheistic practices, though few other changes were made. According to the Qur'an, it was taking the pilgrimage back to its original form, as it was practiced by Abraham.

Many of the pre-Islamic values in Hijaz were also accepted as part of the new religion. On the whole, what the culture considered to be important and of positive value was accepted, for example values such as patience in the face of adversity, which was one aspect of the Bedouin virtue of 'manliness' dating from pre-Islamic times. What the culture normally considered improper or indecent was likewise rejected. This included extravagance, lack of generosity, breach of trust, hypocrisy, suspicion, vanity, boasting, ridiculing of others, slander, cheating in trade, usury, hoarding and gambling. The Prophet was partly successful because his message was couched in terms that people related to and understood. The Qur'an also accepted many of the foods consumed in that culture, with exceptions such as wine.

The Qur'an rejected, accepted or adapted many pre-Islamic Arab practices, all the while making it clear that the Oneness of God (*tawhid*) was the new overarching principle. For instance, the Qur'an recognized some norms surrounding war and peace that existed at that time, although significant changes were made. Aggression was no longer considered a virtue; the Qur'an urged the Muslims to make peace when their opponents surrendered or were inclined to peace. Killing captives was no longer permitted. As alluded to above, the Qur'an's injunctions regarding war and peace need to be understood in the context of Arabian conventions regarding warfare, treaties and alliances, and the idea of tribal protection, as they existed at the time. Slavery also existed, and was accepted as normal, although Islam from the very beginning encouraged the freeing of slaves. The pre-Islamic holy months were also more or less accepted as part of Islam, as was the sacrifice of animals, on the condition that it was dedicated only to the One God, not to other deities.

Ethical language of the Qur'an: context and women

In general, many Muslims consider Qur'anic texts to be legal. If we look at the texts more closely, however, we often find that much of the language of the Qur'an is primarily *ethical*. Later, with the development of Islamic law during the first three centuries of Islam, this ethical language came to be seen as legal in nature. An emphasis on legal matters was needed during this early period, as jurists were seeking an authoritative basis for developing law and devising a system of jurisprudence. This emphasis, however, became excessive when clearly ethical texts came to be regarded as purely legal, and the language and spirit of the Qur'an was lost to the more rigorous legal interpretations.

An example of this is an area that the Qur'an deals with on numerous occasions: the position of women. Distinctions on the basis of gender and class were a part of pre-Islamic and early Islamic society. This is reflected in the way that certain Qur'anic passages refer to women. However, the Qur'an was not entrenching gender discrimination as religious law; in fact, it was doing the opposite. Women, at least in some cases, were disadvantaged in Arabian society. In many instances, the Qur'an improved the position of women in society as a whole and protected their interests, just as it also made advances in the status of other disadvantaged groups in Arabian society, such as slaves and the poor.[15]

For example, the Qur'an expresses strong disapproval of people who did not welcome the birth of a female child.[16] It also prohibited female infanticide,[17] a practice that existed at that time in some parts of Arabia, as sons were considered to be of greater worth and less of a burden on the family. The Qur'an states that in the eyes of God, the only distinction of any consequence among human beings is in their piety – and in this respect, women and men are judged equally.[18] One verse in particular states this beyond doubt:

> For men and women who are devoted to God – believing men and
> women, obedient men and women, truthful men and women, steadfast
> men and women, humble men and women, charitable men and women,
> fasting men and women, chaste men and women, men and women
> who remember God often – God has prepared forgiveness and a rich
> reward.[19]

Women were also given the right to inherit, which was a significant advance-
ment at the time, as, other than a few aristocratic women, most women
could not inherit. The Qur'an also placed a limit on the number of wives a
man was permitted to have, and, in what is arguably an advance, allowed
polygamy only for men (polygyny); it had previously existed for women
also but had degenerated into a form of prostitution. Finally, clear guidelines
for divorce were established which accorded women more rights than they
previously had.

While rejecting some manifestations of discrimination against women, the
Qur'an also appeared to retain certain social and cultural practices. Some
verses suggest that, when viewed from today's perspective, the Qur'an gave
females a lower status than men. For instance, in some financial matters,
the value of a woman's evidence was considered as only half that of a man's
in certain cases:

> You who believe, when you contract a debt for a stated term, put it
> down in writing: have a scribe write it down justly between you . . . Call
> in two men as witnesses. If two men are not there, then call one man and
> two women out of those you approve as witnesses, so that if one of the
> two women should forget the other can remind her.[20]

Several other references in the Qur'an also suggest that, in the social context
of early Islam, women, at least in some areas, were not of the same status
as men. There are other areas where the Qur'an prescribes differential
treatment for men and women: divorce,[21] polygamy,[22] dress codes,[23] the
issue of men 'taking full care of' women,[24] the punishment for immorality,[25]
marrying People of the Book,[26] and inheritance.[27] There are certain other
passages that, upon an initial reading, appear to compare women
unfavourably with men.[28]

Overall, if individual verses are read in isolation, it may appear that the
Qur'an's position on women is rather ambiguous. In most cases it appears
to treat both sexes equally, but at other times the status of women seems to
be lower than that of men. It is clear, however, that the overall effect of the
Qur'an and the Prophet's mission was to give women in the Islamic era
greater rights than they had received in the pre-Islamic Arabia.

However, after the Prophet Muhammad's death, Islam spread into surrounding regions where also, historically, women were often discriminated against. These cultural attitudes and practices rubbed off on Muslims. Islamic exegetical writings thus increasingly displayed views that were patriarchal and patronizing towards women, despite the Qur'an's emphasis on new rights for women and justice and fairness. However, there were always women in Muslim societies who played important roles in Islamic scholarship, and political as well as social life. The negative attitudes and views towards women that existed in much of Islamic scholarship are now being challenged by an increasing number of Muslims, women and men, who argue that such negative attitudes do not reflect the overall Qur'anic message and therefore must be rethought.

Intellectual currents that influenced Muslim engagement with the Qur'an

After the Prophet's death, a period of social and political tension began, and as a result, intense debate among Muslims on a whole range of issues emerged, from political leadership of the community, to religious authority, to interpretation of the Qur'an. These debates led, in the first 150 years or so after the death of the Prophet, to the emergence of several religio-political, theological, mystical and legal orientations. Developments in all these areas were to have a significant impact on how the Qur'an was studied, interpreted, understood and applied. Below we provide a very brief overview of those orientations.

Religio-political orientations

The group known as the Kharijis emerged as a religio-political group within 40 years of the Prophet's death after a serious disagreement among Muslims regarding the legitimate political leadership of the Muslim community during the time of the fourth caliph Ali.[29] Among the key beliefs of the Kharijis was that Muslims who committed grave sins were no longer believers and that the political leader of the Muslim community should never compromise any aspect of religious teachings. Today, Kharijis represent a small minority of Muslims.

The origins of Shi'a, the second group, go back to the time of the death of the Prophet. Some Muslims at the time believed that the family of the Prophet should be given priority in political leadership of the community. Later, this idea was developed further, and the Shi'a as we now know them emerged over the first two centuries of Islam. They argued that Ali, the Prophet's cousin and son-in-law, should have been his immediate political successor and that all subsequent political leadership should have remained within the Prophet's family. The Shi'a gradually developed their own theological system as well as legal school, and today represent a significant minority of Muslims.

Sunnis, the third group, constituted the Muslim 'mainstream', namely those who were not considered Shi'i or Khariji. Sunnis emerged as a distinct group over the first three centuries of Islam, during which time they developed a number of creeds and schools of law. Sunnis were responsible for many of the early hadith collections and the recording of early Islamic history. Once developed, Sunni Islam came to be seen as orthodoxy and still represents the majority of Muslims today.

Theological orientations

Several intellectual trends emerged among Muslims in the first century of Islam.[30] These were not 'schools' as such; rather, they reflected intellectual concerns about the important issues of the time. Much debate existed on issues such as who actually was a Muslim, a believer, a non-believer and a sinner. Definitions of these terms varied among Muslims, depending on the intellectual trend or the religio-political group to which they belonged. Other questions debated in the first two centuries included: What happens to a Muslim who commits grave sins and dies; would he or she end up in Hell forever? Are human actions predetermined by God? Are people free to choose between right and wrong? Some argued for free will, while others argued for God's predetermination of events. Three major theological schools emerged out of these debates: the Mu'tazilis, the Ash'aris and the Traditionists. The Mu'tazilis were rationalist in orientation and argued for free will, while the Traditionists adopted a position that emphasized God's predetermination of events. The Ash'aris were in between these two positions in theological matters.

Mystical orientations

Sufism, or Islamic mysticism, emerged as a separate movement in the second/eighth century, gradually developing into a number of different Sufi orders throughout the Muslim regions.[31] Unlike many other Muslim groups of the time, Sufis tended to be more accommodating of diversity within the Muslim community and were also more accepting of other religious traditions. These views, and the Sufis' esoteric interpretations of Islam, were particularly unpopular among non-Sufi scholars and resulted in the persecution of some leading Sufis.

Legal orientations

In the first 200 years of Islam, the early schools of legal thought also developed. The five major schools still existing today are the Hanafi school, the Maliki school, the Shafi'i school, the Hanbali school and the Ja'fari school.

The Hanafi school is associated with the jurist Abu Hanifa (d.150/767), who lived in Iraq. The Hanafi school placed great importance on the use of reason in interpreting law. Today, it remains the largest Sunni school of law and its followers are found mainly in the Indian subcontinent, Central Asia and Turkey.

In contrast to Abu Hanifa, Malik ibn Anas (d.179/795), with whom the Maliki school is connected, discouraged the excessive use of reason in understanding Islamic law and relied heavily on the foundation texts of the Qur'an and hadith. He considered the customary practice of the people of Medina, where the Prophet and the earliest Muslims lived, to be indicative of practices at the time of the Prophet, and hence authoritative. Teachings of the Maliki school spread across North Africa and Spain. Today, it is the third largest Sunni school of law and its followers are found mainly in North and West Africa.

The Shafi'i school is named after Muhammad ibn Idris al-Shafi'i (d.204/820), a scholar who travelled widely in search of religious knowledge. Shafi'i developed a range of principles of Islamic jurisprudence dealing with questions such as the interpretation of texts and the authority of the sunna. Today, it is the second largest Sunni school of law and its followers are found mainly in Southeast Asia.

The Hanbali school is named after Ahmad ibn Hanbal (d.240/855), a student of Shafi'i. Ahmad ibn Hanbal was known both as a legal scholar and a collector of hadith. The Hanbali school relied heavily on the texts (the Qur'an and sunna) and the opinions of the Prophet's Companions in their interpretation of law. They are often described as literalist and somewhat intolerant of those who hold different opinions to theirs. Today, the Hanbali school is the smallest Sunni school of law and most of its followers are found in Arabia.

The Ja'fari school is the major Shi'a school of law and is followed by Twelver Shi'a Muslims. Ja'fari scholars believe that the Qur'an is the primary source of Islamic law and that only Shi'a imams have the ability to interpret the Qur'an and hadith authoritatively. Although they accept the hadith as a source of law, they only rely on hadith which have been narrated and transmitted by the family of the Prophet or people considered sympathetic to the Shi'a tradition. Other Shi'a have their own systems of law.

These intellectual currents were to have a major impact on how Muslims read and interpreted the Qur'an. In the exegetical writings one can often see clearly how an exegete's religio-political, theological, mystical or legal orientations can shape their interpretation of the Qur'an.

Summary

Some of the important points we have discussed in this chapter include:

- The message of the Qur'an is embedded in the specific context of seventh-century Arabia, and is expressed in a language and symbolism that its first audience understood.
- Many elements of pre-Islamic culture and society were not rejected entirely by the Qur'an, but were accepted in a modified form.
- Many teachings of the Prophet were socially progressive for his time.
- Some of the Qur'an's references to women seem discriminatory today, but should be read in the context of the entire Qur'an and the cultural and social norms of the time of its revelation.

Recommended reading

Karen Armstrong, *Muhammad: Prophet for Our Time*, London: HarperCollins, 2006.

- In this book Armstrong provides insights into the historical context of seventh-century Arabia and the mission of the Prophet Muhammad. Armstrong aims to assist readers in understanding the full measure of Muhammad's achievements. She demonstrates how Muhammad's life and experiences can offer a number of valuable lessons for the world today.

Martin Lings, *Muhammad: His Life Based on the Earliest Sources*, London: George Allen & Unwin, 1983; revised, Rochester, VT: Inner Traditions International, 2006.

- In this book Lings draws on second/eighth- and third/ninth-century Arabic biographies that recount a number of events in the Prophet's life. Some of these passages are translated into English for the first time. The book is written in an easy-to-read, narrative style and the revised edition includes new information about the Prophet's influence in Syria and other surrounding areas.

Tariq Ramadan, *In the Footsteps of the Prophet: Lessons from the Life of Muhammad*, New York: Oxford University Press, 2007.

- In this book Ramadan presents the main events of the Prophet's life in a way which highlights his spiritual and ethical teachings. He describes many of Muhammad's personal traits and also draws attention to the significance of the Prophet's example for issues such as the treatment of the poor, war, racism, the role of women, Islamic criminal punishments, and relations with other religions.

Montgomery Watt, *Muhammad at Mecca*, Oxford: Oxford University Press, 1953; *Muhammad at Medina*, Karachi: Oxford University Press, 1981.

- In these two books, Watt provides a comprehensive history of the life of Muhammad and the origins of the Muslim community. He examines a range of scholarly discussions in relation to topics such as politics, relations with other Arabs and people of different faiths, social reforms and the person of Muhammad himself.

NOTES

1 Karen Armstrong, *Muhammad: Prophet for Our Time*, London: HarperCollins, 2006, pp 24–25.
2 Armstrong, *Muhammad*, p. 27.
3 Michael Sells, *Approaching the Qur'an: The Early Revelations*, Ashland, OR: White Cloud Press, 1999, p. 3.
4 Armstrong, *Muhammad*, p. 101.
5 Montgomery Watt, *Muhammad at Medina*, Oxford: Oxford University Press, 1953, pp. 192–195 and Armstrong, *Muhammad*, pp. 102–103.
6 Marshall G.S. Hodgson, *The Venture of Islam*, Chicago: University of Chicago Press, 1974, vol. 1, p. 159.
7 Qur'an: 82:1–9.
8 Qur'an: 67:1–3.
9 Qur'an: 90:11–17.
10 Qur'an: 17:1.
11 Qur'an: 53:13–18.
12 Watt, *Muhammad at Medina*, p. 201.

13 Qur'an: 3:64.
14 Qur'an: 22:39–40.
15 Abdullah Saeed, *Interpreting the Qur'an: Towards a Contemporary Approach*, London: Routledge, 2006, p. 120.
16 See Qur'an: 16:57–59.
17 Qur'an 17:31. See also Qur'an 81:8–9.
18 Qur'an: 49:13.
19 Qur'an: 33:35.
20 Qur'an: 2:282.
21 Qur'an: 33:49; 2:226–233, 237; 65:4–6.
22 Qur'an: 4:3, 25, 127, 129.
23 Qur'an: 33:59; 24:31, 60.
24 Qur'an: 4:34.
25 Qur'an: 4:15.
26 Qur'an: 5:5.
27 Qur'an: 4:11, 176.
28 Qur'an: 9:87, 93; 3:15.
29 See Chapter 11 for further discussions of religio-political approaches to exegesis.
30 See Chapter 11 for further discussions of theological approaches to exegesis.
31 See Chapter 11 for further discussions of mystical approaches to exegesis.

2 Revelation and the Qur'an

THE QUR'AN IS ONE OF THE MOST SIGNIFICANT religious–literary works in the history of the world. As Islam's holy scripture, it is often compared to the Gospels and the Torah. All three texts are considered by their respective followers to be the Word of God or inspired by God.

In this chapter we will discuss:

- differences in the concept of revelation between Islam, Christianity and Judaism;
- the three types of revelation mentioned in the Qur'an that Muslims believe God uses to speak to humankind;
- the Islamic account of the first revelation to the Prophet Muhammad; and
- a framework for a broader understanding of Qur'anic revelation that takes into account its socio-historical context.

The nature of revelation

The generally held Muslim view of revelation is that it is an initiative of God who reveals His Will to humanity through chosen prophets. Muslims believe in a large number of prophets, including the Prophet Muhammad, who is considered to be the final recipient of divine revelation. Muslims believe that the Prophet Muhammad was a divinely inspired messenger; however, he does not represent God's Being.

For Muslims, the Prophet experienced the presence of the 'voice' of God in his heart and was able to describe it only in metaphorical terms. At times he likened the receiving of revelation to hearing a sound like that of the 'ringing of a bell'.[1] For Muslims, what was revealed was God's Will, not His Being. This Will was conveyed in a human language, Arabic.

The Prophet saw himself as separate to the revelation itself and described his experiences of 'seeing' the angel Gabriel, 'hearing' the voice and comprehending what was said. Muslim tradition tells us that he was quite clear in his mind that he was receiving the content of revelation from a source external to him. He always maintained that he did not have any influence on the actual content of the revelation.

This content is what came to be known as the Qur'an. The Muslim view of revelation affirms the importance of its linguistic content, as distinct from the revelatory experience. Revelation is therefore identical to the Qur'an, whose words are believed to be directly equivalent to the verbal message given to the Prophet. An early Muslim theologian, Nasafi (d.507/1114), describes how Muslims conceptualize the Qur'an as revelation:

The Quran is God's speaking, which is one of His attributes. Now God in all of His attributes is One, and with all His attributes is eternal and not contingent, (so His speaking is) without letters and without sounds, not broken up into syllables or paragraphs. It is not He nor is it other than He. He caused Gabriel to hear it as sound and letters, for He created sound and letters and caused him to hear it by that sound and those letters. Gabriel, upon whom be peace, memorized it, stored it (in his mind) and then transmitted to the Prophet, upon whom be God's blessing and peace, by bringing down a revelation and a message, which is not the same as bringing down a corporeal object and a form. He recited it to the Prophet, upon whom be God's blessing and peace, the Prophet memorized it, storing it up (in his mind), and then recited it to his Companions, who memorized it and recited to the Followers.[2]

The Qur'an in Arabic is at the centre of Muslim faith. Its words are considered divine. Belief in the Qur'an as one of the revealed scriptures is a fundamental article of faith. Its words are memorized and recited. Reciting the Qur'an in Arabic is believed to allow the reader to, in a sense, communicate directly with the divine and hence experience revelation itself.

It is useful to compare this Muslim perspective with that of other faiths, particularly faiths which also have a scripture, such as Judaism and Christianity. The *Encyclopedia of Judaism*[3] states that the 'essential thrust of the [Jewish] Bible' is 'that God is self-disclosing and wishes to be known by human beings',[4] and that most Jews would believe that God revealed Himself both through His deeds and His words, which were communicated through the prophets. The Jewish notion of revelation through prophecy is described as: 'He [God] speaks through their mouths . . . when they speak, "It is I, Yahveh, who speak".'[5] Another way of looking at revelation from a Jewish perspective is that it is:

> evidence of [God's] presence, intuition of His concern and desire to enter into relationship, knowledge of His attributes and, above all, something of His will: His plans, purposes and intentions for the individual, the nation, and mankind.[6]

Some significant branches of Judaism, such as Reform Judaism, which began in nineteenth-century Germany,[7] prefer not to accept supernatural explanations, believing instead that the idea of 'God communicating content of particular commandments to man is sheer miracle and must be rejected.'[8] The dominant Christian views of revelation differ from both Judaism and

Islam, largely due to the central role of Jesus in Christianity. The Christian understanding of revelation is 'the self-communication of God in and through Jesus Christ', which is described as the supreme and unsurpassable self-disclosure of God.[9] Although the Old Testament is viewed as 'a vehicle of revelation', it is believed that 'the Son [Jesus] alone knows the Father [God], and in him the Father is made visible and understandable (Jn. 1:14, 1 Jn. 1:1).'[10] Revelation is viewed as the 'unveiling of the divine plan by which God reconciles the human race to himself in Christ.' Views vary within Christian traditions as to whether the Bible is the direct Word of God.

Some writers have commented that it is perhaps more accurate to compare the place of the Qur'an in Islam not to the Bible, but to the person of Christ himself.[11] The act of reciting the Arabic revelation in its linguistic form can be compared to partaking of the sacrament of the Eucharist in Christianity. By reciting the very words which are believed to have been 'spoken' by God, Muslims in a sense believe they are participating directly in the divine Word, in a somewhat similar way that the bread and wine of the Eucharist allow Christians to partake in the Divine nature of the body of Christ. These views tell us something of how the three faiths – Judaism, Christianity and Islam – understand revelation.

Forms of revelation in the Islamic context

Muslims believe that God has spoken to His creation from the beginning of time. Not only is He believed to have communicated to the Prophets Moses and Muhammad, but also to prophets such as Noah, Abraham, Zechariah, and Jesus. God is also said to speak to the angels and even Iblis (Satan).

The Qur'an describes three forms of communication of God with human beings: 'It is not granted to any mortal that God should speak to him except through revelation or from behind a veil, or by sending a messenger to reveal by His command what He will: He is exalted and wise.'[12] The first form, through revelation, involves communication directly from God to the recipient. In this case, the recipient understands this communication without hearing any sound or having any contact with a messenger (that is, an angel).

The above verse describes the second form of communication as being 'from behind a veil', and refers to a scenario in which God speaks to someone directly using words, but the hearer does not see Him. One of the best examples for this is that of revelation to Moses. The Qur'an tells us that

Moses asked God to reveal or show Himself to Moses, to which God replies: 'You will never see Me, but look at that mountain: if it remains standing firm, you will see Me.'[13] But, of course, neither the mountain nor Moses could stand firm.

Several Muslim scholars believe that the third form, 'through a messenger', is the surest and clearest form of revelation. It is also the method by which Muslims believe the Prophet Muhammad on the whole received the Qur'an. This method involves a messenger – believed to be the angel Gabriel – who brings the Word of God to a prophet. Gabriel is believed to have transmitted the revelation in a form the Prophet could understand – in the Arabic language.[14] This is reiterated through Qur'anic verses such as: 'We [God] have sent it down as an Arabic Qur'an so that you [people] may understand.'[15] More generally, the Qur'an states that: 'We [God] have never sent a messenger who did not use his people's own language to make things clear for them.'[16]

The idea that the Qur'an was transmitted in its linguistic form is also supported by certain Qur'anic concepts and terms. For example, the Qur'an states that it is inscribed on a 'Preserved Tablet' (*al-lawh al-mahfuz*) in the heavens.[17] Muslim theologians hold that the revelation proceeded from God in the first instance to this Tablet, and from there the angel Gabriel brought it to the Prophet. It is worth noting that the Qur'an uses the word *nazala* (to descend), and its derivatives, such as *tanzil* (something sent down), to describe the Qur'anic revelation. The implication of words 'descending' or being 'sent down' is important to understand, and is not fully conveyed by the English word 'revelation'. These Qur'anic terms and concepts form an integral part of the Muslim belief that the words of the Qur'an were 'sent down' verbatim from God to the Prophet Muhammad.

Prophet Muhammad's experience of revelation

Muslim accounts of the first event of revelation for the Prophet Muhammad tell us that he encountered the angel Gabriel while on a retreat to Hira (a cave near Mecca), when he was 40 years old. Prior to this, it is believed that Muhammad had begun to have a series of vivid dreams and premonitions. On the occasion of the first revelation in the cave, we are told that Muhammad felt a presence and then saw an angel in the form of a man, who told him to 'Read!' or 'Recite!' (*iqra'*). When Muhammad replied that he was not a reciter or he could not recite, the angel then held Muhammad so tightly that he thought he was dying. The command to recite was repeated three times. Finally, the angel Gabriel began to recite what we now know as the first five verses of chapter 96 of the Qur'an:[18]

Read! In the name of your Lord who created: He created the human from a clinging form. Read! Your Lord is the Most Bountiful One who taught by [means of] the pen, who taught the human what he did not know.[19]

This experience was not an easy one for Muhammad. He quickly returned home and sought comfort from his wife, Khadija. Muhammad was not quite sure what to make of the experience, and whether what he had received was a revelation from God. It was only slowly that Muhammad came to realize the enormity of the responsibility with which he was entrusted and that he was indeed receiving revelations from God.

The revelations Muhammad began to receive in 610 CE continued over the next 22 years until his death, in 11/632. His experiences of the revelation are described in several hadith, such as the following, narrated by his wife, A'isha (d.58/678):

Al-Harith ibn Hisham asked the Prophet: 'O Allah's Messenger! How is the revelation (wahy) revealed to you?' Allah's Messenger replied: 'Sometimes it is [revealed] like the ringing of a bell; this form of revelation is the hardest of all and when this state leaves me, I remember what was revealed. Sometimes the angel comes in the form of a man and addresses me and I remember what he says.'[20]

Some Muslims believe that the Prophet Muhammad always received the revelation via the angel Gabriel. However, some scholars, like Fazlur Rahman (d.1988), have questioned this view and suggested instead that the Prophet did not necessarily always receive revelation from the angel Gabriel as an external 'other', but that revelation often came to him internally.[21]

Different ways in which Muhammad is referred to by Muslims

Prophet Muhammad
Allah's Messenger
Allah's Apostle
The Prophet
The Messenger

When Muslims refer to Muhammad, they very often recite a blessing or prayer immediately after his name: 'Peace be upon him' or 'Peace and God's blessings be upon him'. Muslims consider it inappropriate to refer to the Prophet by his name alone, without pronouncing this blessing, particularly when speaking. However, in academic discourse it is common to simply refer to him as Muhammad or the Prophet Muhammad.

Revelation: God's speech in human language

The Qur'an asserts its divine origin in several verses, and specifically denies that it includes the speech or ideas of the Prophet. Fazlur Rahman explains that '[n]ot only does the word *Qur'an*, meaning "recitation", clearly indicate this, but the text of the Qur'an itself states in several places that the Qur'an is *verbally revealed* and not merely in its "meaning" and "ideas".'[22] However, the form in which God's Word manifests itself is Arabic, a language embedded in human life and social context.

The importance of God's 'speaking' in the Islamic tradition is summarized by Toshihiko Izutsu (d.1993) who argues:

> And Revelation means in Islam that God 'spoke', that He revealed Himself through language . . . not in some mysterious non-human language but in a clear, humanly understandable language. This *is* the initial and most decisive fact. Without this act on the part of God, there would have been no true religion on earth according to [the] Islamic understanding of the word religion.[23]

Classical and modern Muslim scholars alike recognize the problem inherent in the idea that God has revealed a divine message in a human language such as Arabic. Scholars have asked how the eternal, immutable, non-contingent 'speech' of God could have been transmitted through the vehicle of a contingent, mutable, and context-bound human language. Most have concluded that God's speech would have remained entirely beyond our comprehension unless it was somehow expressed in a form we could understand. The twelfth-century theologian and mystic al-Ghazali (d.505/ 1111) writes:

> He [God] expressed that attribute [of speech] in human images and words to mankind. If the glory and excellence of the Words of God could not have been made understandable in the garb of words, heaven

and earth could not stand to hear His words [in their original form] and all things between them would have smashed to pieces.[24]

Some scholars have emphasized the difference between the essential nature of revelation as God's 'speech', which is a theological mystery incapable of being fully understood by humans, and the way that it appears to us in comprehensible human language. As Izutsu says:

> in so far as it is *God's* speech, Revelation is something mysterious and has nothing in common with ordinary human linguistic behaviour, [but] in so far as it is *speech* it must have all the essential attributes of human speech. In fact, the Koran [Qur'an] uses also other words in reference to Revelation . . . commonly applied to ordinary, commonplace products of speech: *kalimah* meaning 'word' for example in Surat al-Shura.[25]

Exploring the essential nature of God's speech at the level of the Unseen (*al-ghayb*) is said to be similar to attempting to understand the realm of the Hereafter. Though there are many descriptions of the Hereafter, particularly in relation to Paradise and Hell, in the Qur'an, Muslims bear the following saying of the Prophet in mind when reading such descriptions: '[What is in Paradise is] what an eye has not seen, an ear has not heard, and which has not been imagined by the heart.'[26] This saying conveys the idea that, like God's speech, descriptions of the Hereafter are limited by language based in human experience. Such descriptions allow believers to comprehend, in approximate terms, what is essentially beyond human experience and imagination.

Muslim theologians have debated endlessly about whether the Qur'an was 'created' like any other thing that exists in the world. The reasons for this debate are complex and relate to theological discussions about the nature of God and God's attributes. If the Qur'an is the 'speech of God' and 'speech' is an attribute of God, then the Qur'an is linked to God as an attribute. If this is the case, the Qur'an, as an attribute of God, must be eternal, without beginning or end.

Of the two main positions on this issue, the Ash'ari theological school[27] believed that the Qur'an is the Word of God, and, as the Divine Speech, is 'uncreated', that is, co-eternal with God. Meanwhile, the Mu'tazili school,[28] which has largely disappeared today, asserted that there could not be any eternal entity other than God, and therefore that the Qur'an must be 'created'.[29] The difference between the two perspectives is subtle. For instance, they agreed that the Qur'an has a number of levels of existence. The Ash'ari position held that only the Qur'an's 'spirit and meaning' is 'uncreated', while both schools agreed that its 'language and utterance' and 'letters and writing' are 'created'. There is a third view held by those known as the Traditionists,[30] who took less interest in theological debates, which is critical of both the Mu'tazili and Ash'ari perspectives. Proponents of this view argue that Muslims should not discuss whether the Qur'an is 'created' as this was not mentioned in the Qur'an or by the Prophet or the Companions.[31] This brief summary is a simplification of a complex set of theological arguments, which cannot be fully explored here.

The Qur'an as purely divine revelation

The Qur'an denies that it contains the speech or ideas of the Prophet or any other human being. It also asserts that the revelation, in its final Arabic form, came directly from God, without any possibility of human-induced errors or inaccuracies. For example, it states:

> Nor could this Qur'an have been devised by anyone other than God. It is a confirmation of what was revealed before it and an explanation of the Scripture – let there be no doubt about it – it is from the Lord of the Worlds. Or do they [unbelievers] say 'He has devised it'? Say, 'Then produce a *sura* [chapter] like it, and call on anyone you can besides God if you are telling the truth.'[32]

Along with such challenges, the Qur'an also argues that, were it from a source other than God, 'they would have found much inconsistency in it'.[33] Related to this point is the separateness of the Prophet from the source of revelation. This fact is pointed to in the Qur'an itself and was often stressed by the Prophet. As Fazlur Rahman says: 'the Prophet himself was always only too conscious that his prophethood was not of his own making and that even his natural capacities could not *cause* Revelation, which was a sheer mercy of God.'[34] According to Rahman, this separateness is further illustrated by instances where the Qur'an addresses the Prophet directly. For example, the Prophet is chided in the Qur'an for moving his tongue in anticipation of a revelation from God:

> [O Prophet], do not rush your tongue in an attempt to hasten the Revelation: We [God] shall make sure of its safe collection and recitation. When We [God] have recited it, repeat the recitation and We shall make it clear.[35]

Spoken word and written word

The Qur'an refers in many places to itself as spoken word, suggesting that from a Qur'anic point of view, it is first and foremost the 'spoken' Word of God. According to Izutsu:

> It is no wonder, then, that Islam should have been from the very beginning extremely language conscious. Islam arose when God spoke. The whole Islamic culture made its start with the historic fact that man was addressed by God in a language which he himself spoke. This was not a simple matter of God's having 'sent down' a sacred Book. It meant primarily that God 'spoke'. And this is precisely what 'Revelation' means. Revelation is essentially a linguistic concept.[36]

Despite this emphasis on the spoken word in the Qur'an, there are also some verses which suggest that the Qur'an is strongly associated with writing or the written word. For instance, the first verses to be revealed to the Prophet establish the connection of the revelation to 'the pen'.[37] The Qur'an also uses terms denoting the written word to refer to previous revelations, including scripture, pages[38] or tablets.[39] In many cases, the Qur'an refers to revelations given to Moses,[40] Jesus[41] and descendants of Abraham[42] as scriptures of God or simply scripture. The term 'People of the Book' (or 'of the Scripture') is also used in the Qur'an to refer to followers of these revelations, such as Jews and Christians.

Based on what the Qur'an says about itself, we could argue that even before the death of the Prophet Muhammad, the Qur'an came to be conceived of as a written scripture, although it was after the Prophet's death that the entire Qur'an was compiled as a single written document.

Revelation and interpretation

Classical Muslim scholars regarded revelation as the communication of God's Word, and did not consider that the Prophet Muhammad, or his community, could have played a part in the revelation. However, some modern scholars, including Fazlur Rahman, Nasr Hamid Abu Zayd, Farid Esack and Ebrahim Moosa,[43] have begun to develop a slightly different understanding of the notion of revelation, which includes the role of the 'religious personality' of the Prophet Muhammad and his community in the revelatory event. This understanding has some bearing on Qur'anic interpretation. Fazlur Rahman says:

The Qur'an itself certainly maintained the 'otherness', the 'objectivity' and the verbal character of the Revelation, but had equally certainly rejected its externality vis-à-vis the Prophet . . . But orthodoxy (indeed, all medieval thought) lacked the necessary intellectual tools to combine in its formulation of the dogma the otherness and verbal character of the Revelation on the one hand, and its intimate connection with the work and religious personality of the Prophet on the other, i.e. it lacked the intellectual capacity to say both that the Qur'an is entirely the Word of God and, in an ordinary sense, also entirely the word of Muhammad.[44]

Here, Rahman does not argue that the Qur'an is the word or the work of the Prophet. Instead, Rahman emphasizes the close connection between the Qur'an as Word of God, the Prophet and his mission, and the socio-historical context in which the Qur'an was revealed.[45] The idea seems to be that if there is a close connection between the Qur'an and the Prophet and his community, this might allow for a freer interpretation of the Qur'an, taking the socio-historical context into account.

Approaching the understanding of revelation in this way may be very useful. It is important to remember, however, that the classical understanding of revelation, which did not include analysis of the role of the Prophet in the revelation, still allowed for interpretation of the text to occur. Some scholars preferred to limit their efforts to the guidance provided by the Prophet and the earliest Muslims. Others were keen to explore meanings beyond this.

Towards a broader understanding of revelation

From the discussion above, it is possible to construct the following view of revelation: God revealed His Will (not His Being) to the Prophet Muhammad; this revelation to the Prophet occurred through an intermediary known as the angel Gabriel, in Arabic, the language of the Prophet; God's Word continued to be received as revelation until the death of the Prophet Muhammad, after which no new revelation was possible; God's 'Word' and the Prophet's 'word' are clearly distinguished; the 'otherness' of revelation (that is, it is totally external to the Prophet Muhammad) is to be maintained; and, finally, revelation is independent of any socio-historical context and is eternal.

Much of Muslim scholarship concerning the nature of revelation has only considered the process of revelation from God to the Prophet Muhammad. There has been little emphasis on the socio-historical context in which revelation occurred or on the role of the Prophet Muhammad in the revelatory process. The dominant Muslim view has been that the Prophet was a passive receiver, and that the revelation had no connection to the socio-historical context. The following, however, sets out a broader understanding of the concept of Qur'anic revelation that takes into account the role of the Prophet Muhammad and its socio-historical context, while retaining as much as possible from the traditional Muslim view.

Levels of revelation of the Qur'an

Levels of revelation of the Qur'an

God
↓
Preserved Tablet
↓
Heavens
↓
Angel Gabriel
↓
Muhammad
↓
Qur'an is received by the first Muslim community & becomes
a part of Muslims' daily lives
↓
Qur'an continues to be interpreted and applied; God continues
to provide guidance to those who are conscious of Him

It is possible to consider revelation at four different levels:

The first level is that of the Unseen (God–Preserved Tablet–Heavens–Gabriel). At this level, revelation exists beyond human understanding or comprehension.

The second level is that which is uttered in the human context. That is, God's revelation as it is spoken by the Prophet to a community that is subject to various social and historical conditions. As such, God's Word becomes a part of the norms, customs and institutions of a specific society. Through the Qur'an, God addresses both humankind, in general, and the Prophet's community specifically.

The third level of revelation relates to the text that becomes a part of the daily lives of Muslims. That is, the revelation is now both written down and performed or acted upon. It becomes a vital, living part of a community and is used in different ways from society to society. The performance and incorporation of revelation into social life can be called 'actualization'.

After the death of the Prophet, although God's revelations 'were closed', a fourth level involving two further dimensions of revelation occurred. The first is that communities of Muslims have continued to add to, and elaborate upon, the *meanings* of the Qur'anic revelation. Each subsequent community has sought to incorporate the meaning of the Qur'an into their lives. The second aspect is that, from a Qur'anic point of view, God continues to provide guidance to those who are conscious of Him and seek to implement His Word in a just and appropriate manner. Although this last aspect is not linguistic, this level is nonetheless informed by an ongoing interaction with the linguistic forms of revelation as they appear in the Qur'an and as they have been elaborated on by earlier generations of Muslims.

Summary

Some of the important points we have discussed in this chapter include:

- Muslims believe that God revealed the Qur'an in the Arabic language, through the angel Gabriel to the Prophet Muhammad.
- Muslims believe that the Prophet transmitted the Qur'an verbatim to his followers and that the Qur'an still exists in its original form today.
- The most important aspect of revelation for Muslims has been its linguistic content, rather than the Prophet's experience of revelation as such.
- The experience of reciting the Qur'an has a spiritual significance for Muslims, as it is believed to be a type of communication with God.
- A significant issue debated by Muslim theologians is whether the Qur'an is 'created' or 'uncreated'.
- In trying to understand the Qur'an, we need to take into account the Muslim belief that it is the Word of God, its socio-historical context and the way it was interpreted after the Prophet's death.

Recommended reading

John Esposito, 'Muhammad and the Qur'an: Messenger and Message', in *Islam: The Straight Path*, New York; Oxford: Oxford University Press, 1998, pages 1–31.

- In this chapter Esposito discusses Muhammad's role in the revelation of the Qur'an and in conveying its message.

Toshihiko Izutsu, 'Communicative Relation Between God and Man: Non-linguistic Communication', 'Communicative Relation Between God and Man: Linguistic Communication', in *God and Man in the Koran*, Tokyo: The Keio Institute of Cultural and Linguistic Studies, 1964, pages 142–162 and 163–215 respectively.

- In these chapters Izutsu discusses God's communication with human-kind. In the first chapter he explores concepts such as God's 'Signs', divine guidance and worship as a form of communication. In the second chapter he discusses the meanings of concepts such as God's 'Speech', revelation and prayer.

Daniel A. Madigan, 'Revelation and Inspiration', Volume 4; Matthias Radscheit, 'Word of God', Volume 5, in Jane D. McAuliffe (ed.), *Encyclopaedia of the Qur'an*, Leiden: Brill, 2001–2006, pages 437–447 and 541–548 respectively.

- These articles examine the concept of revelation and inspiration in relation to the Qur'an. They also discuss the concept of the Qur'an as the Word of God.

Ahmad von Denffer, 'The Qur'an and Revelation', in *Ulum al-Qur'an: An Introduction to the Sciences of the Qur'an*, Leicester: The Islamic Foundation, 1985, reprint 1994, pages 11–29.

- In this chapter von Denffer provides a basic introduction to the concept of the Qur'an as a divine revelation.

NOTES

1 Bukhari, *Sahih al-Bukhari*, Vols 3–4, Book 54 'The Book of the Beginning of Creation', Chap. 6, No. 3,215, narrated by A'isha, Beirut: Dar al-Kutub al-Ilmiya, 1975–1995, p. 417.

2   Cited in F.E. Peters, *A Reader on Classical Islam*, Princeton, NJ: Princeton University Press, 1994, p. 173.
3   Geoffrey Wigoder, *Encyclopedia of Judaism*, New York: MacMillan Publishing Company, 1989.
4   Wigoder, *Encyclopedia of Judaism*, p. 600.
5   Mircea Eliade, *The Encyclopedia of Religion*, New York: MacMillan Publishing Company, 1987, vol. 12, p. 360.
6   Wigoder, *Encyclopedia of Judaism*, p. 600.
7   'Tzitzit and Early Reform Judaism', *Bluethread*, copyright: Rosemarie E. Falanga, Cy H. Silver, 1997. Accessed: 9 February 2007: http://www. bluethread.com/fringeref1.htm.
8   Eliade, *The Encyclopedia of Religion*, vol. 12, p. 361.
9   Eliade, *The Encyclopedia of Religion*, vol. 12, p. 361.
10 Eliade, *The Encyclopedia of Religion*, vol. 12, p. 361.
11 Seyyed Hossein Nasr, *The Heart of Islam: Enduring Values for Humanity*, New York: HarperCollins, 2004, pp. 22–23.
12 Qur'an: 42:51.
13 Qur'an: 7:143.
14 Qur'an: 26:195.
15 Qur'an: 12:2.
16 Qur'an: 14:4.
17 Qur'an: 85:21–22: 'This is truly a glorious Qur'an, written on a preserved Tablet.'
18 John Esposito, *The Oxford Encyclopaedia of the Modern Islamic World*, New York: Oxford University Press, 1995, p. 386.
19 Qur'an: 96:1–5.
20 Bukhari, *Sahih al-Bukhari*, Vols 3–4, Book 54 'The Book of the Beginning of Creation', Chap. 6, No. 3,215, narrated by A'isha, Beirut: Dar al-Kutub al-Ilmiya, 1975–1995, p. 417.
21 Fazlur Rahman, *Major Themes of the Qur'an*, Minneapolis, MN: Bibliotheca Islamica, 1994, p. 97.
22 Fazlur Rahman, *Islam*, Chicago, IL: University of Chicago Press, 1979, pp. 30–31.
23 Toshihiko Izutsu, *God and Man in the Koran*, Tokyo: The Keio Institute of Cultural and Linguistic Studies, 1964, p. 152.
24 Abu Hamid al-Ghazali, *Ihya Ulum-id-Din*, trans. Fazul-ul-Karim, Lahore: Islamic Publications Bureau, n.d., Book One, p. 268.
25 Izutsu, *God and Man in the Koran*, p. 154.
26 Bukhari, *Sahih al-Bukhari*, Vols 7–8, Book 93 'The Book of the Oneness, Uniqueness of Allah (*Tawhid*)', No. 7,498, narrated by Abu Hurayra, Beirut: Dar al-Kutub al-Ilmiya, 1975–1995, p. 560.
27 Founded by Abu al-Hasan al-Ash'ari (d.324/935–936). The majority of Sunni Muslims follow this school of theology.
28 Founded in the first half of the second/eighth century, by Wasil ibn Ata' (d.131/748).
29 Sabine Schmidtke, 'Mu'tazila', in Jane Dammen McAuliffe (ed.), *Encyclopaedia of the Qur'an*, Leiden: E.J. Bill, 2003, vol. 3, p. 467.
30 The Traditionists were part of a movement referred to as the *Ahl al-Hadith*.

Followers of this movement placed great importance on the Qur'an and hadith, above other Islamic sources such as *qiyas*. They were also known for interpreting these two sources literally.

31 Richard C. Martin, 'Createdness of the Qur'an', p. 471 in Jane Dammen McAuliffe (ed.), *Encyclopaedia of the Qur'an*, vol. 1, pp. 467–472.
32 Qur'an: 10:37–38. Verses such as this will be discussed in greater detail in Chapter 3 – The Qur'an as Scripture – in relation to the Qur'an's inimitability.
33 Qur'an: 4:82.
34 Rahman, *Major Themes of the Qur'an*, p. 91.
35 Qur'an: 75:16–19.
36 Izutsu, *God and Man in the Koran*, p. 152.
37 Qur'an: 96:1–5.
38 Qur'an: 20:133; 53:36; 87:18; 87:19.
39 Qur'an: 7:145; 7:150; 7:154.
40 Qur'an: 37:117.
41 Qur'an: 19:30.
42 Qur'an: 57:26.
43 Rahman, *Major Themes of the Qur'an*; Nasr Hamid Abu Zayd, *al-Nass wa al-sulta wa al-haqiqa*, Dar al-Bayda': al-Markaz al-Thaqafi al-Arabi, 2000; Farid Esack, *Qur'an, Liberation and Pluralism*, Oxford: Oneworld Publications, 1997; Fazlur Rahman (ed. with an introduction by Ebrahim Moosa), *Revival and Reform in Islam*, Oxford: Oneworld, 2000.
44 Rahman, *Islam*, p. 31.
45 Rahman, *Major Themes of the Qur'an*, p. 89.

3

The Qur'an
as scripture

'QUR'AN' IS AN ARABIC TERM WHICH MEANS 'recitation' or 'reading'. It comes from the Arabic root *q-r-'*,[1] which is also the root of the first word that the Prophet Muhammad received as revelation, *iqra'*, meaning 'recite' or 'read'. Muhammad's role as a prophet began when he was commanded to 'recite'. Although the Qur'an uses a range of names to refer to itself, the name 'Qur'an' has become the most common one for the holy scripture of Islam. Other names used by the Qur'an to refer to itself include the Revelation (*tanzil*), the Reminder (*dhikr*), the Criterion (*furqan*) and the Scripture (*kitab*). The Qur'an also attributes a number of characteristics to itself such as Noble (as in the commonly cited phrase 'the Noble Qur'an'), Clear, Glorious and Blessed.

There are several Qur'anic verses which indicate that during the time of the Prophet, the Qur'an came to be conceived of as 'scripture', despite the fact that it had not yet been compiled into a written book. As shown above, the Qur'an often refers to itself as the Book or Scripture (*kitab*). For instance, the Qur'an says, 'God has sent down the Scripture and Wisdom to you, and taught you what you did not know';[2] and 'Now We have sent down to you [people] a Scripture to remind you.'[3] In fact, the Qur'an uses *kitab* to refer to itself more than 70 times in various contexts, indicating that the concept of the Qur'an as a book, or scripture, was well established before the Prophet's death.[4] However, it was not until the time of the third caliph of Islam, Uthman ibn Affan (d.35/656), that the Qur'an was compiled as a book. Muslim tradition also holds that it was Abu Bakr, the first caliph, who initially ordered compilation of the Qur'an and Uthman simply relied on the compilation of Abu Bakr.

In this chapter we will discuss:

- the way in which the Qur'an is structured;
- some views of Muslims and certain Western scholars about the compilation of the Qur'an as a written text;
- the evolution of the Qur'anic script;
- Muslim understandings of the Qur'an's inimitability; and
- other important texts in the Islamic tradition.

Structure of the Qur'an

The Qur'an is made up of 114 chapters (*suras*) of varying lengths. Each chapter comprises a number of verses (*ayas*), the length of which also varies significantly. Some verses may consist of several sentences, while others may only be a short phrase or, in some cases, a single word. For example, '*al-Rahman*'[5] (the Lord of Mercy) is the first verse of a chapter by the same name. In Arabic, it is written as one word. By contrast, verse 282 of chapter 2 (the Cow) is longer than many of the shorter chapters of the Qur'an. In English translation, this verse is over 300 words long. It contains a lengthy discussion of commercial transactions and the requirements for writing a contract between the parties involved.

With the exception of the first chapter, *al-Fatiha* (the Opening), the Qur'an is generally organized according to the length of its chapters. The first chapter is in the form of a prayer, which is seven verses long and is recited several times by Muslims in their daily prayers (*salat*). In addition to *al-Fatiha*, a Muslim is expected to recite a few other verses of the Qur'an during prayer. Although not all verses are in the form of prayers – for instance, some are historical, and others are ethical or legal in nature – any part of the Qur'an can be recited during prayer.

Chapter 1 of the Qur'an: al-Fatiha (the Opening)

In the name of God, the Lord of Mercy, the Giver of Mercy! Praise belongs to God, Lord of the Worlds, the Lord of Mercy, the Giver of Mercy, Master of the Day of Judgment. It is You we worship; it is You we ask for help. Guide us to the straight path: the path of those You have blessed, those who incur no anger and who have not gone astray.

Starting with the second chapter, *al-Baqara* (the Cow), which is the longest and comprises 286 verses, the chapters of the Qur'an gradually become shorter. Thus, the shortest chapters, 110, 108 and 103, all appear towards the end of the Qur'an and comprise only three verses each.

Some chapters of the Qur'an

The following table gives an overview of selected chapters of the Qur'an. The first column refers to the position of the chapter in the order according to the standard numbering of the Qur'an. The number of verses is shown, and the location where the chapter was revealed is provided.

No.	*Sura* name	Translation	Number of verses	Location of revelation
1	*al-Fatiha*	the Opening	7	Mecca
2	*al-Baqara*	the Cow	286	Medina

No.	*Sura* name	Translation	Number of verses	Location of revelation
3	*Al Imran*	the Family of Imran	200	Medina
4	*al-Nisa'*	Women	176	Medina
14	*Ibrahim*	Abraham	52	Mecca
19	*Maryam*	Mary	98	Mecca
24	*al-Nur*	Light	64	Medina
30	*al-Rum*	the Byzantines	60	Mecca
40	*Ghafir*	the Forgiver	85	Mecca
41	*Fussilat*	(Verses) Made Distinct	54	Mecca
42	*al-Shura*	Consultation	53	Mecca
53	*al-Najm*	the Star	62	Mecca
55	*al-Rahman*	the Most Beneficent	78	Medina
67	*al-Mulk*	Sovereignty	30	Mecca
68	*al-Qalam*	the Pen	52	Mecca
71	*Nuh*	Noah	28	Mecca
91	*al-Shams*	the Sun	15	Mecca
92	*al-Layl*	the Night	21	Mecca
113	*al-Falaq*	the Daybreak	5	Mecca
114	*al-Nas*	Humankind	6	Mecca

An example of a short chapter of the Qur'an

97. *Laylat al-Qadr* (the Night of Glory)

This Meccan *sura* celebrates the night when the Qur'an was first revealed.

In the name of God, the Lord of Mercy, the Giver of Mercy

We sent it down on the Night of Glory. What will explain to you what that Night of Glory is? The Night of Glory is better than a thousand months; on that night the angels and the Spirit descend again and again with their Lord's permission on every task; [there is] peace that night until the break of dawn.

Each chapter of the Qur'an has a very short name – in most cases, only one word – which Muslim scholars generally agree was assigned by the Prophet Muhammad under divine instruction. In many cases, this name refers to an issue, event or person found or mentioned in the chapter. 'The Cow' referred to in the name of chapter 2 (*al-Baqara*) appears in connection with a story of the Prophet Moses and the Israelites. This story relates the response of the Israelites to God's command to sacrifice a cow. The name 'Cow' appears to have been chosen because of the significance of the story rather than its length, as the story comprises only seven out of the 286 verses in the chapter.[6] Although this story is not mentioned elsewhere in the chapter, the theme of disobedience to God's commandments, to which the story relates, is touched on repeatedly.

The story of the Cow, from chapter 2: *al-Baqara* (the Cow)

Remember when Moses said to his people, 'God commands you to sacrifice a cow.' They said, 'Are you making fun of us?' He answered, 'God forbid that I should be so ignorant.' They said, 'Call on your Lord for us, to show us what sort of cow it should be.' He answered, 'God says it should neither be too old nor too young, but in between, so do as you are commanded.' They said, 'Call on your Lord for us, to show us what colour it should be.' He answered, 'God says it should be a bright yellow cow, pleasing to the eye.' They said, 'Call on your Lord for us, to show us [exactly] what it is: all cows are more or less alike to us. With God's will, we shall be guided.' He replied, 'It is a perfect and unblemished cow, not trained to till the earth or water the fields.' They said 'Now you have brought the truth,' and so they slaughtered it, though they almost failed to do so. (Qur'an 2:67–73)

At other times, the chapter's name may simply be a prominent word found in the chapter, in some cases the first word of the chapter, which may not be related to a particular narrative. For instance, the title of the thirty-sixth chapter, *Ya'-Sin*, comes from the two Arabic letters *ya'* and *sin*, with which that chapter begins. Several chapters begin with such combinations of letters, which Muslim commentators believe to have a hidden meaning.

Examples of chapters of the Qur'an which begin with combinations of Arabic letters

Twenty-nine chapters of the Qur'an begin with a combination of Arabic letters. The letters are part of the Arabic alphabet, and have no specific meaning by themselves. The following are examples of such chapters:

No.	Sura name	Translation	Beginning letters
2	al-Baqara	the Cow	Alif Lam Mim
3	Al Imran	the Family of Imran	Alif Lam Mim
7	al-A'raf	the Heights	Alif Lam Mim Sad
10	Yunus	Jonah	Alif Lam Ra'
11	Hud	Hud	Alif Lam Ra'
12	Yusuf	Joseph	Alif Lam Ra'
13	al-Ra'd	Thunder	Alif Lam Mim Ra'
14	Ibrahim	Abraham	Alif Lam Ra'
15	al-Hijr	al-Hijr (Stone City)	Alif Lam Ra'
19	Maryam	Mary	Kaf Ha' Ya' Ain Sad
20	Ta Ha	(the Letters) Ta' Ha'	Ta' Ha'
26	al-Shu'ara'	the Poets	Ta' Sin Mim
27	al-Naml	the Ants	Ta' Sin
28	al-Qasas	the Stories	Ta' Sin Mim

Compiling the Qur'an as a single text: the Muslim view

Muslims believe that while the Qur'an was being revealed between 610 and 632 CE, the Prophet reportedly instructed his followers to memorize the verses as they were revealed and also to write them down. However, there was not yet an urgent need to compile them into a single book; the Arab society of the time had a strong oral tradition, and many relied on memory and narration to preserve the most important texts of the culture, such as poetry. The Qur'an, although it is not poetry, had some elements of the poetic style and it was considered a text of very high literary quality. Muslim tradition holds that it was the literary beauty of the Qur'an which initially attracted many people to Islam during the time of the Prophet.

In keeping with this oral tradition, the Prophet and the first Muslim community would often recite parts of the revelation both publicly and in private throughout the 22 years of revelation. From the year 620 CE, once the five daily prayers had been made a religious obligation, Qur'anic verses would also be recited regularly during these prayers. Similarly, all the revelations the Prophet had received up to the beginning of the month of Ramadan (the month of fasting) each year would also be recited during that month, helping to preserve the text in the memory of the community.

Although the Qur'an was not compiled as a single volume before the death of the Prophet, Muslim tradition holds that most, if not all, verses had in fact been written down on a variety of different materials by the time of the Prophet's death in 11/632. It is believed that the Prophet left clear instructions as to how the Qur'an should be organized and read as a single text. These instructions are understood to be the basis of the Qur'an's order as it exists today.

Muslim tradition holds that Abu Bakr (r.11–13/632–634), who reigned briefly as the first caliph, instructed Zayd ibn Thabit (d.45/665), one of the Prophet's foremost scribes of the Qur'an, to compile the text of the Qur'an as a single book. Zayd was assisted by a committee made up of other Companions of the Prophet. This instruction was apparently given in response to the deaths in battle of many Muslims who had retained the Qur'an in their memory. If a large number of these Muslims were to die, there was a danger that parts of the Qur'an could be lost, or disputes could emerge about their authenticity. It is reported that the complete, written text, as it was compiled during Abu Bakr's reign, remained with him until his death. The text was then left in the care of the second caliph, Umar ibn al-Khattab (r.13–23/634–644), and then entrusted to Umar's daughter Hafsa (d.45/666), a wife of the Prophet.

While the sources indicate that the texts of the Qur'an had already been gathered together in some form during the time of Abu Bakr, it was the third caliph, Uthman (r.23–35/644–656), who saw the need to establish a standardized text that could be disseminated widely. The need for a standardized text was based on advice received by Uthman that disputes about the Qur'an and its recitations were emerging throughout the newly expanding Muslim caliphate.[7] Thus, Uthman instructed Zayd and several other Companions to use the first collection of the Qur'an, along with other reliable sources, to compile a single authoritative text. Due to the existence of variant readings, Uthman instructed Zayd and his committee to favour the Quraysh dialect of Arabic (of Mecca) in instances where the reading of a particular text was disputed. This was based on the fact that the Prophet himself was from the tribe of Quraysh, and the Qur'an was revealed in this dialect. The Qur'an says: 'We [God] have never sent a messenger who did not use his people's own language to make things clear for them.'[8]

After Zayd had collected the verses of the Qur'an and checked them with other Companions, copies were made of the final text, which were sent to the provincial centres of the caliphate, such as Damascus, Basra and Kufa, in about 24/645. Uthman then instructed his governors to destroy all other texts of the Qur'an circulating in their provinces, and to establish the codex that was sent to them as the single authoritative text of the Qur'an. In so doing, Uthman unified Muslims around a single text. Today, this text, known as 'the Mushaf of Uthman' (the Uthmanic Codex), is the authoritative text of the Qur'an for all Muslims. In the post-Uthmanic period the Qur'an came to be known not only in its oral form (as it existed at the time of the Prophet) but also as a written codex (*mushaf*) or 'closed official corpus'[9] to which nothing could be added.

In discussing the difference between the Qur'an as an idea at the time of the Prophet and as a standardized codex in the post-prophetic period, William Graham, a scholar of Middle Eastern studies, says:

> It is obvious that 'al-Qur'an' in the later, fixed meaning of God's Word as written down in the *masahif* [plural of *mushaf*] is necessarily a post-Uthmatic, or at the very least a post-Muhammadan, usage. Until the codification of what has since served as the *textus receptus* – or at least until active revelation ceased with Muhammad's death – there could have been no use of 'al-Qur'an' to refer to the complete body of 'collected revelations in written form'. This is not to deny that even in the Qur'an there may be hints of a developing notion of the collective revelation in the use of the words *qur'an* and *kitab*, but rather to emphasize the fallacy involved in 'reading back' the later, concretized meaning of these terms into all of their Qur'anic or other traditional-text occurrences.[10]

Although this view is not considered controversial by most Muslims, it should be noted that it is easy to fall into the trap to which Graham refers in this quote; namely that of understanding the words 'Qur'an' and '*kitab*', as they were used during the time of the Prophet, as referring to a completed and written text during the time of the Prophet. For this reason, the use of terminology is important in any debate about the Qur'an. Use of the word '*qur'an*' during the time of the Prophet should be understood as a reference to the ongoing revelations that were being received and were in fact evolving. Only in the post-Uthmanic period can it also be understood as a physical *mushaf* or codified text.

Important dates of the Qur'an according to Muslim tradition

610:        First verses of the Qur'an revealed.

620:        Five daily prayers are made obligatory and the Prophet experiences his Night Journey to Jerusalem and Ascension to Heaven.

2/624:   Verses revealed which make *zakat* (giving in charity) and fasting in Ramadan compulsory and which change the direction of prayer to Mecca.

3/625:   Verses revealed which prohibit drinking wine.

9/631:   Verses revealed which make Hajj obligatory, and prohibit riba (understood to mean usury or interest).

11/632:   The final Qur'anic revelation occurs, the Prophet Muhammad dies and Abu Bakr becomes the caliph.

11/633:   The first collection of the Qur'an is completed under Abu Bakr.

13/634:   Abu Bakr dies and Umar ibn al-Khattab becomes the caliph;

            Umar is entrusted with the collected texts of the Qur'an which he later entrusts to his daughter Hafsa.

23/644:   Umar dies and Uthman ibn Affan becomes the caliph.

24/645:   Uthman commissions Zayd and his committee to create an official codex of the Qur'an to be circulated through the Muslim provinces.

            The Uthmanic Codex is finalized and disseminated throughout the Muslim lands; any variants are destroyed.

35/656:   Uthman dies and Ali ibn Abi Talib (Muhammad's son-in-law) becomes the caliph.

Although the vast majority of Muslims today from both the Sunni and Shi'i[11] streams of Islam accept this codex, some early Shi'a Muslims disputed the traditional account of its compilation. Some early Shi'a believed that Ali ibn Abi Talib, the Prophet's son-in-law and one of the most revered figures in Shi'ism, transcribed the Qur'an as a single text in the days following the death of the Prophet. This text was said to include not only the text of the Qur'an in chronological order, but also commentary and interpretation by the Prophet, as well as the Prophet's clarifications about which verses of the Qur'an had abrogated others, which were to be understood as 'clear' and which were to be seen as 'ambiguous'.[12] Unfortunately, there is no evidence to suggest that any copies of this reported text of Ali are still in existence.

Muslim tradition holds that the codex compiled during the caliphate of Uthman was accurate and uncorrupted, since it was compiled within a short period after the Prophet's death and in the presence of those who had witnessed the revelation.

Although the Uthmanic Codex is considered accurate, there is some question as to whether it includes everything that was revealed to the Prophet. In fact, some argue that the Qur'an itself points to the possibility that some verses might have been excluded during the Prophet's lifetime. For instance, verse 2:106 says: 'Any revelation We cause to be superseded or forgotten, We replace with something better or similar. Do you [Prophet] not know that God has power over everything?'[13] Some Muslim scholars argue, based on this verse, that certain verses may have been 'abrogated' and erased from the Qur'an altogether by God, or by the Prophet on divine instruction. Even if this were the case, Muslim scholars on the whole reject the notion that the compilers of the Qur'an themselves may have discarded any parts of the revealed text. The early exegete Zamakhshari (d.539/1144) summarizes the general Muslim understanding of abrogation as follows, in his interpretation of verse 2:106:

> To abrogate a verse means that God removes (*azala*) it by putting another in its place. To cause a verse to be abrogated means that God gives the command that it be abrogated; that is, He commands Gabriel to set forth the verse as abrogated by announcing its cancellation. Deferring a verse means that God sets it aside (with the proclamation) and causes it to disappear without a substitute. To cause a verse to be cast into oblivion means that it no longer is preserved in the heart. The following is the meaning [of the verse 2:106]: Every verse is made to vanish whenever the well-being (*maslaha*) (of the community) requires that it be eliminated – either on the basis of the wording or the virtue of what is right, or on the basis of both of these reasons together, either with or without a substitute.[14]

Thus, from a Muslim perspective, the codex of Uthman represents the historical and authentic codification of the revelation to the Prophet Muhammad. Any texts that God may have caused to be superseded or forgotten, or the variant readings which were omitted in the attempt to unify Muslims on one text by Uthman, are not considered as being an essential part of the codified text. As such, this codification has become the basis of Islamic teachings and practices, and the many developments in understanding and interpretation of the Qur'an throughout history. For many Muslims, to question its authenticity and reliability amounts to questioning Islam itself.

Challenges by Western scholars of the Qur'an

A number of Western scholars have criticized the traditional Muslim view of the history of the Qur'an. They include Richard Bell, whose ideas were, to some extent, taken up by other scholars, such as Montgomery Watt. Bell questioned the validity of aspects of the traditional Muslim view, arguing that some Muslim sources include contradictory statements about whether it was Abu Bakr, Umar or Uthman who initiated the task of collecting the Qur'an. He also had doubts about the supposed reasons for initiating the collection of the Qur'an, questioning the truth of reports that a large number of those who memorized the Qur'an were killed in battle. He further suggested that if it were true that the first collection of the Qur'an was, in fact, initiated by Abu Bakr, it was obviously not accorded much authority, as Uthman apparently made a fresh collection only a few years later. Bell's view is that any collection made during Abu Bakr's time was probably only partial and unofficial.

While positions such as Bell's do not question Muslim tradition regarding the collection of the Qur'an in its entirety, other Western scholars have attempted to revisit fundamental aspects of this tradition. Many have argued that the Qur'an was an evolving text, the content of which may not have been fixed, in either oral or written form, until well after the Prophet's death. This position clearly contradicts key aspects of Islamic tradition regarding the Qur'an. Some scholars have also argued that much of the Islamic tradition and literature on issues related to the collection of the Qur'an was fabricated during the second century of Islam. The British scholar John Wansbrough was one of the foremost proponents of this approach. His main ideas are found in his work, *Quranic Studies: Sources and Methods of Scriptural Interpretation*, which has influenced numerous scholars in the West.

One of the most controversial aspects of Wansbrough's work was that he approached the Qur'an as a literary work, in the tradition of the Hebrew and Christian scriptures, and regarded it as a purely man-made product. Wansbrough made a number of 'conjectural' proposals, as he called them, among them that Islam could be more accurately defined as a sect which grew out of the Judaeo-Christian tradition during a period of fierce debate between existing Jewish and Christian groups. He suggested that during this time, Arab tribes adapted Judaeo-Christian texts to their own cultures, eventually developing their own 'Islamic' scriptures over the first/seventh and second/eighth centuries.[15] This argument was supported by Wansbrough's assertion that no textual evidence existed regarding the concept of 'Islam', or the collection of the Qur'an as a text, until 150 years after the Prophet's death.[16]

Wansbrough's use of methods of biblical criticism led him to conclude that the Islamic tradition is a 'salvation history' – a term used in biblical studies to describe a theologically and evangelically motivated myth related to a religion's origins that is projected back in time.[17] However, his main aim was not to identify why the Qur'an was compiled. Rather, Wansbrough's focus was on determining how and when the Qur'an came to be accepted and canonized as 'scripture'; something he believed did not occur until the Umayyad caliphate, over 100 years after the Prophet's death.[18]

Wansbrough's work inspired other scholars in the revisionist tradition, such as Michael Cook and Patricia Crone, who attempted to reconstruct the history of the origins of Islam. In *Hagarism: The Making of the Islamic World*,[19] Cook and Crone proposed that Islam was actually a messianic Arab movement allied with Judaism, which attempted to reclaim Syria and the Holy Land from the Byzantine empire. Wansbrough himself was critical of the book's methodological assumptions, and the authors themselves have since moved away from some of their initial theories.

According to a British scholar, Gerald Hawting, Wansbrough was mainly concerned to separate the link typically made between the Qur'an and the life of the Prophet Muhammad, who he believed to be merely an idea created by the Islamic tradition, just as some biblical scholars believe Jesus to be a product of Christianity.[20] Hawting suggests that many scholars do not approach Islam seriously – instead of examining the religion with academic rigour, many refrain from questioning issues such as the origins of the Qur'an, possibly out of a desire not to offend Muslims. In contrast, he argues that Wansbrough took Islam seriously by subjecting the Qur'an to the same critical historical analysis used in the study of Christian and Jewish texts.

However, for many Muslims, the views of scholars like Wansbrough are highly controversial and, indeed, unpalatable. An example of the Muslim response to this scholarship is the work of Muhammad Azami, who, in his work *The History of the Qur'anic Text from Revelation to Compilation*,[21] attempts to defend the historical reliability of the Qur'an. Azami cites traditional Muslim sources in arguing that approximately 65 Companions served as scribes for the Prophet for varying periods, and were reported to have written down entire sections of the Qur'an before the Prophet's death.[22] He also suggests that written documents were, in fact, already part of early Muslim culture, and that many Companions reportedly had their own records of parts of the Qur'an.[23] Azami argues that, based on available records, the only variations of Qur'anic verses known at the time were minor and did not alter the meaning of the texts. For instance, minor variations in vowels sometimes occurred, or there was a shift from the second person to the third person, with little or no impact on meaning.[24]

A criticism of this traditional response is that many of these arguments are circular. While revisionist Western scholars like Wansbrough have questioned the very authenticity of the Qur'an and the traditions concerning its collection and compilation, Azami's counter-arguments are based almost entirely on these traditions and the Qur'an itself. As a scholar of hadith, he seems to rely on an authentication of these traditions, using the traditional approach to hadith criticism, which a number of Western scholars have also rejected.

However, other scholars of the Qur'an, including some Western scholars, have cited debates among Muslim communities from the first/seventh century about the content of the Qur'an as evidence of the Qur'an's early compilation. For example, it is reported that during this time the Kharijis rejected the twelfth chapter of the Qur'an, and that some early Shi'a accused the official compilers of excluding certain verses, which supported their views, from the complete official text.[25] Other scholars, such as John Burton, have also argued that the Prophet himself had 'sanctioned' a complete 'edition' of the Qur'an by the time of his death.[26]

An American scholar, Estelle Whelan, has also criticized aspects of Wansbrough's analysis for assuming that the Qur'an's compilation followed a similar path to that of Hebrew scripture.[27] Whelan refers to evidence of Qur'anic inscriptions at the Dome of the Rock, in Jerusalem, that date from around 65–86/685–705, only half a century after the Prophet's death. Some of the most prominent inscriptions appear to be drawn from Qur'anic verses. While most match the standard Uthmanic Codex, some appear to contain slight modifications, and at one point two verses are conflated.[28]

Whelan argues that the best explanation for the modifications is that they were introduced to allow the inscription to flow as a single text. She comments that although there were 'efforts to establish and preserve a standard version [of the Qur'an] . . . there has [also] been a tradition of drawing upon and modifying that text for a variety of rhetorical purposes.'[29] This practice was 'dependent upon recognition of the text by the listeners, or readers'.[30] This implies that for creative use of Qur'anic texts to have occurred, they must already have been the 'common property of the community'.[31] Further, had the codex still been undergoing revision at this early stage, it is difficult to believe that the variations in such a prominent inscription would not have influenced the final version.[32]

Other evidence cited by Whelan includes Qur'anic inscriptions from the Prophet's mosque, in Medina, that seem to indicate that the order of at least chapters 91–114 had been established by the end of the first/seventh century.[33] She also cites evidence from a number of sources about the existence of professional Qur'an copyists in Medina at a similar time, which indicates a demand for copies of an established text.[34] Further discussion of Western scholarship on the Qur'an can be found in Chapter 6.

Evolution of the script of the Qur'an and its presentation

The earliest copies of the Qur'an were written in what is referred to as 'Uthmanic orthography' (al-rasm al-uthmani). Uthman's committee for the compilation of the Qur'an, led by Zayd, wrote the first complete codex of the Qur'an using this orthography. The original manuscript of the Uthmanic Codex was written in an early Arabic script, known as Hijazi. In its first/seventh-century form, this script did not mark any vowels and it was difficult to differentiate between certain consonants. For example, the Arabic letters ba', ta' and tha' could only be distinguished from one another based on their context, as the letters themselves were written in exactly the same way. Although this may seem problematic, it is unlikely that these features caused difficulties for the first generation of Muslims, who were predominantly Arabic-speaking and had a reasonable knowledge of the Qur'an.

However, as the number of non-Arabic-speaking Muslims began to grow, reliance on this basic script became increasingly difficult. Consequently, from the end of the first/seventh through to the third/ninth centuries, continual improvements were made to the script in order to facilitate reading of the Qur'an by both Arab and non-Arab Muslims. These changes to the script also came about because of the interest of early caliphs in 'Arabizing' the bureaucracy of the Muslim state, particularly under the Umayyad caliphate. In order to achieve this, it was necessary to develop a more efficient and readable script for use in official documentation and correspondence. As the script was improved, reading of the Qur'an also became easier.

Improvements to the Arabic script included the addition of dots to differentiate between certain consonants with the same basic form, and the addition of short and long vowels.[35] Other improvements specific to the Qur'an included signs to indicate the end of a verse, parts of a sentence where reciters might pause, and parts where they should continue in order to avoid reading a partial section which may convey an incorrect meaning.

Given that Arabic words without vowel markings can be read in a number of different ways, their inclusion helped greatly to guide readers of the Qur'an who were unfamiliar with the text in its oral form, or were not Arabic speakers. Copies of the Qur'an published today contain full vowel markings in order to allow both Arabic and non-Arabic speakers to read the Qur'an with greater ease. Many printed copies also contain recitation marks, as described above. Because vowel and recitation markings are not necessary for comprehension, they are not found in other modern Arabic texts, such as newspapers or books.

Despite all these improvements, the underlying form of the original Uthmanic orthography of the Qur'an has not been altered significantly. This fact reflects the desire of early Muslims to retain the original wording and script of the Qur'an. This desire has persisted until modern times and, in the early twentieth century, attempts to transcribe the Qur'an using scripts such as the Latin alphabet were vigorously opposed by Muslim scholars, who argued that this might lead to distortion of the Qur'anic text.

For ease of reference, modern copies of the Qur'an also include verse numbers. Unlike the numbering of chapters, which is fixed, there is more than one method for numbering the verses, although the actual text remains the same. Hence, the total number of Qur'anic verses may range from 6,212 to 6,250, depending on the system used. The reasons for such differences are varied. Richard Bell and Montgomery Watt have suggested that the 'varying systems of verse-numbering depend to some extent, though not entirely, upon varying judgement as to where the rhyme was intended to fall in particular cases.'[36] In other cases, the reasons for differences are more straightforward. For instance, some Indo-Pakistani systems count the *basmala* phrase (which reads 'In the name of God, the Lord of Mercy, the Giver of Mercy', and is found at the beginning of every chapter except chapter 9, *al-Tawba*, Repentance) as part of the number of verses. Most other numbering systems around the world only include this phrase as part of the first chapter (the Opening or *al-Fatiha*), while some do not include it at all. Other variations are less predictable, as in one Indian system that divides verse 6:73 into two, while it combines verses 36:34–35 into one.[37]

The Egyptian numbering system, first introduced under King Fu'ad and originally published in 1925,[38] has become the standard used throughout most of the Muslim world today. However, other variations, such as those mentioned above, are still in circulation.[39] One of the better-known variations in the West was devised by the German Orientalist Gustav Flügel in 1834. Flügel is believed to have created his numbering system based on his reading of the rhyming endings of phrases in the Qur'an. However, it does not correlate exactly with any known Muslim tradition. Despite this, his system has served as the basis for many European translations and other works on the Qur'an.[40]

The final method of partitioning the Qur'an to be discussed here is based on the common Muslim practice of reciting the full text of the Qur'an over 30 days during the month of Ramadan. This division involves separating the Qur'an into 30 parts, of roughly equal length, each known as a *juz'* (part). Each *juz'* is named after the first word or phrase that appears in it. The first *juz'* is a slight exception to this rule, as it is named *alif lam mim* after the three-letter beginning of chapter 2, rather than the first chapter with which it begins.

The nature of the Qur'anic text: the idea of inimitability

For Muslims, the Qur'an is considered the most perfect expression of the Arabic language; a unique piece of writing that is comparable to no other and which, as the Qur'an itself states, can be matched by no human composition.[41] This aspect of the Qur'an, referred to generally as its 'inimitability' (*i'jaz al-qur'an*), has been the subject of major works by Muslim linguists, interpreters of the Qur'an and literary critics.

The idea of the Qur'an's inimitability is supported by a number of Qur'anic verses,[42] which challenged the Prophet Muhammad's opponents in Mecca to produce a literary compilation similar to the Qur'an. These challenges came in response to accusations by the Prophet's opponents that the Qur'an was composed by the Prophet himself rather than God. In one such challenge, the Qur'an states, 'Say: "Even if all humankind and *jinn*[43] came together to produce something like this Qur'an, they could not produce anything like it, however much they helped each other".'[44] In other places it explicitly challenges people to produce ten chapters like it, saying: 'If they say, "He [Muhammad] has invented it [the Qur'an] himself," say, "Then produce ten invented *suras* like it, and call in whoever you can beside God, if you are truthful".'[45] As the Meccans continually failed to meet this challenge, it was later reduced to producing just one chapter like the Qur'an.[46] According to Muslim tradition, the Qur'an's inimitability is supported by the fact that no Meccan was ever able to meet this challenge, despite their general reputation as masters of Arabic expression.

Another important idea associated with the inimitability of the Qur'an is the belief that the Prophet Muhammad was illiterate, and thus incapable of producing a work as eloquent as the Qur'an by his own efforts. Some suggest that the Prophet's illiteracy is supported by at least two Qur'anic verses,[47] but the meaning of the word translated as 'illiterate' (*ummiy*) was often debated by early Muslims. Although it can mean illiterate, *ummiy* can also be translated as 'gentile', reflecting the fact that the Prophet was an Arab, not a Jew. Some Muslim scholars believed that the Prophet was able to read and write, though not proficiently.[48]

Muslim views regarding the basis for the Qur'an's inimitability vary considerably. Some suggest that the impossibility of producing anything like the Qur'an is because God prevented anyone from doing so. The majority of Muslims, however, believe it is because of the Qur'an's unique style and content. This argument is generally related to the presumably unsurpassable eloquence and unique style of the Qur'an. The content of the Qur'an, particularly its inclusion of historical information about earlier prophets and their communities that would have been impossible for any person of the Prophet's period to know, is also seen as evidence of the Qur'an's inimitability, as is the apparent lack of contradictions found in the text.

In recent years, some Muslims have also approached the Qur'an's inimitability from a mathematical perspective. One view claims that certain permutations of the number 19 can be found in the words and phrases of the Qur'an. For instance, a number of key phrases in the Qur'an are said to contain 19 letters, or appear 19 times, or a multiple thereof.[49] The recurrence of the number 19 and its multiples is said to be evidence of God's handiwork. It is argued that, without access to computers, the Prophet could not have independently composed a work of the Qur'an's significance, while inserting such a numerical pattern into the text.

A number of modern theorists cite scientific 'facts' found in the Qur'an that were not discovered until the modern era as a basis of this inimitability. For example, proponents of this theory claim that the following verse refers to the Big Bang: 'Are the disbelievers not aware that the heavens and the earth used to be joined together and that We ripped them apart, that We made every living thing from water?'[50] This so-called scientific inimitability of the Qur'an has been a source of much debate in the modern period.

These two approaches, the 'mathematical' and 'scientific', are indicative of some of the new ways that Muslims today are attempting to demonstrate the 'truth' of the Qur'an. These approaches have a certain level of popular appeal.

Connection between the Qur'an and the traditions of the Prophet

The Qur'an occupies a central place in Islam's textual tradition, but it is not the only source from which Islamic laws, principles and traditions are drawn.

The second most important textual source of Islam is hadith. Hadith refers to the reports by the Prophet's contemporaries about the Prophet's speech and conduct. These hadith were initially narrated informally, before being collected and compiled by hadith scholars. Hadith are considered to be a crucial part of the Islamic textual tradition, as a result of the importance of the relationship between the Qur'an and the normative behaviour of the Prophet (which is referred to as his sunna). As we will see later, the Qur'an itself provides relatively few explicit instructions about how to live as a Muslim, that is, in submission to God. A large number of the Qur'an's ethical teachings are expressed in general terms and were only put into practice by early Muslims after they were given a practical interpretation by the Prophet. Thus, the Prophet is often referred to in Muslim tradition as the 'walking Qur'an', and his sunna, or his ways of doing things, was regarded as a practical commentary on the Qur'an. Adherence to the sunna constitutes the practical element of what it means to be a Muslim. A Muslim's knowledge of the Prophet's sunna comes from the hadith.

There are two components to a hadith: its *matn* or textual content, and its *sanad* or chain of transmission. An important field of study in Islamic scholarship is the analysis of hadith and their chains of transmission. In the first two centuries of Islam a large number of hadith of questionable origin were in circulation. In response to this situation, scholarly efforts were made to collect and evaluate all available hadith according to several criteria. These criteria related either to the reliability of the narrators of hadith, or the internal consistency of their textual content. One of the most important and reliable narrators of hadith was the Prophet's wife, A'isha.

Two of the most important collections of hadith were made in the third/ninth century by Bukhari (d.256/870) and Muslim ibn Hajjaj (d.261/875). Bukhari's hadith collection, called *Sahih* (meaning 'The Authentic'), is considered by Sunni Muslims to be the most authentic collection. Bukhari is said to have considered over 600,000 hadith circulating during his time. After stringent analysis, only about 7,000 of the 'soundest' narrations were eventually included in his collection. Sunnis also consider the multi-volume hadith collection by Muslim, also called *Sahih*, to be highly accurate. Other, less reliable hadith collections also exist, and Shi'a Muslims also have their own collections of hadith.

Despite the stringency of the hadith collectors' methods, questions still remain about the authenticity of many hadith. In particular, the authenticity of hadith which seem to contradict core Islamic teachings, such as those which support sectarian or misogynistic views, is now being questioned. Some Western scholars, such as Joseph Schacht, have questioned the authenticity of the entire corpus of hadith.[51] Many Muslim scholars today, while rejecting the idea that all hadith are fabrications, have also called for a re-examination of the hadith literature in the light of new methods of textual analysis and criticism.

An example of a hadith related to the Qur'anic injunction to pray is as follows:

> A man entered the mosque and started praying while the Messenger of God was sitting somewhere in the mosque. Then (after finishing the prayer) the man came to the Prophet and greeted him. The Prophet said to him, 'Go back and pray, for you have not prayed.' The man went back, and having prayed, he came and greeted the Prophet. The Prophet after returning his greetings said, 'Go back and pray, for you did not pray.' On the third time the man said, '(O Messenger of God!) teach me (how to pray).' The Prophet said, 'When you get up for the prayer, perform the ablution properly and then face the Qibla [direction of prayer] and say "God is the Greatest", and then recite of what you know of the Qur'an, and then bow, and remain in this state till you feel at rest in bowing, and then raise your head and stand straight; and then prostrate till you feel at rest in prostration, and then sit up till you feel at rest while sitting; and then prostrate again till you feel at rest in prostration; and then get up and stand straight, and do all this in all your prayers.'[52]

This hadith provides details about how the Prophet actually prayed. The injunction to pray is repeated several times in the Qur'an, as in the following verse: 'Keep up the prayer, pay the prescribed alms, and bow your head [in worship] with those who bow theirs.'[53] But the Qur'an does not provide any details as to how a Muslim should perform the prayer. These practical details are found in hadith. Hence, the hadith form a critical part of the development of Islamic practice and are also highly relevant to the practice of Qur'anic interpretation.

Summary

Some of the important points we have discussed in this chapter include:

- The word Qur'an means 'recitation' or 'reading'.
- According to Islamic sources, a complete codex of the Qur'an was compiled within 25 years of the Prophet's death.
- Original copies of the Qur'an did not have vowel markings; today copies of the Qur'an often include vowel and other markings to assist with recitation.
- Muslims believe that, as the Word of God, the Qur'an is inimitable, and its style cannot be reproduced by humans.
- Reports of the Prophet's sayings and deeds, known as hadith, are an important component of the Islamic textual tradition.

Recommended reading

Muhammad Mustafa Al-Azami, *The History of the Qur'anic Text from Revelation to Compilation*, Leicester: UK Islamic Academy, 2003.

- In this book Azami provides insights into the history of the Qur'anic text, with a view to refuting historical and contemporary attacks on the Qur'an. He also assesses a number of alternative Western theories regarding the Qur'an and questions their motivation and accuracy.

Farid Esack, 'Gathering the Qur'an', in *The Qur'an: A Short Introduction*, Oxford: Oneworld, 2001, pages 77–99.

- In this chapter Esack traces the collection and documentation of the Qur'an as a book, from the time of revelation until the period of the third caliph, Uthman.

William Graham, *Beyond the Written Word*, Cambridge: Cambridge University Press, 1993.

- In this book Graham re-examines the concept of 'scripture' by analysing the traditions of oral use and sacred writings of religions around the world. He suggests that there is a need for a new perspective on understanding the words used to describe 'scripture' in the Qur'an, and the way in which scripture has been used by people throughout history.

Daniel A. Madigan, *The Qur'an's Self-Image: Writing and Authority in Islam's Scripture*, Princeton, NJ: Princeton University Press, 2001.

- In this book Madigan explores the ways in which the Qur'an refers to itself. His first chapter in particular, 'The Qur'an as a Book', explores the concept of the Qur'an as a book or scripture. Throughout the book, Madigan makes reference to the Qur'an's own perspective as expressed through a number of Qur'anic verses.

NOTES

1 As with other Semitic languages, most words have a root, which consists of three consonants that are then combined with other vowels and letters to produce derivates of the root meaning. The last root consonant of Qur'an - ' - represents a glottal stop in Arabic transliteration.
2 Qur'an: 4:113; see also 2:231; 4:105.
3 Qur'an: 21:10.
4 Qur'an: 16:64; 6:155; 6:154–157; 2:176; 3:7; 4:105; 29:47.
5 Qur'an: 55:1.
6 Qur'an: 2:67–73.
7 Caliphate: a system of governance that combines both religious and political rule.
8 Qur'an: 14:4.
9 Mohammed Arkoun, *Rethinking Islam*, trans. Robert D. Lee, Boulder: Westview Press, 1994, p. 37.
10 William Graham, *Beyond the Written Word*, Cambridge: Cambridge University Press, 1993, p. 89.
11 See Chapter 1 for further discussion of religio-political groups in Islam.
12 Ali Abbas (ed.), 'The Quran Compiled by Imam Ali (AS)', *A Shi'ite Encyclopedia*, Chapter 8. Accessed 20 February 2007: www.al-islam. org/encyclopedia/.
13 Qur'an: 2:106.
14 Zamakhshari, *al-Kashshaf*, in Helmut Gatje, *The Qur'an and its Exegesis*, trans. and ed. Alford T. Welch, Oxford: Oneworld, 1997, p. 58.
15 See John Wansbrough, *Qur'anic Studies: Sources and Methods of Scriptural Interpretation*, New York: Prometheus Books, 2004, pp. 78–81.
16 See Wansbrough, *Qur'anic Studies*, pp. 43–50.
17 Toby Lester, 'What is the Qur'an?', *The Atlantic Monthly*, January 1999, vol. 283, no. 1, p. 55.
18 See Wansbrough, *Qur'anic Studies*, p. 202.
19 Cambridge: Cambridge University Press, 1977.
20 Stephen Crittenden, 'John Wansbrough Remembered: Interview with Gerald Hawting', 26 June 2002, ABC, Radio National – The Religion Report. Accessed 20 August 2007: http://www.abc.net.au/rn/talks/8.30/relrpt/stories/s591483.htm.
21 Muhammad Mustafa Al-Azami, *The History of the Qur'anic Text from Revelation to Compilation*, Leicester: UK Islamic Academy, 2003.
22 Azami, *The History of the Qur'anic Text*, p. 68.
23 Azami, *The History of the Qur'anic Text*, p. 69.

24   Azami, *The History of the Qur'anic Text*, p. 97–105.
25   Farid Esack, *The Qur'an: A Short Introduction*, Oxford: Oneworld, 2001, p. 91. Note – the Kharijis were an early school of Islamic thought that has largely disappeared today; the Shi'i stream of Islam is still in existence today. For more information on these groups see Chapter 11.
26   John Burton, *The Collection of the Qur'an*, Cambridge and New York: Cambridge University Press, 1977, pp. 239–240.
27   Estelle Whelan, 'Forgotten Witness: Evidence for the Early Codification of the Qur'an', *Journal of the American Oriental Society*, vol. 118, no. 1 (Jan–Mar 1998), p. 3.
28   Whelan, 'Forgotten Witness', pp. 4–6.
29   Whelan, 'Forgotten Witness', p. 8.
30   Whelan, 'Forgotten Witness', p. 8.
31   Whelan, 'Forgotten Witness', p. 8.
32   Whelan, 'Forgotten Witness', pp. 5–6.
33   Whelan, 'Forgotten Witness', pp. 8–10.
34   Whelan, 'Forgotten Witness', pp. 10–13.
35   The vowels that were added to the script are still used today. These are 'a', 'i' (pronounced like the English 'ee') and 'u' (pronounced like the English 'oo').
36   Montgomery Watt and Richard Bell, 'The External Form of the Quran', *Introduction to the Quran*, Edinburgh: Edinburgh University Press, 1995, pp. 70–71.
37   'Different verse numbering systems in the Qur'an'. Accessed 20 February 2007: http://www.answering-islam.de/Main/Quran/Text/numbers.html.
38   Ahmad von Denffer, 'Introduction to the Qur'an: A Rendition of the Original Work Titled *Ulum al Qur'an*', A.E. Souaiaia (ed.), *Studies in Islam and the Middle East (SIME) Journal*, SIME ePublishing (majalla.org), 2004. Accessed 5 September 2007: http://www.islamworld.net/UUQ/.
39   von Denffer, 'Introduction to the Qur'an'.
40   A. Jeffery and I. Mendelsohn, 'The Orthography of the Samarqand Codex', *Journal of the American Oriental Society*, vol. 63, New Haven: American Oriental Society, 1943, pp. 175–195.
41   See Qur'an: 2:23; 11:13; 10:38.
42   See Qur'an: 2:23; 11:13; 10:38.
43   *Jinn* are imperceptible spirits who, like humans, are capable of both good and evil. They are said to be created from fire.
44   Qur'an: 17:88.
45   Qur'an: 11:13.
46   See Qur'an: 10:38.
47   Qur'an: 7:157; 7:158.
48   For instance, Rashid al-Din Fadl Allah (d.718/1318) argued that it was highly unlikely that 'the best of created beings' would not have known the art of writing (*al-Madjmu'a al-rashidiyya al-sultaniyya*, in E. Geoffroy, 'Ummi', p. 864, P.J. Bearman et al. (eds), *Encyclopaedia of Islam*, vol. 10, Leiden: Brill, 2000, pp. 863–864).
49   Edip Yuksel, *www.19.org*, cited in Dave Thomas, 'Code 19 in the Quran?', *New Mexicans for Science and Reason*. Accessed 18 February 2007: http://www.nmsr.org/code19.htm.

50 Qur'an: 21:30.
51 See Joseph Schacht, *The Origins of Muhammadan Jurisprudence*, Oxford: Oxford University Press, 1950.
52 Bukhari, *Sahih al-Bukhari*, Vol. 8, Book 78 'The Book of Oaths and Vows', Chap. 15, No. 660, narrated by Abu Hurayra, in *The Translation of the Meanings of Sahih Al-Bukhari*, trans. Muhammad Muhsin Khan, Ankara, Turkey: Hilal Yayinlari, 1977, pp. 429–430.
53 Qur'an: 2:43. See also 2:110, 277; 11:114; and 22:78.

4

Major themes and text types

SEVERAL MAJOR THEMES APPEAR IN THE QUR'AN, all of which revolve around the central theme of God's relationship to human beings. Creation, the early prophets, and life after death are other major themes that make up the Qur'anic text. Because references to each of the major themes appear throughout the Qur'anic text, they are not always easy to separate. Each time one of these themes is mentioned the Qur'an highlights a different facet of it in the particular wording of passages.

Although there are many different themes in the Qur'an, the reader will quickly notice the constant invocation of God's names that occurs throughout the text. This repeated invocation consistently and subtly invites the reader to reflect on two of the Qur'an's most important themes, namely the nature of God and the essential relationship between the Creator and His creation.

In this chapter we will discuss:

- some of the most important themes in the Qur'an, including God, spiritual beings, Satan, God's creations, early prophets, the Qur'anic view of other religions, historical events of the Prophet's time, life after death, and ethical and moral guidelines for human behaviour; and
- the main types of text in the Quran.

God

During the Prophet Muhammad's time, many of the Arabs in Mecca and Medina were polytheists; they believed in both higher and lesser gods. Like monotheists of the time, they also believed in a single higher God (*al-ilah* or Allah, 'the God'). Unlike monotheists, however, they believed that Allah existed in the heavens, and lesser gods existed to serve as intermediaries between Allah and human beings. One of the primary themes of the Qur'an is its rejection of these polytheistic ideas and its affirmation of the concept of one God.

There are numerous references to and descriptions of God in the Qur'an. For instance, the Qur'an states that God possesses innumerable names that refer to His attributes. Some of the names mentioned in the Qur'an include the Merciful, the Compassionate, the Creator, the Omnipotent, the Dispenser of Rewards, the Reckoner and the Wise. Ninety-nine of God's 'most beautiful names' are known, although the most common one, which encompasses all His attributes, is simply 'Allah'.

The names of God

Muslims believe God has 99 'names' or 'beautiful names', or attributes. These are found in the Qur'an and hadith. The most frequently used name is simply *Allah*, 'the God'. Some of His other names are as follows:

Lord of Mercy	Creator	Tremendous
Giver of Mercy	Forgiver	Eternal
True King	Ever Giving	Ever Living
Holy One	All Knowing	Self-Subsistent
Source of Peace	All Seeing	Truth
Guardian	Most Forbearing	Giver of Life
Almighty	Most Loving	

Further references to God are found throughout the Qur'an, from which we are able to form an idea of who God is. For instance, God is described as the Creator of everything in the universe, including life and death. It is also said that all things belong to Him alone. He is just, and rewards handsomely those who are virtuous but punishes those who reject His guidance. We are told that He has complete knowledge of all things and cannot be restricted or limited in any way. The Qur'an also states that God has no sons or daughters: 'He fathered no one nor was He fathered.'[1] We are reminded that God is 'the Compassionate' and that He hears the prayers of believers and watches over everyone.

As we read the Qur'an, it becomes quickly apparent that God is one of its most prevalent themes. In fact, we would be unlikely to find a page of the Qur'an without a reference to God. One of the most important aspects of this theme is that, although the Qur'an at times uses anthropomorphic terms to describe God (such as references to His 'hand' or 'face'), it also emphatically denies that there are any similarities between God and human beings. It reminds us that He is like nothing that we know. Below is the famous 'Verse of Light', which uses complex imagery to convey to us some idea about who or what God is:

> God is the Light of the heavens and earth. His Light is like this: there is a niche, and in it a lamp, the lamp inside a glass, a glass like a glittering star, fuelled from a blessed olive tree from neither east nor west, whose oil almost gives light even when no fire touches it – light upon light – God guides whoever He wills to His light; God draws such comparisons for people; God has full knowledge of everything.[2]

In another verse, the Qur'an says:

> He is God: there is no other god but Him. It is He who knows what is
> hidden as well as what is in the open, He is the Lord of Mercy, the Giver
> of Mercy. He is God: there is no other god but Him, the Controller, the
> Holy One, Source of Peace, Granter of Security, Guardian overall,
> the Almighty, the Compeller, to whom all greatness belongs; God is far
> above anything they consider to be His partner.[3]

Spiritual beings

The Qur'an acknowledges the existence of beings belonging to the spiritual
realm, which are beyond our immediate human experience. For instance, the
Qur'an often refers to angels, some of whom have specific functions, such as
bringing revelation to prophets or forewarning death. Some of the angels are
mentioned by name, such as Gabriel and Michael. The importance of belief
in angels is such that it is one of six 'pillars of faith' in Islam. The Qur'an
says: 'The Messenger [Muhammad] believes in what has been sent down to
him from his Lord, as do the faithful. They all believe in God, His angels,
His scriptures, and His messengers.'[4]

As well as the angels, who are always and without exception obedient to
God, the Qur'an also refers to beings called *jinn*. Muslim theologians hold
that *jinn* are imperceptible beings, created of smokeless fire; they have free
will and may or may not be obedient to God; in this regard they are similar
to human beings. Reflecting this similarity, *jinn* are often referred to in the
Qur'an in conjunction with human beings. For example, the Qur'an says:
'Say [Prophet]: "I have created jinn and mankind only to worship Me. I want
no provision from them, nor do I want them to feed Me."'[5]

Satan – the symbol of evil and disobedience

The Qur'anic symbol of evil and disobedience to God is Satan (Shaytan), also
called Iblis. Iblis is a creature described in the Qur'an as being of the *jinn*
in origin, who somehow came to be regarded as an angel.[6] In the Qur'anic
story of creation, God informs the angels that He intends to create a
vicegerent on earth. Some of the angels protest that this being will create
havoc on earth and cause bloodshed. God rejects their protests and creates
the first human being, Adam. God teaches Adam the 'names' of all things
and then commands the angels to bow down to Adam.[7]

All the angels obey, but Iblis objects to God's command and argues that he is superior to Adam because he is created from fire, while Adam is a creature of clay.[8] Iblis is condemned for rebelling against God, but is given a temporary reprieve until the Day of Judgement. At that time, he and those who follow his misguidance will be punished for their open rebellion against God.

Thus, in the Qur'an, the forces of good are aligned with and follow the guidance of God, whereas the forces of evil, represented by Satan, are those that oppose Him and seek to lead people away from Him. The singular 'Satan' (shaytan) generally refers to Iblis, while its plural (shayatin) refers to those who follow in his footsteps. The shayatin may include both jinn and human beings. The Qur'an says: 'And do not follow Satan's footsteps, for he is your sworn enemy.'[9] And: 'In the same way, We assigned to each prophet an enemy, evil humans and evil jinn [shayatin]. They suggest alluring words to one another in order to deceive.'[10]

Creation

The Qur'an includes numerous references to the creation of the heavens and the earth, and what is 'in' or 'between' them.[11] Although it does not specify exactly when creation took place, some verses suggest that it occurred over several 'days'. However, the Qur'an explains that 'days' as we know them are not the same as 'days' in the sight of God. For example, the Qur'an says: 'A Day with your Lord is like a thousand years by your reckoning.'[12] This suggests that Qur'anic references to a single day may correspond to a much longer period of time according to human understanding.

The Qur'an speaks about the creation of the sun, the moon, the stars and other celestial bodies. It also speaks of the creation of life on earth and of everything needed to sustain life; for example, water, from which, in the Qur'anic account, life itself originates, and air. It also refers to the changing seasons and the creation of trees and foodstuffs such as fruits and grains, and calls upon the reader to reflect on these 'Signs' of God.

In the Qur'an, human beings are considered to be among the most noble creations. As we have seen, in the Qur'an's description of the creation of humanity, God commanded the angels to bow down to Adam, the first human, in recognition of the importance of humankind. Although humans have a high status in the eyes of God, they also have the potential for both good and evil. One of God's first 'actions' in relation to human beings after the creation of Adam and his companion (Eve) was to test them by means of the forbidden tree. According to the Qur'an, both fail God's test, but He accepts their repentance, forgives them and then commands them to live on earth, where they are instructed to convey the message of God's guidance to their offspring. We are also told that it is from this pair that the human family emerges. Thus, from the Qur'anic perspective, Adam was the first teacher, guide and prophet.

Part of God's promise to Adam and Eve was that He would send prophets and messengers to their descendants, bringing guidance from God. The Qur'anic account of the creation and 'fall', therefore, depicts God honouring, forgiving and maintaining a close relationship with humanity from the very beginning. Since God also intended from the beginning to create a 'vicegerent on the earth', the 'fall' is seen as part of the divine plan.

Earlier prophetic figures

Approximately one-fifth of the Qur'an deals with narratives of past prophets, their messages, their communities and how those communities responded to God's call to recognize His Oneness and follow His guidance. These narratives vary in length and detail, and are scattered throughout the Qur'an. For instance, although a particular chapter is named after a prophetic figure, it will not provide a biography of that person. As with the majority of the Qur'an's narratives, the primary objective of references to prophetic figures is to highlight particular teachings, rather than to present a full account of their lives. As a result, in order to fully understand the Qur'anic account of a particular figure, the reader must undertake the task of bringing together texts from various parts of the Qur'an.

Of all the narratives related to prophets, the most detailed are about Moses, Jesus and Joseph. The narratives about Jesus, for example, recount the events surrounding his birth, some of his miracles and teachings, his relationship to his community, and what happened to him at the end of his life. These narratives usually focus on particular issues which illustrate a broad lesson, and do not include historical specifics of names, places or times.

The Qur'an mentions the names of 25 prophets. However, Muslim tradition holds that the total number of prophets from the very beginning of humanity may well be over a hundred thousand. This is a view supported by Qur'anic statements such as: '[earlier] communities each had their guide'.[13] Among the prophets named in the Qur'an are familiar biblical figures such as Adam, Noah, Abraham, Jacob, Joseph, Moses, David, Solomon and Jesus. According to the Qur'an, all of them taught the same basic message of belief in the One God, Creator and Sustainer of the universe, and that human beings should recognize God's Oneness and lead an ethical and moral life.

Names of prophets mentioned in the Qur'an

Listed roughly in chronological order, with biblical equivalent, where relevant, given in parentheses.

Adam	Harun (Aaron)
Idris (Enoch)	Da'ud (David)
Nuh (Noah)	Sulayman (Solomon)
Hud	Dhu'l-Kifl (probably Ezekiel)
Salih (Shelah)	al-Yasa' (Elisha)
Lut (Lot)	Ayyub (Job)
Ibrahim (Abraham)	Yunus (Jonah)
Isma'il (Ishmael)	Zakariyya (Zechariah)
Ishaq (Isaac)	Yahya (John)
Ya'qub (Jacob)	Ilyas (Elijah)
Yusuf (Joseph)	Isa (Jesus)
Shu'ayb (probably Jethro)	Muhammad
Musa (Moses)	

The primary purpose of these narratives does not seem to be simply to tell a story, but rather to relate the struggles of the Prophet Muhammad to those of earlier prophets. When Muhammad was having difficulties in his mission, these stories would remind him that earlier prophets had to face similar challenges. Thus, Muhammad was encouraged to persevere, be patient and have faith that God would provide the help and support he needed in his mission, as He had done for his predecessors. The narratives also provided reassurance that those who do good deeds and are faithful to God will ultimately succeed.

Example of Mary, mother of Jesus

One of the most important figures connected to a prophet is Mary, mother of Jesus. Although she was not a prophet, the Qur'an had a lot to say about her. As with other important figures in the Qur'an, the narrative of Mary is not found in one chapter, even though a chapter of the Qur'an is named after her. In order to compile the story of Mary as it is found in the Qur'an, it is necessary to bring together sections from seven different chapters, including the following verses from chapter 19 (Mary), which describes the annunciation of Jesus' birth:

> Mention in the Qur'an the story of Mary. She withdrew from her family to a place to the east and secluded herself away; We [God] sent Our Spirit to appear before her in the form of a perfected man. She said, 'I seek the Lord of Mercy's protection against you: if you have any fear of Him [do not approach]!' But he said, 'I am but a Messenger from your Lord, [come] to announce to you the gift of a pure son.' She said, 'How can I have a son when no man has touched me? I have not been unchaste,' and he said 'This is what your Lord said: "It is easy for Me – We shall make him a sign to all people, a blessing from Us".'
>
> And so it was ordained: she conceived him. She withdrew to a distant place and, when the pains of childbirth drove her to [cling to] the trunk of a palm tree, she exclaimed, 'I wish I had been dead and forgotten long before all this!' But a voice cried to her from below, 'Do not worry: your Lord has provided a stream at your feet and if you shake the trunk of the palm tree towards you, it will deliver fresh ripe dates for you, so eat, drink, be glad, and say to anyone you may see: "I have vowed to the Lord of Mercy to abstain from conversation, and I will not talk to anyone today".'
>
> She went back to her people carrying the child, and they said, 'Mary! You must have done something terrible! Sister of Aaron! Your father was not an evil man; your mother was not unchaste!' She pointed at him [the child]. They said, 'How can we converse with an infant?' [But] he [Jesus] said: 'I am a servant of God. He has granted me the Scripture; made me a prophet; made me blessed wherever I may be. He commanded me to pray, to give alms as long as I live, to cherish my mother. He did not make me domineering or graceless. Peace was on me the day I was born, and will be on me the day I die and the day I am raised to life again.' Such was Jesus, son of Mary.
>
> [This is] a statement of the Truth about which they are in doubt: it would not befit God to have a child. He is far above that: when He decrees something, He says only 'Be', and it is.[14]

Mary is one of a number of women who are highly venerated in Islam. She is also one of very few people to have a chapter of the Qur'an named after her. Mary is described in another verse of the Qur'an as being chosen by God above all other women, and is known to Muslims as the essence of virtue and a model for all people to aspire to.[15]

As illustrated by the excerpt above, Muslims believe that Mary's conception of Jesus was by divine miracle. The verses go on to describe Jesus' birth, the reaction of Mary's community on discovering that she has given birth out of wedlock, and the words spoken by Jesus at the time of his birth, predicting his prophethood and life to come. Other events of Mary's life which are described in the Qur'an include her time as a young woman when she was assigned into the care of a priest named Zechariah.[16]

Other important female figures in Islam, who are referred to in the Qur'an, include the wives of the Prophet; Eve, the first woman; the mother of Moses; Bilqis, the Queen of Sheba; and the mother of Mary.

Faith and other religions

Much of the content of the Qur'an centres on the themes of faith in the One God and rejection of all other deities or objects of worship. Terms relating to belief, unbelief, hypocrisy, monotheism and polytheism abound. In fact, the core message of the Qur'an relates to faith, so it is not surprising that numerous verses relate not only to Islam, but also to other religious traditions.

While the Qur'an clearly rejects the idea that there are many gods, it does recognize that other prophets and traditions existed before Muhammad. In particular, it often refers to Christians and Jews, and, as we have already seen, confers on them the title 'People of the Book', thus recognizing the scriptures which Christians and Jews had received from God.

This recognition of Christians and Jews does not mean that the Qur'an is not critical of them. In fact, members of the Jewish tribes that opposed Muhammad in Medina are sometimes censured harshly. Similarly, the Qur'an condemns those Christians who claim that God is 'the third of three' instead of recognizing only one God.[17] When the Qur'an criticizes a Jewish, Christian or even Muslim community, Muslim scholars have generally understood this as referring to the specific conduct of certain individuals or groups within the community. In some cases this view is based on the traditional interpretation of a verse. In other cases it is reflected in the specific wording of the Qur'anic verse; for example: 'Some Jews distort the meaning of [revealed] words: they say, "We hear and disobey".'[18] And: 'Those We gave Scripture know it as well as they know their sons, but some of them hide the truth that they know.'[19]

The Qur'an appears to be somewhat ambivalent towards the recipients of previous revelations, and some verses are difficult to reconcile with others. In order to understand these verses we must read these passages in a highly nuanced way and with an understanding of their individual contexts. At times the Qur'an appears harshly critical of the failure of older religious communities (such as the Jews and Christians) to accept the prophethood of Muhammad, and the new guidance given by God to Muhammad.[20] At other times, however, it clearly affirms the righteous among those of other faiths: 'For the [Muslim] believers, the Jews, the Sabians,[21] and the Christians – those who believe in God and the Last Day and do good deeds – there is no fear: they will not grieve.'[22]

Similarly, the Qur'an censures religious exclusionism,[23] and also points to a higher, divinely ordained purpose in the diversity of human religions, as in the following verse:

> We [God] have assigned a law and a path to each of you. If God had so willed, he would have made you one community, but He wanted to test you through that which He has given you, so race to do good: you will all return to God and He will make clear to you the matters you differed about.[24]

Historical events of the Prophet's time

Based on passages of the Qur'an and volumes of historical reports, a great deal is known about the Prophet Muhammad's life. Muhammad's role as a prophet of God required him to be involved in public life not only as a religious teacher and recipient of revelation, but also as a statesman, an arbitrator of disputes, a commander in battles and a friend and relative of many. His experiences varied greatly, ranging from his first teachings in Mecca about the Oneness of God, to his establishment and leadership of the first Muslim community in Medina.

There are numerous references in the Qur'an to events that took place during the Prophet's lifetime, particularly during the time of revelation (610–632). References to some of these events are usually brief, while a few are described in more detail. The relatively succinct nature of most references reflects the fact that they are not included as a historical account, but serve to highlight certain aspects from which a moral lesson can be drawn.

An example of a seemingly insignificant event in the life of the Prophet which is used to convey a higher moral teaching can be seen in the chapter 'He Frowned' (*Abasa*, chapter 80). The opening ten verses of this chapter describe an incident when the Prophet was talking to some Meccan notables, in the hope of attracting them to Islam. While talking to these people, who were relatively uninterested in his message, he was approached by a blind man who was eager to learn about Islam. The moral teaching of this story is clearly expressed in the following verses:

> He frowned and turned away when the blind man came to him – for all you know, he might have grown in spirit, or benefited from being taught. For the self-satisfied one you go out of your way – though you are not to be blamed for his lack of spiritual growth – but from the one who has come to you full of eagerness and awe you allow yourself to be distracted. No indeed! This [Qur'an] is a lesson from which those who wish to be taught should learn.[25]

Many of the Qur'an's references to events in the Prophet's life also relate to his time in Medina, when the Prophet undertook the task of establishing the first Muslim community. It was during this period that several battles took place between the Muslim community and their enemies. The Qur'an refers to these battles and the moral lessons which can be drawn from the way the different parties behaved during times of conflict. For example, in relation to the Battles of Badr and Uhud, which took place in the years 2/624 and 3/625 respectively, the Qur'an states:

> [O Prophet], remember when you left your home at dawn to assign battle positions to the believers: God hears and knows everything. Remember when two groups of you were about to lose heart and God protected them – let the believers put their trust in God – God helped you at Badr when you were very weak. Be mindful of God, so that you may be grateful. Remember when you said to the believers, 'Will you be satisfied if your Lord reinforces you by sending down three thousand angels? Well, if you are steadfast and mindful of God, your Lord will reinforce you with five thousand swooping angels if the enemy should suddenly attack you!' And God arranged it so, as a message of hope for you [believers] to put your hearts at rest – help comes only from God, the Mighty, the Wise.[26]

The first part of this excerpt refers to the Battle of Uhud and reminds the Prophet of two groups among his forces who were 'about to lose heart', because of the Muslims' numerical weakness, before they decided to continue following the Prophet into battle. This is followed by a reference to the Battle of Badr, when the Muslims were weak but God helped them to win the battle against the superior Meccans. The reference here includes reminders of moral teachings, such as the injunction to be mindful of God in order to be grateful. It also states that God will help and reinforce those who are mindful of Him, and reminds its audience that help comes from God alone; thus, only in Him should they put their trust.[27]

Life after death

The afterlife is also a significant theme in the Qur'an. The Qur'an insists on the reality of a life after death, stating a number of times that the life of this world is both short and temporary. The primary purpose of this life is to serve God and prepare for the hereafter by having faith in Him, doing good deeds and leading an ethical and moral life. This life is also important in that it gives human beings the opportunity to contribute to the building of life on earth, to work towards the well-being of others, and to acknowledge and recognize the One God.

The Qur'an emphasizes the importance of being accountable for one's thoughts, sayings and actions. We are told that a complete record is kept of what everyone does and says in this world, and that God will use this to determine each individual's fate on the Day of Judgement. This day, also referred to as the Day of Reckoning, is described in the Qur'an as a momentous event. Passages depict the collapse of the heavens and the destruction of the mountains, and the masses of human beings gathered to receive judgement. The Qur'an also describes how God will dispense His justice, and reiterates that all human beings will be questioned about their earthly lives.[28]

Several verses in the Qur'an describe the afterlife itself. Although these descriptions are often quite vivid, many Muslims understand them as metaphorical, remembering the statement attributed to the Prophet that '[What is in Paradise is] what an eye has not seen, an ear has not heard, and which has not been imagined by the heart'.[29]

In the Qur'an, Hell is described as a place for those who do not acknowledge and believe in God, do not follow the path of the prophets, and are tyrannical and unjust. Hell is a place of fire, torment and punishment – often described in specific and vivid terms – and it is watched over by powerful angels. For instance, the Qur'an says:

> Hell lies in wait, a home for oppressors to stay in for a long, long time, where they will taste no coolness nor drink except one that is scalding and dark – a fitting requital, for they did not fear a reckoning, and they rejected Our messages as lies. We have recorded everything in a Record. 'Taste this: all you will get from Us is more torment.'[30]

On the other hand, Paradise is for those who believe in One God, do good deeds, and are just and kind. It is described as a garden full of comfort and luxury, where rivers flow, every type of food is available for enjoyment and there is no sadness. For example, the Qur'an says:

> And reward them, for their steadfastness, with a Garden and silken robes. They will sit on couches, feeling neither scorching heat nor biting cold, with shady [branches] spread above them and clusters of fruit hanging close at hand. They will be served with silver plates and gleaming silver goblets according to their fancy, and they will be given a drink infused with ginger from a spring called Salsabil. Everlasting youths will attend them – if you could see them, you would think they were scattered pearls – and if you were to look around, you would see bliss and great wealth: they will wear garments of green silk and brocade; they will be adorned with silver bracelets; their Lord will give them a pure drink.[31]

Human behaviour

A significant part of the Qur'an deals with commandments, prohibitions, instructions and guidance to humans about how they should behave. For instance, the commandments related to religious practice which are commonly referred to as the 'five pillars of Islam' come from the Qur'an. These include instructions for Muslims to believe in one God,[32] pray regularly,[33] give generously to support the poor, needy and disadvantaged,[34] fast in the month of Ramadan,[35] and, if possible, perform the pilgrimage to Mecca.[36] In regard to interactions with other people, the Qur'an instructs Muslims to be patient, fair and just, to respect one's parents and support them in their old age, to be chaste and modest, and to forgive others instead of taking revenge. Similarly, as general guidelines for life, Muslims are told to take 'a middle path' by avoiding excess and extremism, and to refrain from improper conduct such as mistreating parents, backbiting or being tight-fisted.

There are also teachings on etiquette and socially acceptable norms in the Qur'an. For instance, the Qur'an advises Muslims not to visit people when they are resting and provides guidelines on how to greet one another, dress appropriately and how to interact with the Prophet.

In contrast to the general guidance given above, more detailed teachings are included to complement a general principle. For example, given the difficult moral issues associated with war, very clear guidelines are offered in this area, such as what forms of combat are permitted, when hostilities should cease and how to distribute any gains from battle. Similarly, detailed instructions are given in relation to legal matters such as marriage, divorce, child custody and inheritance.

The Qur'an also contains a number of prohibitions. Forbidden actions include drinking wine, theft, adultery, fornication, murder and causing injury to others. Several punishments are specified in connection with certain forbidden actions, such as amputation of a hand for stealing, and 100 lashes for fornication. The Qur'an also prohibits misappropriation of property, gambling, giving false testimony, particularly in legal cases, and usury or interest (*riba*). Some examples of verses of prohibition are as follows:

> You who believe, intoxicants and gambling, idolatrous practices, and [divining with] arrows are repugnant acts – Satan's doing: shun them so that you may prosper. With intoxicants and gambling, Satan seeks only to incite enmity and hatred among you, and to stop you remembering God and prayer. Will you not give them up?[37]

And:

> Do not kill your children for fear of poverty – We shall provide for them and for you – killing them is a great sin. And do not go anywhere near adultery: it is an outrage, and an evil path. Do not take life – which God has made sacred – except by right. If anyone is killed wrongfully, We have given authority to the defender of his rights, but he should not be excessive in taking life, for he is already aided [by God].[38]

Although legal injunctions such as those mentioned above are important, they must also be put into perspective. The number of legal verses in the Qur'an is estimated to be between 100 and 500, depending on the definition of the term 'legal'. In the context of the entire Qur'an, this is a relatively small proportion of the entire text, which has close to 6,300 verses. Despite this, these legal verses are given a lot of attention, and their interpretation has often been a source of debate. The issues involved in these debates will be discussed further in Chapter 9.

Types of texts in the Qur'an

Related to the idea of 'themes' is that of 'text types'. There are several identifiable types of texts in the Qur'an. These include theological, historical, ethical and legal texts, as well as those that convey spiritual or religious wisdom, and those which are formulated as supplications. Gaining a basic understanding of these different types of texts allows the reader to better understand the intended purpose of different verses.

Several early Qur'anic scholars attempted a basic classification of the Qur'an's texts that focused on factors other than the type of text, as we have done here. Tabari (d.310/923), for instance, classified texts from the perspective of 'authority to interpret'. First he identified those verses he believed could only be interpreted by the Prophet. These included verses related to various commandments and prohibitions. The second category included verses whose interpretation is known only to God. Such verses are concerned with future events such as the time of the 'Hour',[39] the 'Day the Trumpet is blown',[40] or the return of Jesus.[41] Tabari's third category comprised verses whose interpretation is open to anyone familiar with the Arabic language.[42]

By contrast, Ibn Abbas (d.68/687), one of the earliest commentators of the Qur'an, reportedly divided the verses of the text into four categories from the perspective of 'knowability': those which Arabs could know or understand because they were in their own language; those which anyone could interpret and come to understand; those that only scholars could understand; and those known only to God.[43] These attempts at classifying the Qur'anic text reflected that early Muslims understood that not all Qur'anic texts should be treated the same way.

Theological texts

Many verses in the Qur'an refer to two types of entities that exist in the 'Unseen' realm, and are thus beyond human experience and comprehension. The first type of entity includes God and His Being, including His attributes and works. The second type includes concepts such as 'God's Throne', Paradise, Hell, angels and the 'Preserved Tablet'. Since Qur'anic references to the Unseen are not directly related to anything within human experience, it is an open question whether such references can truly be understood or explained. For instance, despite containing numerous descriptions of God and His attributes, the Qur'an also refers to our inability to fully understand God in passages such as 'There is nothing like Him'[44] and 'No one is comparable to Him'.[45]

The Qur'an emphasizes that it was revealed in the Arabic language,[46] and so it is likely that the words of these theological verses were largely familiar to the early Muslims. However, in the context of references to the Unseen, the literal meaning of these words may not convey their full significance.

Rather than being terms which can be understood literally, these references are believed to convey, through the language and images of human experience, approximate understandings of things that cannot be fully known. As a classical Qur'anic scholar, Zamakhshari, explains, texts related to metaphysical concepts are conveyed 'through a parabolic illustration, by means of something which we know from our experience, of something that is beyond the reach of our perception'.[47]

Historical texts

Many verses of the Qur'an contain historical elements, which are often included in order to highlight a particular moral teaching. The references to historical events and figures are often very brief. In most cases, they lack specific details of names, places or time. It is, however, possible to supplement these references using other sources. Muslim theologians have viewed the task of understanding these historical details in various ways. Some suggest that the Bible is a useful tool in understanding the historical elements of the Qur'an, as it provides additional information on the prophets that are part of both Judaeo-Christian and Muslim traditions. However, particularly in the later centuries of Islam, several Muslim scholars of the Qur'an argued against using the Bible for additional insights, as they believed that this would put the Bible on an equal footing with the Qur'an, which they thought was unacceptable.

Prior to the fourth/tenth and fifth/eleventh centuries, it was common for scholars to refer to Jewish and Christian sources, known as *isra'iliyyat*, in order to better understand some of the historical references of the Qur'an. From the sixth/twelfth century onwards, this practice gradually began to be challenged by prominent scholars, who claimed that it was not appropriate for Muslims to rely on such sources. Slowly, the use of Jewish and Christian sources was marginalized in Islamic scholarship. Eventually, the use of such extra-Islamic sources in attempting to understand the Qur'an came to be understood by some as tantamount to acting against Islam itself.

Despite these developments, the lack of specific details with regard to historical information within the Qur'an is not seen as problematic, as the Qur'an itself does not purport to be a record of history. Historical figures and events in the Qur'an often serve primarily as examples of ethical behaviour. Thus, these references serve as both ethical parables and fragments of larger historical accounts. For example, the story of Noah and his people is mentioned briefly in 13 different chapters of the Qur'an.[48] Each time the narrative appears, a different teaching is emphasized. Although the exact details of the story are not necessary to convey its moral teaching, many of these figures and events would have been familiar to early Muslims and, thus, would have served as a powerful rhetoric.

The Qur'anic references to the story of the Prophet Shu'ayb and his people are another example. The main issue for the reader appears not to be exactly who Shu'ayb was, but rather how his people responded to the message of God. A section of the story reads as follows:

> To the people of Midian We sent their brother, Shu'ayb. He said, 'My people, serve God: you have no god other than Him. A clear sign has come to you from your Lord. Give full measure and weight and do not undervalue people's goods; do not cause corruption in the land after it has been set in order: this is better for you, if you are believers. Do not sit in every pathway, threatening and barring those who believe in God from His way, trying to make it crooked. Remember how you used to be few and He made you multiply. Think about the fate of those who used to spread corruption. If some of you believe the message I bring and others do not, then be patient till God judges between us. He is the best of all judges.'
>
> His people's arrogant leaders said, 'Shu'ayb, we will expel you and your fellow believers from our town unless you return to our religion.' He said, 'What! Even if we detest it? If we were to return to your religion after God has saved us from it, we would be inventing lies about Him: there is no way we could return to it.'[49]

As with other stories of the Qur'an, only those details which are relevant to the teaching of the reference are included.

Parables

There are several texts that can be referred to broadly as 'parables' or 'illustrations' (*mathal*). These are indicated by Qur'anic references such as 'We offer people such imagery (*mathal*) that they may reflect.'[50] Like historical texts, the parables also make use of a literary style and imagery that would have been familiar to the first generation of Muslims. Parables from the pre-Islamic era were often adapted in order to convey Islamic principles and ethical teachings more easily. Such texts are often used in the Qur'an to convey its teachings in a vivid manner. These types of text often contain metaphors that convey positive examples of human conduct, for example:

> [Prophet], do you not see how God makes comparisons? A good word is like a good tree whose root is firm and whose branches are high in the

sky, yielding constant fruit by its Lord's leave – God makes such comparisons for people so that they may reflect.[51]

Others may be used to discourage negative traits such as arrogance:

> You who believe, do not cancel out your charitable deeds with reminders and hurtful words, like someone who spends his wealth only to be seen by people, not believing in God and the Last Day. Such a person is like a smooth rock with earth on it: heavy rain falls and leaves it completely bare. Such people get no rewards from their works: God does not guide the disbelievers.[52]

Metaphor is used in a number of places throughout the Qur'an to convey similar moral messages, the teachings of which can often be understood on several different levels.

Ethical-legal texts

Another important type of text in the Qur'an are the ethical-legal texts. Many Muslims regard these texts as having the greatest impact on their daily lives. Such texts relate to a range of different teachings, including the Muslim system of belief, devotional practices, essential values such as protection of life, and legal instructions such as those on inheritance and the punishment of crimes. This category of texts can at times be difficult to interpret, and interpretation of them requires a careful consideration of both the text and the context. For example, one of the Qur'an's verses on inheritance is set out below:

> They ask you [Prophet] for a ruling. Say, 'God gives you a ruling about inheritance from someone who dies childless with no surviving parents. If a man leaves a sister, she is entitled to half of the inheritance; if she has no child her brother is her sole heir; if there are two sisters, they are entitled to two-thirds of the inheritance between them, but if there are surviving brothers and sisters, the male is entitled to twice the share of the female. God makes this clear to you so that you may not make mistakes: He has full knowledge of everything.'[53]

In interpreting ethical-legal texts, the historical context of the Prophet's time needs to be considered. For instance, in pre-Islamic Mecca and Medina, women, in many cases, did not receive an inheritance. To suggest that a woman would receive part of an inheritance herself, as the above verse does, was an important concept and one which was not easily accepted at the time. Another consideration is the Qur'an's own instruction that men are obliged to provide financially for their families, and that, in general, the Qur'an places greater financial responsibilities on men. In this context, the Qur'an's stipulation that a man receive a larger share of inheritance, so that he can meet his greater financial responsibilities, is more comprehensible.

Although this example of inheritance does not convey all the different understandings and connections between various aspects of the interpretation of ethical and legal texts, it provides some insight into the issues associated with that area. We will discuss this important category of texts in more detail in Chapter 9.

Summary

Some of the important points we have discussed in this chapter include:

- God is a core theme of the Qur'an, and His many 'beautiful names' or attributes are referred to frequently.
- The Qur'an describes Satan as the archetype of evil and as leading humans away from God's path.
- God's creations are referred to as 'Signs' for humans to reflect upon.
- Around one-fifth of the Qur'an is devoted to stories of the prophets or earlier communities.
- Jews and Christians are referred to in the Qur'an as 'People of the Book' because they have received scriptures from God.
- Muslim belief in the afterlife and accountability for our own actions are both important messages of the Qur'an.
- The Qur'an contains a number of ethical prescriptions, among them that Muslims should take a 'middle path' in life by avoiding extremes.
- There are various different types of Qur'anic texts, including theological, historical and ethico-legal texts.

Recommended reading

Muhammad Abdel Haleem, *Understanding the Qur'an: Themes and Styles*, London: I.B. Tauris, 2001.

- In this book Abdel Haleem discusses some major themes of the Qur'an and presents those themes that are pertinent to modern debates on

Qur'anic interpretation. This work is easy to understand and provides the reader with useful insights into difficult verses through its thematic approach.

Kenneth Cragg, 'The Qur'an in its Themes: the Logic of Selection', in *Readings in the Qur'an*, London: HarperCollins, 1988, pages 29–45;

'The Trouble of Man', 'The Seeking of Forgiveness', 'No God but Thou . . .', 'The Sacramental Earth' and 'Desiring the Face of God', in *The Mind of the Qur'an*, London: George Allen & Unwin, 1973, pages 93–181.

- These chapters by Cragg, found in separate works, look at the reasoning behind the Qur'an's focus on particular themes. The chapters from *The Mind of the Qur'an* provide an in-depth discussion of some important Qur'anic themes, how they are presented and their significance.

Fazlur Rahman, *Major Themes of the Qur'an*, Minneapolis, MN: Bibliotheca Islamica, 1994.

- In this book Rahman explores the theological, moral and social teachings and principles of Islam. He does so by engaging in a systematic study of the sacred text according to specific themes, rather than focusing on individual verses.

Faruq Sherif, *A Guide to the Contents of the Qur'an*, Berkshire, UK: Ithaca Press, 1985; revised, Reading, UK: Garnet Publishing, 1995.

- In this book Sherif systematically arranges the contents of the Qur'an according to its major themes. Each of the 68 theme-related sections contains a list of relevant Qur'anic verses. The index lists verses individually and also according to their theme or subject matter.

NOTES

1 Qur'an: 112:3.
2 Qur'an: 24:35.
3 Qur'an: 59:22–23.
4 Qur'an: 2:285.
5 Qur'an: 51:56–57.
6 Qur'an: 18:50.
7 See Qur'an: 2:31 and 2:34.
8 See Qur'an: 7:11–18; 2:30–38.
9 Qur'an: 2:168.
10 Qur'an: 6:112.
11 See for example: Qur'an: 15:85; 2:29.

12 Qur'an: 22:47. Also see Qur'an: 70:4 where a day is referred to as 50,000 years.
13 Qur'an: 13:07. Also see Qur'an: 4:163–164; 40:78.
14 Qur'an: 19:16–35.
15 See Qur'an: 3:42.
16 See Qur'an: 3:37.
17 Qur'an: 5:73.
18 Qur'an: 4:46.
19 Qur'an: 2:146.
20 For example, see Qur'an: 2:120–121.
21 The Sabians appear to have been a monotheistic religious group which emerged after Judaism but before Christianity. They may have been followers of John the Baptist. See Muhammad Asad, *The Message of the Qur'an*, Gibraltar: Dar al-Andalus, 1980, p. 14, fn. 49.
22 Qur'an: 5:69.
23 Qur'an: 2:111.
24 Qur'an: 5:48.
25 Qur'an: 80:1–12.
26 Qur'an: 3:121–126.
27 Asad, *The Message of the Qur'an*, pp. 85–86, fn. 90. See Chapter 1, this volume, for more discussions of historical events in the Prophet's time.
28 For example, see Qur'an: 56:5–12; 84:1–12.
29 Bukhari, *Sahih al-Bukhari*, Vols 7–8, Book 93 'The Book of the Oneness, Uniqueness of Allah (*Tawhid*)', No. 7,498, narrated by Abu Hurayra, Beirut: Dar al-Kutub al-Ilmiya, 1975–1995, p. 560.
30 Qur'an: 78:21–30.
31 Qur'an: 76:12–22.
32 For example, see Qur'an: 7:158; 20:98.
33 For example, see Qur'an: 2:177; 22:41.
34 For example, see Qur'an: 2:271; 76:8.
35 For example, see Qur'an: 2:185; 33:35.
36 For example, see Qur'an: 3:97; 2:196.
37 Qur'an: 5:90–91.
38 Qur'an: 17:31–33.
39 See Qur'an: 7:187; 79:42. This is also referred to as the Day of Judgement and denotes a time when all people will be held accountable for their lives before God.
40 See, for example, Qur'an: 6:73; 18:99; 78:18. This refers to a trumpet that will be blown to herald the coming of the 'Hour' (the Day of Judgement).
41 See for example Qur'an: 19:15; 19:33. Muslim scholars generally believe that Jesus will return to this world some time close to the end of the world; during this time he will rule benevolently.
42 Abu Ja'far Muhammad ibn Jarir al-Tabari, *Jami' al-Bayan an Ta'wil ay al-Qur'an*, Beirut: Dar al-Fikr, 1988, I, p. 33.
43 Tabari, *Jami'*, I, p. 34.
44 Qur'an: 42:11.
45 Qur'an: 112:4.
46 Qur'an: 14:4.

47 Zamakhshari, *Kashshaf*, II, p. 532, cited in Asad, *The Message of the Qur'an*, p. 990.
48 Qur'an: 7:59–64; 9:70; 11:25–48; 14:9; 22:42; 25:37; 26:105–122; 38:12; 40:5, 31; 50:12; 51:46; 53:52; 54:9–17.
49 Qur'an: 7:85–89.
50 Qur'an: 59:21.
51 Qur'an: 14:24–25.
52 Qur'an: 2:264.
53 Qur'an: 4:176.

5 The Qur'an in daily life

THROUGHOUT THE HISTORY OF ISLAM, THE QUR'AN has always been much more than a legal or religious text used mainly by scholars and preachers. From its revelation in the seventh century, the Qur'an has been memorized, recited and to a lesser extent copied by people at all levels of society, from scholars to young children. Recitation of the Qur'an has always been a central part of Muslim religious practice. Muslims will usually learn how to memorize and recite parts of the Qur'an from a young age. A select few reach the level of international competitions, where the beauty of their Qur'anic recitation is put on show, although this is a relatively recent development. Whether it is in daily prayer, or to open formal meetings or informal social gatherings, parts of the Qur'an are recited daily by Muslims throughout the world.

The Qur'an, in its written form, is also found throughout the public and private spheres of Muslim communities. Since the advent of printing, it has become increasingly common for Muslims to own a written copy of the Qur'an, and today there would be one in most Muslim households. References to the Qur'an are found in the language and literature of most Muslim countries, and excerpts are commonly printed in newspapers, on formal invitations, and in religious documents. Today, the decorative art of Qur'anic calligraphy can be found everywhere from a mosque or mausoleum, to the wall of a Muslim household or the screensaver of a computer.

Given the strong presence of the Qur'an in the lives of many Muslims, various norms and practices concerning interaction with the Qur'an have developed over time. Some of these practices are universal, known to most Muslims, regardless of the time or place in which they live, while others may be specific to a certain culture or time. The common thread in all these practices is a sense of respect and reverence for the Qur'an as the Word of God and hence as a sacred object.

In this chapter we will discuss:

- the contexts in which the Qur'an is most commonly recited, and some of the chapters and verses usually associated with them;
- the importance of memorization and recitation of the Qur'an – both historically and to Muslims today;
- general etiquette for Muslims in relation to handling the Qur'an, including the issue of ritual purity and whether non-Muslims may handle the Qur'an; and
- calligraphy as a common artistic expression of the Qur'an.

Reciting the Qur'an

Muslims will recite at least one chapter of the Qur'an – 'the Opening', *al-Fatiha* – from memory each time they perform one of their five daily prayers. In addition, most will recite a few other verses or one of the shorter chapters of the Qur'an. The recitation itself will be in Arabic, even though it may not be a person's mother tongue. Thus, it is common for Muslims from all linguistic and cultural backgrounds to know at least a small section of the Qur'an by heart.

There is a long history of recitation of the Qur'an as a form of worship, not only as part of daily prayers, but also in its own right. This tradition is based on certain passages of the Qur'an as well as numerous well-known sayings of the Prophet. For instance, the Qur'an describes itself by saying that 'it is a recitation that We have revealed in parts, so that you [Prophet] can recite it to people at intervals.'[1] In other places, recitation of the Qur'an is mentioned alongside prayer and giving in charity as an important act of worship.[2]

The Qur'an enjoins Muslims to 'recite the Qur'an slowly and distinctly'[3] and a saying of the Prophet instructs: 'Beautify the Qur'an with your voices.'[4]

Given the importance placed by the Qur'an itself on recitation, it is not surprising that a number of traditions regarding recitation developed in the early centuries of Islam. For instance, according to Islamic sources, the Prophet used to recite the entire Qur'an (as it had then been revealed) from memory at least once a year, during the fasting month of Ramadan. This practice was continued by later generations of Muslims, and today many Muslims still attend the mosque each night during Ramadan to pray together and listen to the recitation of one *juz'*, or a thirtieth, of the Qur'an. This practice of public recitation brings the Muslim community together and, by the end of Ramadan each year, the entire Qur'an will have been recited by thousands of groups and individuals in mosques around the world.

In Muslim communities people often recite the Qur'an as part of their personal religious practice, and children often start learning to recite the Qur'an from an early age. As they recite they are also encouraged to memorize sections of it; some are able to memorize the entire Qur'an before reaching adolescence. Whether they are able to memorize it or not, a child's successful recitation of the entire Qur'an is considered to be a significant community event and is celebrated in many Muslim cultures by family, teachers and community. Anyone who is able to memorize the Qur'an, whether as a child or later in life, is accorded special status in the community and referred to as a *hafiz*, meaning someone who has preserved the Qur'an in their heart.

In the modern age, the task of memorizing such large amounts of text may seem daunting. However, in most parts of the Muslim world today there are still many who have committed the entire Qur'an to memory. Historically, memorization of the Qur'an was a standard part of an Islamic education, and it remains part of the curriculum in many Islamic schools and seminaries today. In some countries, memorization of part of the Qur'an is still a prerequisite for gaining entry into Islamic studies in higher education.

The recitation of the Qur'an itself is a well-developed form of religious art, with rules for correct pronunciation and varying styles between different regions. As an art form, it is solemn, measured and meditative. Its ability to evoke emotions is closely linked to the beauty and majesty of the Qur'an itself. It is not considered to be music, which is a distinct and rich genre of Islamic art in its own right. However, in modern times, reciters with particularly beautiful voices can often become semi-professional, producing recordings of the Qur'an which are sold around the world or downloaded from the Internet. For both children and adults, there are local and national competitions in Qur'an recitation, as well as major international events held regularly throughout the Muslim world.

Commonly recited verses

As mentioned above, parts of the Qur'an are often recited on both private and public occasions. For instance, a formal speech or important gathering will often be opened and closed with a short reading from the Qur'an. This reading acts as a form of prayer or blessing on the occasion. Often people will choose a number of verses which they feel are appropriate for the occasion, but there are verses that are read more often than others.

For example, the opening chapter of the Qur'an (*al-Fatiha*) is often recited to open a meeting or gathering. At the end, the short chapter 'the Declining Day' (*al-Asr*, chapter 103) is often recited as a prayer, and as a reflection on the shortness of life and the importance of remembering one's most important priorities in life: 'I swear by the declining day, that man is [deep] in loss, except for those who believe, do good deeds, urge one another to the truth, and urge one another to steadfastness.'[5] At a wedding, it is common for the following passage from the chapter entitled 'the Byzantines' to be recited: 'Another of His signs is that He created spouses from among yourselves for you to live with in tranquility: He ordained love and kindness between you. There truly are signs in this for those who reflect.'[6] When someone is on their deathbed, or after they have passed away, family members will often gather and read the Qur'an, in particular the chapter *Ya'-Sin,* which is often referred to as 'the heart of the Qur'an'. This chapter is said to ease a person's suffering and describes both creation and death.

Certain passages of the Qur'an are also used as a form of protection, like a talisman. For instance, some people believe that the last two chapters of the Qur'an, and certain passages from the second chapter, in particular the 'verse of the Throne', have powers of protection which can keep away evil. The verse of the Throne reads as follows:

> God: there is no god but Him, the Ever Living, the Ever Watchful. Neither slumber nor sleep overtakes Him. All that is in the heavens and in the earth belongs to Him. Who is there that can intercede with Him except by His leave? He knows what is before them and what is behind them, but they do not comprehend any of His knowledge except what He wills. His throne extends over the heavens and the earth; it does not weary Him to preserve them both. He is the Most High, the Tremendous.[7]

Such passages may be written down, displayed on a wall or recited when someone feels that they are in danger. Similarly, reading or reciting of the Qur'an is used in some Muslim cultures for curative purposes. When a person is ill, they are often encouraged to read the Qur'an, or to have someone read it for them.

Aside from the significant events and occasions described above, many Muslims also use phrases from the Qur'an on a daily basis, often without even thinking about it. Such phrases range from short personal prayers, often based on prayers which were offered by Qur'anic prophets, such as the well-known prayer of Moses which asks God to give a person confidence to speak clearly: 'Lord, lift up my heart and ease my task for me, and untie my tongue so that they may understand my words.'[8] Other phrases are much shorter, such as the often repeated 'If God wills' – used after mention of any plan for the future – or 'Glory be to God' – a common exclamation.

Handling the Qur'an

As the Qur'an is also a physical text, a whole range of additional norms and practices regarding the etiquette of interacting with the Qur'an as a book have developed over time. These norms are underpinned by the Muslim belief that the Qur'an is the Word of God, and, as such, should be treated with the utmost respect at all times.

Before examining the practices of Muslims today, we will look first at a summary of a classical approach to 'Qur'anic etiquette'. Most Muslims today would still accept these guidelines, which were compiled by the Qur'anic scholar Qurtubi (d.671/1273) in the seventh/thirteenth century, as forming some of the key elements of Qur'anic etiquette, although many would not observe all the recommendations.

Qurtubi suggests that, in preparation for reciting the Qur'an, a person should brush their teeth with a *siwak* (twig used for brushing the teeth) and rinse their mouth with water, so that the mouth will be fresh before recitation. People should also sit up straight, dress as if intending to visit a prince, and place the Qur'an on their lap or on something that is off the floor. They should then find a quiet place, facing Mecca, where they will not be interrupted, or where they will need to intersperse their recitation with human words. Recitation should not be done in marketplaces or places of frivolity, and when they start to recite, people should seek refuge in God from Satan.

Qurtubi also recommends that Muslims should recite an entire section of the Qur'an, rather than just a few verses here and there. He further suggests that they should recite at a leisurely pace to allow time to concentrate, pronounce every letter clearly, and use their 'chair for the Qur'an' or a book holder. This helps to avoid situations where the Qur'an may end up on the floor or where it might be thrown around. After reading the Qur'an, many people will return it to a high position, often separate from other books, as a further sign of respect. Qurtubi's suggestion that people should face towards Mecca when reading the Qur'an is also a part of some cultures, although most regions do not follow this custom strictly.

Ritual purity and cleanliness

Many Muslims believe that before someone touches or carries the Qur'an, they should be ritually pure. This involves going through the same purification ritual that a Muslim would undertake before performing the five daily prayers. Some will also attempt to ensure that their clothing is clean and that they are dressed modestly as a further sign of respect.

Although most Muslims will agree on the importance of ritual purity before touching the Qur'an, there are different opinions regarding the exact details. There are two forms of ritual impurity recognized in Islam: major and minor ritual impurities. The most common form of major ritual impurity is associated with sexual intercourse, or, in the case of women, menstruation. If a Muslim is in a state of major ritual impurity, they are required to wash from head to toe in order to purify themselves ritually for prayer. Most Muslims would agree that this form of ritual purity is required before either touching or carrying the Qur'an. Minor ritual impurity, which is brought about by bodily functions such as urinating, need only be purified through *wudu'* (ablution). This normally involves washing the hands, face, arms and feet, and wiping the hair and ears with water. Opinions vary considerably as to whether this form of ritual purity is required before touching or reciting the Qur'an and depend on local cultures and individual beliefs. The following *fatwa* (Islamic legal opinion) from Saudi Arabia's Permanent Committee for Scholarly Research and Legal Rulings provides an example of a ruling that ritual purity is required in both instances:

> Question:
> Yesterday, we had a discussion on the permissibility of reciting the Holy Qur'an without holding the Qur'an, or from a book that contains some verses of the Holy Qur'an, in case the person is not ritually pure . . . What is the legal ruling on that act?

> Answer:
> Praise be to God alone, and prayers and peace be upon the last Prophet Muhammad.

> When a Muslim wishes to touch the Qur'an, he has to purify himself from minor and major impurities . . . As for reciting it without holding the *mushaf* [physical copy of the Qur'an], it is permissible to do so if one is in a state of minor ritual impurity. As for a person with major ritual impurity, he should not recite the Holy Qur'an with or without holding the *mushaf*.[9]

However, most Muslims believe that a person does not have to perform ablution or be ritually pure in order to recite the Qur'an, as long as they are reciting it from memory and are not physically touching it. Many scholars also believe that a menstruating woman may recite the Qur'an without touching it. In relation to digital recordings of the Qur'an on CDs, disks or tapes, the general view is that such material may be handled without any concern about ritual purity. The following *fatwa* from the same Saudi Arabian scholarly committee provides an example of this view.

> Question:
> I heard that it is permissible for a menstruating woman to analyze the syntax of the Holy Qur'an. I teach Muslim women the rules of

recitation. They come from distant places and their time is limited. Is it permissible for me to teach them the rules of recitation, correct [their recitation of] some verses of the Holy Qur'an, and recite it for them while I am in menstruation? Is it permissible for the learning woman in menstruation to receive her lessons or should she wait until she is purified? Please, point out the legal ruling on these acts. May God reward you for it. Besides, I read *tafsir* [Qur'anic exegesis] books when I am in menstruation. Is such an act permissible? Or should not I do so?

Answer:
Praise be to God Alone, and prayers and peace be upon the last Messenger Muhammad.

It is permissible for you to recite the Holy Qur'an while being in menstruation, and also to teach recitation and its rules during menstruation, but without touching the *mushaf* [physical copy of the Qur'an]. The woman in menstruation can also touch *tafsir* books and recite the verses in them, according to the most sound opinion of scholars.[10]

Non-Muslims and the Qur'an

Muslims differ as to whether a non-Muslim may touch or carry the Qur'an. The main argument against it is that non-Muslims are not ritually pure, as they do not follow Muslim regulations regarding ritual purity. Much of this debate is nowadays rather theoretical. It relies mainly on classical Islamic opinions formed largely before the advent of the printing press, when each Qur'an required a great deal of effort to produce and most, if not all, were published in parts of the world where most people were Muslim.

Some Muslims also debate whether it is permissible to take the Qur'an to non-Muslim countries. Such ideas are still current among a small section of Muslims, but are highly problematic, given the large number of Muslims who are born and live in non-Muslim majority countries. In current times this debate is also largely irrelevant, since the Qur'an is readily available in bookshops throughout the world. Even if it were desirable, in many parts of the world it would be almost impossible to restrict people of any religious persuasion from purchasing or reading the Qur'an if they wished.

The general view among most contemporary Muslims is that everyone should be able to handle or touch the Qur'an, but they would expect all who do so to show an appropriate level of respect.

Desecration of the Qur'an

As a sacred object, there are a number of general guidelines regarding the ways in which people are not supposed to handle the Qur'an. For instance, there are religious rulings that state that the Qur'an should not be taken into places that are considered unclean, such as a rubbish dump or toilet. Many Muslims also remove jewellery and other objects which may have texts from the Qur'an or the name of God written on them before entering such places. These guidelines, like many other rituals surrounding the Qur'an, are deeply embedded in Muslim culture. It was for this reason that global protests occurred in April 2005, when it was reported that American soldiers in Guantanamo Bay had flushed parts of the Qur'an down a toilet.[11]

Similarly, inappropriate use of any material that may contain Qur'anic verses, such as newspapers, is also discouraged. A common view among Muslims is that such material should not be thrown out with or put in the same place as rubbish. Instead, it should be burnt or buried. Although respectful of the Qur'anic text, this view can create practical problems in some countries, such as in the Middle East, where inclusion of Qur'anic phrases in the newspaper is very common. In these situations it may not be possible to regularly burn or bury large quantities of newspapers or similar materials. Hence, most Muslims consider paper recycling or shredding to be an acceptable alternative, as long as paper is not mixed with general waste. Some Muslims, however, have argued that recycling Qur'anic material is forbidden. The following *fatwa* states that the recycling of newspapers with Qur'anic texts, either through recycling bins or through personal use, is not permissible in any circumstances. Unfortunately, the *fatwa* does not go on to suggest a practical alternative.

Question:
The opening verse [of the Qur'an] 'In the Name of God, the Most Beneficent, the Most Merciful' is written on some newspapers which are sometimes thrown in the streets. Some people use them for cleaning. What is the legal ruling on both acts?

Answer:
Praise be to God Alone, and prayers and peace be upon the last Prophet Muhammad.

Writing 'In the Name of God, the Most Beneficent, the Most Merciful' at the beginning of religious books and research works is permissible, as the Prophet (peace be upon him) used to do so in his correspondence, and so did his Companions and Successors, and people have followed this until now.[12] Therefore, glorifying and holding this phrase in reverence is obligatory, and dishonouring it is prohibited. Whoever dishonours it [the phrase] is a sinner, because it is a verse of the Holy Book of God, the Exalted, and a part of a verse in the chapter *al-Naml* ['the Ants', chapter 27, verse 30]. Therefore, it is not permissible for anyone to use it [the paper] for cleaning, as a tablecloth, or for wrapping belongings. Moreover, it is not permissible to throw it in a recycle or waste bin.[13]

Qur'anic texts and calligraphy

Arabic calligraphy is considered one of the most important forms of Islamic artistic expression. Patterns based on Qur'anic texts are often displayed in mosques, tombs and palaces, as well as in homes, on walls, furniture, tapestries and ornaments, and in secular manuscripts throughout the Muslim world. Such calligraphy appears on a range of surfaces, including metalwork, pottery, stone, glass, wood, textiles and often in a different style depending on the surface. Calligraphy is highly valued for its strong association with the Qur'an and also because it enables free artistic expression without needing to produce images of sentient beings, a practice which many Muslims believe is discouraged.[14]

Over time, Muslim artists have developed a variety of styles of calligraphy, which differ from country to country and time to time. Common features across different styles include the interplay of curves and lines, the articulation of words and letters in floral or geometric designs, and a distribution of colours over the whole or part of the text. The subject of calligraphy tends to focus on Qur'anic verses, the names of God, the names and titles of the Prophet and, in the case of Shi'i Islam, the names of the infallible imams.[15]

An example of the artistic use of calligraphy is to be found in one of the world's most famous monuments, the Taj Mahal in India, which was built by the Mughal emperor, Shah Jahan (d.1076/1666), as a tomb for his wife, Mumtaz Mahal (d.1039/1630) and later himself. The tombs are decorated with exquisite floral patterns, which are offset by extensive calligraphic inscriptions. It is suggested that the monument is a representation of the Throne of God above the Garden of Paradise.[16]

Summary

Some of the important points we have discussed in this chapter include:

- Recitation of the Qur'an is an important Islamic practice dating back to the time of the Prophet.
- A *hafiz*, someone who has memorized the Qur'an, is accorded a place of high respect in the Muslim community and may become a professional reciter.
- Passages from the Qur'an are often recited as part of daily prayers, weddings, funerals and other important occasions, for the purpose of protection or healing, and as part of daily life for many Muslims.
- Muslims show respect to the Qur'an by being ritually pure before touching it and by not placing it on the floor or in a place which is considered unclean.
- Calligraphy, often based on Qur'anic texts, is an important Islamic art form which has developed into many different styles and can be observed in all spheres of Muslim life.

Recommended reading

Muhammad Abul Quasem (trans.), 'The Excellence of the Qur'an and the People Concerned with it', 'External Rules of Qur'an Recitation', 'Mental Tasks in Qur'an Recitation', in *The Recitation and Interpretation of the Qur'an: Al-Ghazali's Theory*, London, Boston and Melbourne: Kegan Paul International, 1982, pages 18–85.

- In these chapters Abul Quasem provides a valuable insight into the great importance placed by Muslims on study and recitation of the Qur'an. He also explores the skill and accuracy required for recitation, as well as the importance of reading and memorizing the Qur'an as an act of respect towards the holy text.

Kenneth Cragg, 'Having the Text by Heart', in *The Mind of the Qur'an*, London: George Allen & Unwin, 1973, pages 26–37.

- In this chapter Cragg discusses the spiritual merits and elements of memorizing the Qur'an.

Kristina L. Nelson, *The Art of Reciting the Qur'an*, Austin: University of Texas Press, 1985.

- This book was among the first dissertations of its kind in the West. Here, Nelson provides a comprehensive study of the art of Qur'anic recitation. Based on fieldwork conducted with some of the leading reciters of the Qur'an in Egypt, Nelson looks at the historical, cultural, linguistic and spiritual aspects of reciting the Qur'an, as well as the etiquette of its recitation.

Ahmad von Denffer, 'Reading and Studying the Qur'an', in *Ulum al-Qur'an: An Introduction to the Sciences of the Qur'an*, Leicester: The Islamic Foundation, 1985, pages 165–182, reprint 1994.

- In this chapter von Denffer provides an introduction to the general etiquette of reading and studying the Arabic text of the Qur'an.

NOTES

1 Qur'an: 17:106.
2 Qur'an: 73:20.
3 Qur'an: 73:4.
4 Abu Da'ud Sulayman ibn al-Ash'ath Al-Sijistani, *Sahih Sunan Abi Dawud*, Vol. 1, No. 1,468, narrated by Al-Bara' ibn Azib, Riyadh: Maktabat al-Ma'arif li al-Nashr wa al-Tawzi', 1998, p. 404.
5 Qur'an: 103:1–3.
6 Qur'an: 30:21.
7 Qur'an: 2:255.
8 Qur'an: 20:25–28.
9 Reciting Qur'an by a *junub* (ritually impure) person. *Fatwas Issued by the Permanent Committee for Scholarly Research and Ifta', Saudi Arabia*. Reference: Question No. 4, Fatwa No. 2,217, Volume IV, Page 72. 13 February 2005. Accessed 24 August 2007: http://www.qurancomplex.org/qfatwa/display.asp?f=51&l=eng&ps=subFtwa.
10 What is [the] judgment of a menstruating woman who reads in the books of Tafsir? *Fatwas Issued by the Permanent Committee for Scholarly Research and Ifta', Saudi Arabia*. Reference: Question No. 2, Fatwa No. 4,902, Volume IV, Page 75. (The English of the text has been modified to a certain extent to make it more readable.) 13 February 2005. Accessed 8 February 2007: http://www.qurancomplex.org/qfatwa/Hits.asp?f=10-20&l=eng.
11 *Newsweek*, 30 April 2005.
12 The term 'Successors' refers to the second generation of Muslims after the Prophet Muhammad.
13 The legal ruling on throwing newspapers in the recycle bins. *Fatwas Issued by the Permanent Committee for Scholarly Research and Ifta', Saudi Arabia*. Reference: Fatwa No. 49, Volume IV, Page 5. 13 February 2005. Accessed 24 August 2007: http://www.qurancomplex.com/qfatwa/display.asp?f=49&l=eng&ps=subFtwa.

14 'Introduction', *Islamic Art*. Accessed 8 February 2007: http://www.lacma. org/islamic_art/intro.htm.

15 Shi'i Islam is one of the two major branches of Islam. The infallible imams are male descendants of Prophet Muhammad and are believed by Shi'a to be the rightful leaders of the Muslim community. They are believed to be sinless, religiously inspired and the interpreters of God's Will. Although not prophets, their sayings, writings and deeds are considered to be authoritative religious texts in addition to the Qur'an and sunna.

16 'The Taj Mahal', *Islamic Architecture*. Accessed 8 February 2007: http:// www.islamicart.com/library/empires/india/taj_mahal.html

6

Western scholarship and the Qur'an

WESTERN SCHOLARSHIP ON ISLAM HAS HISTORICALLY been considered as being an example of 'Orientalist' scholarship. The term 'Orientalism' itself traces its origins, in part, back to medieval studies of Islam and the Qur'an. It is derived from the Latin *oriens*, referring to the rising of the sun, to imply the 'East'[1] and generally refers to the study of Eastern cultures and traditions by Western scholars. It became popular during the colonial period of the nineteenth and early twentieth centuries when the term 'Orientalists' referred both to Western artists inspired by the Orient, and to Western scholars who specialized in the study of Oriental languages, religions and cultures. It was from an 'Orientalist' perspective that much of the early Western scholarship on the Qur'an developed.

In modern times, some scholars, such as the well-known socio-political critic and commentator Edward Said, have argued that the distinction between the Orient ('the East') and the Occident ('the West') does not represent a 'natural' division; rather it is the result of 'imaginative geography',[2] and must be examined as a product of cultural history. In contemporary society, although 'Orientalism' still retains much of its original meaning, the prejudices and stereotypes which have traditionally accompanied this 'Orient/Occident' distinction have meant that the term 'Orientalism' has come to have a pejorative meaning, referring to Western scholarship that ostensibly lacks objectivity and reflects a bias towards Western thought and culture. Because of this perceived bias, Muslims themselves have not often held Orientalist scholarship in high regard.

However, such scholarship has undeniably had a significant impact on historical and contemporary understandings of the Qur'an in the West. In order to gain a better understanding of the Qur'an's place in both Muslim and non-Muslim scholarship, this chapter will present a brief overview of Muslim and non-Muslim scholarly interactions, and of the development of Western scholarship on the Qur'an.

In this chapter we will discuss:

- the historical context surrounding Western scholarship on the Qur'an;
- the range of approaches to the Qur'an by Western scholars;
- alternative Western scholarly views on the Qur'an's origin and compilation; and
- outlines of the contributions of some key Western scholars.

Early Western scholarship on Islam and the Qur'an: eighth to fourteenth centuries

Historical periods and events

8th–15th century CE
- Muslim Spain (or Andalusia, 711–1492). A period of largely peaceful co-existence between Muslims, Jews and Christians.

11th–13th century
- The Crusades (1095–1291). Military conflicts took place, generally aimed at recapturing the holy land of Jerusalem from Muslim rule.

12th–14th century
- Large quantities of translation into Latin of Arabic texts on science, medicine, and philosophy, as well as translation of the Qur'an and refutations of its text.

14th century
- Council of Vienna (1311–1312). Universities of Rome, Bologna, Paris, Oxford and Salamanca ordered to teach Oriental languages, though this had little practical effect initially.

Significant scholars and scholarship

8th century CE
- John of Damascus (d.135/753). Syrian monk who wrote *Heresy of the Ishmaelites*, one of the first polemical writings against Islam.

9th century
- al-Kindi's *Risala*, first complete refutation of the Qur'an; supposedly written by a Jacobite or Nestorian Christian.

12th century
- Robert of Ketton (fl.1136–1157). Englishman who produced the first known Latin translation of the Qur'an.

14th century
- Raymond Lull (d.1316). Wrote voluminous Arabic writings devoted to converting Muslims to Christianity; known as the founder of Western Orientalism.
- Riccoldo da Monte Croce (d.1320). Dominican priest who wrote an influential Christian denunciation of the Qur'an.

Muslim Spain 711–1492

Extensive interaction between Muslims, Jews and Christians in Europe was first recorded in Muslim-ruled Spain, during the period popularly referred to by Muslims as the Andalusian period. During this time, Islamic, Christian and Jewish cultures and religions co-existed for nearly eight centuries. For a significant part of this period, the inhabitants of Spain on the whole co-existed peacefully, knowledge of Arabic language and literature was widespread even among Christians and Jews, and religious debate and dialogue were common. Examples of interaction include a gathering of the Muslim scholar and doctor, Ibn al-Kattani (d.420/1029), the Jewish doctor, Hasdai ibn Shaprut (d.380/990) and the Christian bishop, Rabi' ibn Zayd (fl.350/961), at the royal palace to study 'the book of Dioscorides' – *De Materia Medica*, an ancient Greek medical text.[3] The strong focus on scholarship at the time was reflected in the existence of over 70 libraries and hundreds of thousands of books in the Andalusian capital, Cordoba. This period of largely peaceful co-existence began to decline in 1031 when the Cordoba Caliphate ended. Muslim rule gradually came to an end in the fifteenth century, when the whole of Spain came under the control of Christian rulers, and Muslim and Jewish inhabitants were either forced to leave or convert to Christianity.[4]

Early polemic translations and knowledge of Islam outside Spain

Around the period of Cordoba's decline, Europeans from outside Spain began to come into increasing contact with Islam and Muslim culture. It was after the capture of Toledo in 1085 by Christian forces that the Catholic archbishop, Don Raymundo (r.1125–1151), and the Benedictine Abbot of Cluny, Peter the Venerable (d.1156), began to commission scholars to work on the translation of various Arabic texts into Latin, including the scientific and philosophical texts of Andalusia, and religious works such as earlier refutations of the Qur'an and, importantly, the Qur'an itself.[5]

Translations of early works on Islam and the Qur'an were largely polemical. These translations were produced in an environment where Christians and Muslims competed to show the superiority of their respective faiths, as well as the alleged lack of authenticity of their counterparts. Many Christian scholars hoped to refute Islam through translations which aimed to show that the Qur'an was a fabricated document, concocted by Muhammad and based on what he knew of Christianity and Judaism. Peter the Venerable was of the opinion that Christians should proceed against Muslims 'not as our people often do, by arms, but by words.'[6]

Among the translated texts was a document named 'al-Kindi's *Risala*', believed to have been written by a Jacobite or Nestorian Christian in the third/ninth century under the pseudonym, al-Kindi.[7] This text, alleged to be the first complete refutation of the Qur'an, claimed that the Qur'an was unoriginal and was influenced by a Christian monk named Sergius, or Nestorius, who wanted to imitate the Gospels. Another text, known as the 'Bahira legend', claimed that Sergius taught Muhammad and was, in fact, the real inspiration behind the Qur'an.[8] One of the first known Christian polemical writings against Islam, written by the second/eighth-century Christian theologian John of Damascus (d.135/753) was also translated. This work's chapter on the 'heresy of the Ishmaelites' (Islam) focused on Qur'anic texts relating to polygamy and divorce and set a precedent for later Christian arguments against Islam, many of which would focus on issues of polygamy and divorce.[9]

During this period, the Crusades continued to fuel Europe's view of Islam as the great adversary of Christianity. Despite the growing body of knowledge about Islam, this view continued to be sanctioned by the Roman Catholic Church and anti-Islamic sentiment continued to grow. Thus, alongside translations of earlier polemic works, a flood of new anti-Islamic writings began to be produced. One of the earliest was Robert of Ketton's (fl.530–551/1136–1157) highly influential and hostile Latin translation of the Qur'an, which remained the most widely available Western translation until the seventeenth century.[10]

Other influential works of the period included Raymond Lull's (d.715/1316) voluminous Arabic writings, which were largely devoted to converting Muslims to Christianity.[11] Lull fiercely advocated the teaching of Arabic as part of the church's missionary effort and has come to be referred to by some as the founder of Western Orientalism.[12] The Dominican priest Riccoldo da Monte Croce (d.719/1320), a preacher, also produced a 'classic' denunciation of the Qur'an which systematically summarized Christian objections to the Qur'an and was highly influential.[13]

For a long time to come these attacks represented the greatest obstacle to any genuine understanding or appreciation of Islam, Muslims or the Qur'an at a popular level by European Christians. However, in academia, it was around this time that Lull's persistent calls for the teaching of Arabic were finally heard, and in 1311 the Council of Vienna ordered the universities of Rome, Bologna, Paris, Oxford and Salamanca to teach Oriental languages, thus institutionalizing the scholarly study of Arabic in Europe. This institutional change had remarkably little effect in practical terms at the time, but led the way for future understanding of Islam based on original Arabic texts. [14]

Later Western scholarship on Islam and the Qur'an: fifteenth to nineteenth centuries

Historical periods and events

15th–20th century
- Muslim Ottoman empire. Ottoman Turkish state that spanned three continents, including Europe; spurred the study in Europe of Islam and Muslim societies for military, political, economic and missionary purposes.

16th century
- Arabic printing presses installed in Venice and Rome.
- Oriental studies established at University of Leiden (1575); increase in the number of Western scholars with a knowledge of Arabic.

17th century
- Pope Alexander VII (1655–1667) forbade production of the Qur'an in Latin.

18th–19th century
- Orientalist period. Western scholars began to specialize in the study of Oriental languages, religion and culture.

Significant scholars and scholarship

15th century
- John of Segovia (d.1458). Spanish Catholic theologian; produced a Castilian translation of the Qur'an with Muslim jurist, Isa Dha Jabir (or Yça Gidelli, fl.1450).
- Nicholas of Cusa (d.1464). German cardinal; wrote *Shifting the Quran*; argued the Qur'an was a beneficial introduction to the Gospel.

16th century
- Complete Arabic Qur'an printed in Italy around 1538.

17th century
- William Bedwell (d.1632). English priest and scholar; produced a catalogue of the standard Muslim naming and numbering of Qur'anic chapters.
- Joseph Justus Scaliger (d.1609). A leading Arabist; argued the Qur'an should be read to understand language and history.
- Abraham Wheelock (d.1653). English minister and professor of Arabic; produced a translation and refutation of the Qur'an.

18th century
- George Sale (d.1736). Produced first published English translation of the Qur'an made directly from Arabic.

19th century
- Gustav Flügel (d.1870). Translated the Qur'an and introduced a Western numbering system for Qur'anic verses.

The early Ottoman period, 1450–1700

The Muslim Ottoman empire's presence in Europe from the fifteenth to the twentieth centuries spurred Europe to greatly increase its knowledge about Islam and Muslim societies for military, political and economic reasons. As in earlier times, this learning was to a large extent also designed to further the Christian missionary effort. In this drive to learn about Islam, there were both positive and negative examples of interaction. For instance, some Europeans, such as the Spanish theologian and cardinal John of Segovia (d.1458), were motivated to deepen their understanding of Islam so as to facilitate living in harmony and peace with Muslims. To this end, John of

Segovia studied the Qur'an, and became aware of the many imperfections of Robert of Ketton's earlier translation. Working with the Muslim jurist Isa Dha Jabir (or Yça Gidelli, fl.1450) for four months during the winter of 1455/56, he produced a new Castilian translation of the Qur'an, which included significant criticism of Robert of Ketton's translation.[15]

In the sixteenth century, the continued Ottoman presence, combined with the beginning of European colonization of parts of the Muslim world, provided a further motivation in the West to continue the study of Islam and the Qur'an. The centre for Islamic and Arabic studies at the time was in Italy, where Arabic printing presses were installed in Venice and Rome. The press was used around 1538 not for the purpose of missionary activity, but for commerce. The first complete Arabic Qur'an was published by Paganino de Paganinis for what turned out to be the largely unsuccessful venture of selling printed copies of the Qur'an to Muslims.[16]

The sixteenth century also saw the beginning of a more extensive programme for the study of Islam and Arabic in universities. For instance, Oriental studies were established at the University of Leiden in 1575, and, in 1593, Joseph Justus Scaliger was appointed professor of Arabic. Scaliger argued that scholars should engage with the Qur'an in order to understand Muslim culture and the Arabic language for their own sake, rather than solely for polemical purposes.[17]

This trend continued into the seventeenth century when scholars such as John Selden (d.1654), John Gregory (d.1646), Abraham Wheelock (d.1653), André du Ryer (d.1660) and Ludovico Marraci (d.1700) used their knowledge of the Qur'an in its original Arabic form in their scholarship. For instance, in Britain, Selden often quoted directly from the Arabic and referred to the original when critiquing Ketton's earlier Latin translation; and Wheelock produced both an English translation of the Qur'an and an Arabic refutation of the text.[18] Later in Italy, Marraci had to produce a lengthy refutation of the Qur'an before he was able to publish his own, highly accurate Italian translation.[19] These translations, and many others, were produced in the seventeenth century, despite a decree by Pope Alexander VII (1655–1667) officially forbidding the publication of the Qur'an in Latin.[20]

The Orientalist period, eighteenth to nineteenth centuries

The eighteenth century saw continued colonization of the Muslim world by Europeans, the presence of the Ottomans in Europe and the beginning of the Enlightenment. During this time sections of the Qur'an began to be published more widely and the term 'Orientalism' was coined. Western thinkers began to question publicly the very foundations of religion, particularly Christianity and the church. It was in this environment that the French philosopher Voltaire (d.1778) wrote his play *Mahomet: tragédie* (1741) and described the Qur'an as both illogical and undecipherable.[21]

Meanwhile, other efforts were being made to further European understanding of Islam and the Qur'an. New teaching institutions began to appear in Paris and Vienna which provided courses in both language and Islamic culture. In England, George Sale (d.1736) published the first English translation of the Qur'an to be made directly from Arabic; it remained influential well into the twentieth century. The introduction to Sale's translation was nearly 200 pages long, and discussed the Prophet's life, as well as Islamic history, theology and law. It was Sale's translation which was read and cited in the works of Thomas Jefferson (d.1826), one of America's founding fathers.[22]

During the nineteenth century, bilingual editions of the Qur'an became more common, and European universities began to expand their programmes of Arabic and Islamic studies to include analysis of the Qur'an. Also in Europe, a German scholar, Gustav Flügel (d.1870), published a significant translation of the Qur'an (1834) that introduced a new numbering system for its verses. For a long time, this would be used as the standard numbering system in the West.[23] His translation was later criticized, particularly by Muslims, for adopting a system which did not correspond with any known Islamic numbering system at the time.[24]

As the quantity of scholarship continued to increase, the study of Islam moved from being a subset of Oriental studies to an independent field of academic knowledge. With these developments came an increase in the study of Arabic, which led to numerous publications on Islamic religious, political and cultural history, and a growing number of translations and analyses of its religious and historical texts.

Contemporary Western scholarship on Islam and the Qur'an: twentieth to twenty-first centuries

---

Significant scholars and scholarship

20th–21st centuries
- Theodor Nöldeke (d.1930), first to arrange Qur'anic *suras* chronologically.
- Richard Bell (d.1952) believed the Qur'an was compiled before Prophet Muhammad's death.

- John Wansbrough (d.2002), foremost proponent of the 'revisionist' approach, believed the Qur'an was compiled approximately 150 years after the Prophet's death.
- Montgomery Watt (d.2006) believed the Qur'an was the Word of God for a certain time and place.
- Christoph Luxenberg believes the Qur'an was based on an Aramaic Christian liturgical document.
- Patricia Crone and Michael Cook, in their early scholarship, claimed Islam was a form of Judaism known as Hagarism.
- Gerd Puin believes parts of the Qur'an may be hundreds of years older than Islam.
- Andrew Rippin believes that the Qur'an must be understood within a broader monotheistic, rather than purely Arabian environment.
- Jane Dammen McAuliffe, editor of the *Encyclopaedia of the Qur'an*, who edited one of the most important works on the Qur'an bringing Muslim and non-Muslim thought together.

By the twentieth century, the study of Islam and Muslim societies had emerged as a significant area of Western scholarship. It is this most recent period which has seen a proliferation of Western scholarship on Islam and the Qur'an.

The twentieth and twenty-first centuries have seen a breaking down of the traditional divide between the Western and Muslim worlds. This has resulted in an increasing number of scholars collaborating across different faiths and countries of origin, and combining traditional Islamic and Western approaches in their study of Islam and the Qur'an. As the number of Muslims living in the West has increased, so too has the general level of understanding of Western scholars towards Islam and the Qur'an. Since the Second World War in particular, Islamic studies at universities throughout the Western world has been developed and extended to include a large number of programmes related to Islamic languages, history and social sciences.

Western scholarship on Islam over the twentieth century has approached the study of the Qur'an in a variety of ways. Many scholars have explored general areas related to the Qur'an without questioning Muslim accounts of its origins. Others have questioned the traditional Muslim understandings of the origins of the Qur'an by applying similar methods to those used in studies of the Bible.

Some Western scholars, such as John Wansbrough, whose work was briefly discussed in Chapter 3, have adopted an approach to the study of the

Qur'an that makes use of critical historical analysis, which is now the norm for studies of Christian and Jewish scriptures. It is worth noting that many Muslims have objected to this treatment of the Qur'an. This can be explained partly because, as discussed previously, the Qur'an has a similar role in Islam to that of Christ in Christianity – as a manifestation of the divine. Thus, for Muslims, to question the origin of the Qur'an is akin to questioning the divine nature of Jesus for Christians.

As suggested by Edward Said in his two major studies *Orientalism*[25] and *Culture and Imperialism*,[26] it is also important that we understand that any study of the Qur'an, by a Muslim or a Western scholar, must always be examined as a product of each scholar's own cultural history. According to Said, any scholarly work on Islam will reflect the cultural understandings, subjectivities and prejudices of the scholar. Thus, when discussing the various scholarly views on this topic, or for that matter any other topic, whether Muslim or non-Muslim, it is worth attempting to discern how a scholar's subjectivities or prejudices may have affected their work. It is important to remain aware of our own understandings and subjectivities, and the influence they may be having on our views of such scholarship.

In the following we will briefly examine the work of a few Western scholars of the Qur'an. We also make note of other scholars who have adopted similar approaches, for students who wish to explore the issues in more depth.

Theodor Nöldeke

The German scholar Theodor Nöldeke (d.1930) describes the Qur'an as a book 'composed of unstable words and letters, and full of variants' which, as a result, could not possibly be divine.[27] Perhaps as a result of his poor view of the Qur'an in the form as it is accepted by Muslims, Nöldeke became one of the foremost scholars to work on rearranging the Qur'an into a more chronological order. His reordering of the chapters of the Qur'an, which Richard Bell drew on in his own later rearrangement, assumes a 'progressive deterioration of style beginning with exalted poetical passages, and gradually becoming more prosaic'.[28] Nöldeke accepted the structural coherence of major units of texts, but examined the phraseology, manner and style of passages within a given chapter in order to determine their likely sequence.[29]

Nöldeke's work has been praised by some as 'the first truly scientific study of the Qur'an'[30] and by others as being a useful first approximation.[31] Bell suggests that Nöldeke relied too heavily on style in deciding the order of chapters and that his assumption that Muhammad's initial emotion and enthusiasm gradually waned was too simplistic. He also criticizes Nöldeke's failure to recognize that short passages within a given chapter may have been dated differently.[32]

John Wansbrough

The British scholar John Wansbrough (d.2002) was one of the foremost proponents of the 'revisionist' approach to the Qur'an. His work examined the evidence for the acceptance and canonization of the Qur'an. Among his claims was the assertion that the Qur'an was not completed until around 150 years after the Prophet's death, and that traditional accounts of its compilation were a 'salvation history' or myth that was projected backwards by Muslims of the Umayyad period (41–132/661–750).[33] Wansbrough thought that Islam was more likely to have been a sect which grew out of debates within the Judaeo-Christian tradition.[34]

Other scholars who adopted a somewhat similar approach to the Qur'an include Gerald Hawting, Patricia Crone, Michael Cook, Christoph Luxenberg, and Gerd Puin. However, Muslims in general have been critical of Wansbrough's approach, given its lack of recognition of core Islamic beliefs about the Qur'an. His approach has also been criticized by a number of Western scholars, who have noted that the gap between the time of the Prophet and the earliest evidence of a Qur'anic text is much shorter than he suggests;[35] they have also questioned the assumption that the process of the Qur'an's compilation was similar to that of the Bible, which spanned a much longer time.[36]

Patricia Crone and Michael Cook

Like Wansbrough, Patricia Crone and Michael Cook have also questioned the origins of the Qur'an and suggested a possible link with Judaism. In their controversial book *Hagarism: The Making of the Islamic World*,[37] Crone and Cook refer to Islam as 'Hagarism', based on Muhammad's claim to be a descendant of the Prophet Abraham's slave wife, Hagar. They also claim that the term 'Muslim' was not commonly used in early Islam and that the religion was originally a form of Judaism practiced by the 'Hagarenes'.[38] They suggest that the Qur'an first began to be compiled under the governor al-Hajjaj of Iraq, around 85/705,[39] and that the idea of the *hijra*, or migration, of Muhammad and the early Muslim community to Medina in 622, may have evolved as an idea long after Muhammad's death.[40]

Although their work presented some interesting new ideas, on its publication it came under immediate attack from Muslim and non-Muslim scholars alike due to its heavy reliance on hostile sources.[41] Wansbrough himself appears to have been critical of Crone and Cook's methodological assumptions.[42] So too was Stephen Humphreys, who criticized it for its 'use (or abuse) of its Greek and Syriac sources',[43] and others who describe it as not only bitterly anti-Islamic in tone, but anti-Arabian.[44] In their later works, Crone and Cook have moved away from some of their more controversial claims, but still question both the Muslim and Western orthodox views of Islamic history.[45]

Andrew Rippin

Andrew Rippin is also known for his questioning of traditional accounts of Islamic history. He has been described as 'perhaps the most widely read exponent of Wansbrough',[46] a connection which is demonstrated by his recent editing of Wansbrough's well-known *Qur'anic Studies: Sources and Methods of Scriptural Interpretation*.[47] Rippin's arguments regarding Qur'anic history and interpretation include that the Qur'an must be understood within a broader monotheistic, rather than purely Arabian environment, and that it should be situated within its literary tradition and at the focal point of a reader-response study.[48] Much of Rippin's earlier work is consolidated in his 2001 publication *The Qur'an and Its Interpretative Tradition*,[49] which includes 22 of Rippin's articles, covering topics from analyses of John Wansbrough's work, to examinations of the nature and development of the *tafsir* tradition.

Responses to Rippin's work have varied. It has been suggested that some scholars have effectively accused Rippin of 'arbitrarily ditch[ing] history in favour of literary analysis'.[50] His work has also been praised, for example by Norman Calder[51] and Andreas Christmann, who describe him as 'one of the most prolific and well-known scholars of early Tafsir'.[52] In general, Rippin's work on early *tafsir* scholarship has been well received and is recognized as providing a valuable contribution to Qur'anic scholarship.

Christoph Luxenberg

'Christoph Luxenberg' appears to be the pseudonym of a German scholar who also disputes the orthodox Muslim account of the Qur'an, arguing that the Qur'an is based on a Christian liturgical document written in a language closer to Aramaic than Arabic.[53] These arguments are based on Luxenberg's knowledge of early Semitic languages and his study of the earliest available copies of the Qur'an.[54] Luxenberg suggests that understandings of the Qur'an today are based on an incorrect understanding of its original context and function. Perhaps one of his best-known claims is that the word *huri*, often understood as referring to young companions or maidens in heaven, is actually the Aramaic word for 'white raisins' or 'white grapes'.[55]

Luxenberg's study has been described as 'arbitrary' by Gerald Hawting, a scholar who has also questioned the orthodox Muslim understanding. Hawting describes Luxenberg's proposed recomposition of the Qur'an as allowing too much scope for superimposing his own preconceptions of what may be found in the text.[56] Luxenberg's persistent attempts to identify underlying Aramaic or Syriac readings of the Qur'an have also been viewed with suspicion by other scholars and his methodology as 'presuppos[ing] its very results'.[57] Despite these and other criticisms, his study has also been described as 'introducing a whole new era of Qur'anic study' in the West.[58]

Gerd Puin

In contrast to the suggestion that the Qur'an was written after the time of Muhammad, the German scholar Gerd Puin suggests that parts of the Qur'an 'may even be a hundred years older than Islam itself' and that the Qur'an is most probably 'a kind of cocktail of texts that were not all understood even at the time of Muhammad'.[59] These assertions are based on Puin's study of some of the 15,000 ancient sheets of paper discovered in Yemen in 1972 and said to contain sections of the oldest known extant record of Qur'anic verses.[60] Puin claims that the Qur'anic texts found in Yemen show unconventional verse orderings and textual variations. He believes that a fifth of the Qur'anic text is 'incomprehensible' and that by proving that the Qur'an 'has a history', he claims that he will enable Muslims to engage in a discussion of the Qur'an which does not assume it is 'just God's unaltered word'.[61]

Puin's view of the potential of the Yemeni manuscripts is shared by other scholars of the Qur'an, who recognize the potential impact that variant readings and verse orders will have on modern understandings of its early history.[62] However, given the lack of availability of the Yemeni manuscripts at this stage, it is difficult for anyone to offer an evaluation of Puin's claims.

Richard Bell and William Montgomery Watt

Two scholars of Islam and the Qur'an who have had a significant impact on Western understandings of the Qur'an are Richard Bell (d.1952) and Montgomery Watt (d.2006). Both scholars are responsible for a significant work, the *Introduction to the Qur'an*, a book written by Bell and later considerably revised by Watt.[63] This work outlined the historical background of the life and character of the Prophet Muhammad and also explained the views of Muslim and Western scholars on the history, form and chronology of the Qur'an.[64]

Bell was a scholar of Islam and a minister of the Church of Scotland. He devoted much of his life to examining possible Christian influences on Islam, and the structure, chronology and composition of the Qur'an. His major work was *The Qur'an Translated, with a Critical Rearrangement of the Surahs*,[65] and he is best known for reordering the text of the Qur'an, in part based on the earlier orderings of Gustav Flügel and Theodor Nöldeke. Bell recognized the Qur'an as a complex text worthy of serious study, and commented that few books 'exercised a wider or deeper influence upon the spirit of man'.[66] He also suggested that the 'present form of the Qur'an . . . rests upon written documents that go back to Muhammad's lifetime',[67] and that modern study of the Qur'an had not 'raised any serious question of its authenticity'.[68]

Bell did, however, question the Islamic belief that the Qur'an is the direct Word of God. He believed that Muhammad played a significant role in its composition and that in writing the Qur'an, Muhammad was 'aiming at giving his followers something similar to the Scripture read . . . by other monotheists'.[69] Bell further believed that the revelation underwent considerable revisions during the Prophet's lifetime and emerged as a finalized written scripture during what he referred to as the 'Book period', namely the last eight years of Muhammad's time at Medina (ca.2–11/624–632).[70]

In general, many regard Bell's work as an extremely valuable contribution to the field, which has helped to move the focus of Western scholarship away from theories about the Qur'an to studies of the actual text itself.[71] Responses to specific aspects of his scholarship have varied. For instance, his translation of the Qur'an has been recognized as a useful tool for demonstrating his theories, but has also been criticized by scholars such as Andrew Rippin, who describes it as 'extremely difficult to just "read"', due to Bell's failure to attempt to 'convey directly the sense of the text'.[72]

Like Bell, the Scottish priest and scholar Montgomery Watt committed many years of his life to the scholarly study of Islam and was responsible for a major revision of Bell's *Introduction to the Qur'an* in 1970. In contrast to Bell, Watt believed that 'the Qur'an came from God [and] that it is Divinely inspired'.[73] Watt believed that the Qur'an was the Word of God for a particular time and place and that, like the Bible, the commands given in the Qur'an were valid for the society to which it was primarily addressed.[74] He did not support the comparison of the Qur'an to the Bible, arguing that the Qur'an was received by Muhammad 'in a period of less than 25 years, whereas from Moses to Paul [there] is [a period of] about 1,300 years'.[75] His respect for the Qur'an was reflected in his reported practice of using passages from the Qur'an and other Islamic texts in his daily meditation.[76] Watt was known as the 'last Orientalist'[77] and was regarded as a key figure and key Western contributor to the study of Islamic history.

Muslim scholars in Western settings

As an increasing number of Muslim scholars are taking up positions at Western universities, new approaches to the Qur'an – which combine traditional Islamic methodologies with modern theories in fields such as linguistics and feminism – are beginning to emerge. Among these scholars are figures such as Fazlur Rahman, who focused much of his work on considering the importance of context to Qur'anic interpretation; Amina Wadud, a feminist scholar of the Qur'an; Mohammed Arkoun, who has combined knowledge from a range of disciplines in his study of Qur'anic hermeneutics; and Khaled Abou El Fadl, a Muslim jurist who is highly critical of literalist readings of the Qur'an. The work of these scholars will be examined in greater depth in Chapter 12. Other Muslim scholars based at Western institutions who have contributed to contemporary understandings of the Qur'an include the Pakistani-born American scholar, Asma Barlas, and the Egyptian-born Nasr Hamid Abu Zayd, who at the time of writing is based in the Netherlands.

Jane Dammen McAuliffe and the *Encyclopaedia of the Qur'an*

The increasing amount of collaborative research now being undertaken into the study of the Qur'an is perhaps best reflected in the existence of the *Encyclopaedia of the Qur'an*, an online and hardcopy encyclopaedia which was first published by E.J. Brill in 2001. The *Encyclopaedia* draws on extensive scholarly work by Muslim and non-Muslim scholars in areas such as the linguistic, rhetorical and narrative analysis of the Qur'an. It provides extensive data on terms, concepts, places and history, and exegesis on subjects within the scope of Qur'anic studies. This five-volume work represents the first comprehensive, multi-volume reference work on the Qur'an to appear in a Western language.[78]

The *Encyclopaedia's* general editor, Jane Dammen McAuliffe, gained a PhD in Islamic studies in 1984, and since then has written extensively on topics in this area. Much of her work has focused on the Qur'an and its interpretation, as well as early Islamic history and relations between Islam and Christianity. For instance, in her 1991 publication *Qur'anic Christians: An Analysis of Classical and Modern Exegesis*,[79] McAuliffe analyses positive

Qur'anic references to Christians through a close examination of ten centuries of Muslim exegesis.

Summary

Some of the important points we have discussed in this chapter include:

- There was significant scholarly interaction between Muslims, Jews and Christians in Muslim Spain.
- Broader Western interest in Islam began around the eleventh century, when numerous Arabic works began to be translated into Latin.
- Early Western scholarship on the Qur'an was largely polemical.
- Alternative Western theories about the origins of the Qur'an have questioned when it was composed, the identity of its author and what language it was originally written in.
- Today, the number of collaborative scholarly works on the Qur'an is increasing, as is the number of Muslim scholars based in Western institutions who combine traditional and modern approaches in seeking to understand the Qur'an.

Recommended reading

Jane Dammen McAuliffe (ed.), *Encyclopaedia of the Qur'an,* 5 volumes plus index, Leiden: E.J. Brill, 2001–2006.

- This *Encyclopaedia* includes nearly 1,000 articles on Qur'anic terms, concepts, history, personalities and exegesis. A range of Muslim and non-Muslim scholars have contributed essays on the most important themes and subjects of Qur'anic studies. It is the first comprehensive, multi-volume reference work on the Qur'an to appear in a Western language.

Andrew Rippin, *Muslims: Their Religious Beliefs and Practices*, third edition, London: Routledge, 2005.

- In this book Rippin provides an overview of Islamic history and thought from its formative period to the present day. He adopts a critical approach to Islam, paying particular attention to the Qur'an and hadith. Rippin also examines the impact of Muslim interaction with these sources on the development of theology and law, from the medieval period to modern times.

John Wansbrough, *Quranic Studies: Sources and Methods of Scriptural Interpretation*, Oxford: Oxford University Press, 1977; reprinted, New York: Prometheus Books, 2004 with a new foreword and annotations by Andrew Rippin.

- In this book Wansbrough uses techniques of biblical criticism to analyse the Qur'an. He proposes that the study of Islam should be divided into scriptural canon, prophetology and sacred language. Wansbrough then focuses on analysis of the Qur'an as he develops a kind of Islamic scriptural exegesis based on form analysis. In the 2004 reprinted edition, Andrew Rippin has added a foreword and a substantial number of useful annotations which make the text more accessible.

Montgomery Watt and Richard Bell, *Introduction to the Qur'an*, Edinburgh: Edinburgh University Press, 2001.

- In this introductory book Watt and Bell examine the Qur'an's historical background as well as the character of the Prophet Muhammad. They provide the views of both Muslim and non-Muslim scholars and explain the history, form and chronology of the Qur'an.

NOTES

1 J.A. Simpson and E.S.C. Weiner (eds), 'Orient', *The Oxford English Dictionary*, second edition, Oxford: Clarendon Press, vol. 10, 1989, p. 929.
2 Edward W. Said, *Reflections on Exile and Other Literary and Cultural Essays*, London: Granta, 2000, p. 199.
3 Mohamed Benchrifa, 'The Routes of al-Andalus – Tolerance and Convergence', *UNESCO* (page was last updated on: 7/6/2001). Accessed 15 February 07: http://www.unesco.org/culture/al-andalus/html_eng/benchrifa.shtml.
4 Peter N. Stearns (ed.), *The Encyclopedia of World History*, sixth edition, Boston: Houghton-Mifflin, 2001, p. 179. Accessed 30 April 2007: http://www.nmhschool.org/tthornton/mehistorydatabase/umayyad_spain.php.
5 J.D.J. Waardenburg, 'Mustashrikun', in P. Bearman et al. (eds), *Encyclopaedia of Islam*, Brill Online, 2007. Accessed 27 August 2007: http://www.encislam.brill.nl.ezproxy.lib.unimelb.edu.au/subscriber/entry?entry=islam_COM-0818.
6 John Allen Jr., 'Seeking Insight from Muslim/Christian History', *National Catholic Reporter: NCRonline.org*, 3 November 2006. Accessed 26 August 2007: http://ncronline.org/NCR_Online/archives2/2006d/110306/110306m.php.
7 Hartmut Bobzin, 'Pre-1800 Preoccupations of Qur'anic Studies', p. 236 in Jane Dammen McAuliffe (ed.), *Encyclopaedia of the Qur'an*, vol. 4, Leiden: E.J. Brill, 2004, pp. 235–253.

8 Richard J.H. Gottheil, 'A Syriac Bahira Legend', p. 237 in 'Proceedings at Boston, May 11th, 1887', *Journal of the American Oriental Society*, vol. 13, 1889, pp. 151–203.

9 Bobzin, 'Pre-1800 Preoccupations of Qur'anic Studies', pp. 28–32.

10 G.J. Toomer, *Eastern Wisedome and Learning: The Study of Arabic in Seventeenth-century England*, Oxford: Clarendon Press; New York: Oxford University Press, 1996, p. 9.

11 Toomer, *Eastern Wisedome and Learning*, p. 9.

12 Bobzin, 'Pre-1800 Preoccupations of Qur'anic Studies', p. 240.

13 Bobzin, 'Pre-1800 Preoccupations of Qur'anic Studies', p. 241.

14 Toomer, *Eastern Wisedome and Learning*, p. 10.

15 *Encyclopaedia of the Qur'an*, p. 9.

16 Toomer, *Eastern Wisedome and Learning*, p. 20.

17 Toomer, *Eastern Wisedome and Learning*, p. 43.

18 Toomer, *Eastern Wisedome and Learning*, pp. 89, 224.

19 Toomer, *Eastern Wisedome and Learning*, pp. 24–25.

20 P. Bearman et al. (eds), *Encyclopaedia of Islam*, p. 12.

21 Dave Hammerbeck, 'Voltaire's *Mahomet*: The Persistence of Cultural Memory and Pre-Modern Orientalism', *AgorA: Online Graduate Humanities Journal*, vol. 2, no. 2, 27 May 2007. Accessed 27 August 2007: http://www.humanities.ualberta.ca/agora/Articles.cfm?ArticleNo=154.

22 Kevin J. Hayes, 'How Thomas Jefferson Read the Qur'an', *iviews.com*, 27 January 2007. Accessed 27 August 2007: http://www.iviews.com/Articles/articles.asp?ref=IV0701-3221.

23 Montgomery Watt and Richard Bell, *Introduction to the Qur'an*, Edinburgh: Edinburgh University Press, 1970, p. 58.

24 The differences between Flügel's system and the now standard Egyptian numbering system can be seen in Richard Bell's *Introduction to the Qur'an*, Edinburgh: Edinburgh University Press, 1953, p. ix.

25 New York: Pantheon Books, 1978.

26 New York: Knopf, 1993.

27 Theodor Nöldeke, 'The Qur'an', *Sketches from Eastern History*, trans. J.S. Black, Beirut, Khayats, 1963.

28 Bell, *Introduction to the Qur'an*, p. 101.

29 Andrew Rippin, 'Review: Reading the Qur'an with Richard Bell', *Journal of the American Oriental Society*, vol. 112, no. 4, Oct–Dec 1992, pp. 639–647.

30 Todd Lawson, 'Review: The Origins of the Koran: Classic Essays on Islam's Holy Book', *Journal of the American Oriental Society*, vol. 122, no. 3, Jul–Sept 2002, p. 658.

31 Bell, *Introduction to the Qur'an*, p. 102.

32 Bell, *Introduction to the Qur'an*, p. 103.

33 John Wansbrough, *Qur'anic Studies: Sources and Methods of Scriptural Interpretation*, New York: Prometheus Books, 2004, pp. 43–50, 202.

34 Wansbrough, *Qur'anic Studies*, pp. 78–81.

35 See, for example, Peter von Sivers, 'The Islamic Origins Debate Goes Public', *History Compass* 1 (November 2003), p. 11; Estelle Whelan, 'Forgotten Witness: Evidence for the Early Codification of the Qur'an', *Journal of the*

American Oriental Society, vol. 118, no. 1 (Jan–Mar 1998), pp. 1–14; Leor Harevi, 'The Paradox of Islamization: Tombstone Inscriptions, Qur'anic Recitations, and the Problem of Religious Change', *History of Religions*, vol. 44 (2004), pp. 127–128.

36 See, for example, Estelle Whelan, 'Forgotten Witness', p. 2.

37 Cambridge; New York: Cambridge University Press, 1977.

38 Toby Lester, 'What is the Koran?', p.46, *The Atlantic Monthly*, January 1999, vol. 283, no. 1, pp. 43–56.

39 Patricia Crone and Michael Cook, *Hagarism: The Making of the Islamic World*, Cambridge; New York: Cambridge University Press, 1977, p. 18.

40 Lester, 'What is the Koran?', p. 46.

41 Lester, 'What is the Koran?', p. 46.

42 John Wansbrough, 'Review', *Bulletin of the School of Oriental and African Studies, University of London*, vol. 41, no. 1, 1978, pp. 155–156.

43 R. Stephen Humphreys, *Islamic History: A Framework for Inquiry*, revised edition, Princeton: Princeton University Press, 1991, p. 85.

44 http://www.islaam.net/main/display.php?part=2&category=&id=910.

45 See Peter von Sivers, 'The Islamic Origins Debate Goes Public', *History Compass*, vol. 1 (2003), ME 058, pp. 1–16, and Liaquat Ali Khan, 'Hagarism – The Story of a Book Written by Infidels for Infidels', *The Daily Star*, vol. 5, no. 680, 28 April 2006. Accessed 25 May 2007: http://www.thedailystar.net/2006/04/28/d60428020635.htm.

46 Jawid A. Mojaddedi, 'Taking Islam Seriously: The Legacy of John Wansbrough', p. 108, *Journal of Semitic Studies*, vol. 45, no. 1, Spring 2000, pp. 103–114.

47 Wansbrough, *Quranic Studies*.

48 Issa J. Boullatta (ed.), *Literary Structures of Religious Meaning in the Qur'an*, London: Curzon Press, 2000, p. 145.

49 Andrew Rippin (ed.), *The Qur'an and its Interpretative Tradition*, Aldershot: Variorum Publishing, 2001.

50 Norman Calder, 'Review', *Bulletin of the School of Oriental and African Studies, University of London*, vol. 50, no. 3, 1987, pp. 545–546.

51 See, for example, Norman Calder, 'Review', *Journal of Semitic Studies*, vol. 35, no. 2, 1990, pp. 333–335.

52 Andreas Christmann, 'Review', p. 375, *Journal of Semitic Studies*, vol. 47, no. 2, 2002, pp. 374–375.

53 Stefan Theil, 'Challenging the Quran: Scholar's New Book, A Commentary on the Qur'an's Early Genesis', cited in Nerina Rustomji, 'American Visions of the *Houri*', *The Muslim World*, vol. 97, January 2007, p. 88.

54 Alexander Stille, 'Radical New Views of Islam and the Origins of the Koran', *New York Times*, 2 March 2002.

55 Theil, 'Challenging the Quran', p. 88.

56 Angelika Neuwirth, 'Qur'an and History – A Disputed Relationship. Some Reflections on Qur'anic History and History in the Qur'an', *Journal of Qur'anic Studies*, vol. V, no. I, 2003, pp. 1–18.

57 Neuwirth, 'Qur'an and History', pp. 1–18.

58 Theil, 'Challenging the Quran', p. 88.

59 Lester, 'What is the Koran?', p. 283.

60   Lester, 'What is the Koran?', p. 43–44.
61   Lester, 'What is the Koran?', p. 44.
62   Lester, 'What is the Koran?', p. 45.
63   Watt and Bell, *Introduction to the Qur'an*, 2001.
64   Watt and Bell, *Introduction to the Qur'an*.
65   Richard Bell, *The Qur'an Translated, with a Critical Rearrangement of the Surahs*, Edinburgh: T & T Clark, 1937–1939.
66   Bell, *Introduction to the Qur'an*, p. 1.
67   Bell, *Introduction to the Qur'an*, cited in Ibn Warraq (ed.), *What the Koran Really Says*, New York: Prometheus Books, 2002, p. 549.
68   Bell, *Introduction to the Qur'an*, p. 44.
69   Bell, *Introduction to the Qur'an*, p. 129.
70   Ibn Warraq, 'Introduction to Richard Bell', in Ibn Warraq (ed.), *What the Koran Really Says*, p. 518.
71   Rippin, 'Review: Reading the Qur'an with Richard Bell', pp. 639–647.
72   Rippin, 'Review: Reading the Qur'an with Richard Bell', p. 643.
73   Bashir Maan and Alastair McIntosh, 'Interview: William Montgomery Watt', *The Coracle*, 3(51), 2000, pp. 8–11, cited at *Alastair McIntosh*. Accessed: 13 May 2007: http://www.alastairmcintosh.com/articles/2000_watt.htm.
74   Maan and McIntosh, 'Interview: William Montgomery Watt'.
75   Maan and McIntosh, 'Interview: William Montgomery Watt'.
76   Richard Holloway, 'Obituary: William Montgomery Watt', *The Guardian*, 14 November 2006.
77   Maan and McIntosh, 'Interview: William Montgomery Watt'.
78   Jane Dammen McAuliffe (ed.), *Encyclopaedia of the Qur'an*, Leiden: E.J. Brill, 2001–2006.
79   Jane Dammen McAuliffe, *Qur'anic Christians: An Analysis of Classical and Modern Exegesis*, New York: Cambridge University Press, 1991.

7 Translation of the Qur'an

TRANSLATION OF THE QUR'AN IS ONE OF the most important topics in Qur'anic studies today. Primarily, this is because the first book that many non-Arabic speakers will encounter in their attempts to under-stand Islam and its holy text is a translation of the Qur'an. However, most Muslims would not consider a translation of the Qur'an to be equivalent to the Qur'an itself. Since Muslims believe the Qur'an was directly revealed to the Prophet Muhammad in Arabic, the preservation of the linguistic form of the original Arabic is considered paramount. Thus, although parts of the Qur'an have been translated into other languages from the very beginning of Islam, translation has until relatively recently occupied a minor position in Islamic scholarship; Muslim scholars have always considered it more effective to learn Arabic and engage with the original text than to study it in translation.

In this chapter we will discuss:

- the history of translation of the Qur'an by Muslims and non-Muslims;
- the Muslim debate for and against translation;
- the different approaches to translation among Muslims;
- a case study concerning the translation of a particularly contested verse of the Qur'an; and
- a short guide to some of the most commonly available contemporary English translations of the Qur'an.

Early Muslim interest in Qur'anic translation

This question has concerned Muslims since the beginning of Islam in the first/seventh century. Although the early Muslim community consisted pre-dominantly of Arabic speakers, the number of non-Arab converts to Islam, including speakers of Persian, Berber and Syriac, continued to grow. In these early stages, Arab Muslims were central to the community and held powerful political positions; often they were its caliphs, rulers, governors and generals. Thus, Arabic became the language of administrators, scholars and religious leaders, and gradually its influence permeated all corners of the expanding Muslim caliphate. This led to a situation in which most early converts to Islam did not seek translations of the Qur'an. Instead, when they became Muslim, they learnt Arabic and, in many senses, were also 'Arabized'.

Islamic history, however, provides evidence to suggest that, even during the time of the Prophet, there was already some interest in translating at least parts of the Qur'an. The earliest attempts focused on translation from Arabic into Persian. This is understandable given that, after the Arabs, Persians played the most important cultural and intellectual role in the formation of early Islamic civilization. They also constituted the second largest linguistic group to become Muslims after Arabs. Tradition tells us that one of the earliest Persian converts to Islam and a Companion of the Prophet, Salman al-Farisi (d.35/656), translated the first chapter of the Qur'an, consisting of seven verses, into Persian.[1]

In relation to ritual prayer (*salat*), a famous view attributed to one of the key figures of the Hanafi school of Islamic law, Abu Hanifa (d.150/767), is that in certain circumstances a Muslim may recite the Qur'an in Persian.[2] This allowed Persian-speaking Muslims, who were not yet able to recite the Qur'an in Arabic, to recite its meaning in their own language during prayer. Abu Hanifa believed that since prayer is an obligation and one of the five pillars of Islam, a person should not fail to pray simply because they may not yet be able to recite the first chapter of the Qur'an – a minimum requirement for daily prayers – in Arabic. This view was shared by later scholars such as Ibn Taymiyya (d.728/1328) and is also reflected in the following contemporary *fatwa* of 2005:

Question:
Is it permissible for a Muslim to recite or memorize the Holy Qur'an in a language other than Arabic?

Answer:
If a Muslim cannot recite or memorize the Holy Qur'an in Arabic, it is permissible for him to do so in any other language; this is better than abandoning it altogether. Allah said: 'Allah burdens not a person beyond his scope' (Q.2:286).[3]

Muslim tradition also suggests that it was common practice in early Islam for the meaning of the Qur'an to be paraphrased in the local vernacular after it was recited in Arabic.[4] Some Arab rulers of newly conquered lands appear to have occasionally taken an interest in translating parts of the Qur'an into local languages. However, no attempt appears to have been made to translate the entire Qur'an into another language during this early period of Islamic history.

Non-Muslims and translation of the Qur'an

Non-Muslim interest in translating the Qur'an began during the very early period of Islam, when some Christians, based in places such as what is now

Syria, began to translate parts of the Qur'an into Syriac. These were probably the first translations made for polemical purposes and they formed a precedent for later non-Muslim interest in translating the Qur'an in Europe.

The first European translation of the Qur'an is thought to have taken place in the twelfth century. At this time, Peter the Venerable, Abbot of Cluny (d.1156), became concerned with countering Islam, both theologically and intellectually. At the time, many Europeans viewed Islam as both an intellectual and political threat. Thus, he commissioned a team of translators to produce a number of works, including a Latin translation of the Qur'an. This translation was completed in 1143 by the Englishman Robert of Ketton (fl.1136–1157), and later published in 1543, after the advent of the printing press in Europe.[5]

In the sixteenth and seventeenth centuries, translations into European vernaculars began to increase. The oldest known complete translation of the Qur'an into a European vernacular was an Italian paraphrase of Ketton's earlier Latin translation, by Andrea Arrivabene in 1547.[6] These early translations formed the basis for subsequent translations of the sixteenth, seventeenth and eighteenth centuries. For example, the German pastor, Salomon Schweigger (d.1622), completed a translation in 1616. Based on Schweigger's text, a Dutch edition by an unknown translator was printed in 1641, and a few years later, in 1647, André du Ryer (d.1660) produced a French translation of the Qur'an. By the middle of the seventeenth century, in 1649, the first English translation was published by Scottish author Alexander Ross (d.1654),[7] with the title: *The Alcoran of Mahomet translated out of Arabique into French, by the Sieur Du Ryer . . . And newly Englished, for the satisfaction of all that desire to look into the Turkish vanities* (London, 1649). Ross had no knowledge of Arabic and a less than thorough understanding of French.[8] His translation has been described as crude and reflecting his 'rabidly anti-Islamic' feelings and Orientalist approach.[9]

In the eighteenth century, translations directly from Arabic began to appear again. Among the first of these translations was that of the English jurist and Orientalist, George Sale (d.1736), first published in 1734. This was followed by Claude E. Savary's (d.1788) French translation, in 1786, and Friedrich E. Boysen's (d.1800) translation into German, in 1773.[10] In contrast to previous Christian translations, Sale's *The Qur'an: Commonly Called the Alkoran of Mohammed* (London, 1734) is still in circulation today, and has been printed in more than 120 editions.[11] Despite being criticized by some Muslims as containing a number of omissions and incorrect translations, as well as being intended for missionary purposes,[12] Sale's work remained the standard reference for English readers until almost the end of the nineteenth century.[13]

In the nineteenth and early twentieth centuries translations into other languages also appeared, including Swedish (1843), Italian (1843), Polish (1849), Hebrew (1857), Russian (1877), Portuguese (1882) and Spanish (1907). It was only in the late nineteenth and the twentieth centuries that Western scholars such as Richard Bell (d.1952), Henry Palmer (d.1882), and Arthur J. Arberry (d.1969) began to undertake the task of producing better translations of the Qur'an as part of their scholarly pursuits.[14] Arberry's translation in particular remains highly regarded by both Muslim and non-Muslim scholars.

Muslims and translation of the Qur'an

As indicated earlier, from the first century of Islam, indigenous languages have been used to convey the meaning of the Qur'an to non-Arabic-speaking Muslims. The first major translation of the full Qur'anic text is considered to be the tenth-century CE translation into Persian of Tabari's monumental commentary, *Jami' al-bayan*, which included the full text of the Qur'an; this was subsequently translated into Turkish.[15] While translation has continued since that time, it has also been accompanied by ongoing debates, and, in some cases, vocal opposition to the translation of the Qur'an.

Going against the then prevailing view that the Qur'an should not be translated, the eighteenth-century Indian scholar Shah Wali Allah Dihlawi (d.1762) produced a Persian-language work of exegesis,[16] which included a full translation of the Qur'an. A number of decades later, translations by Muslims in regional Indian languages, such as Urdu (1828), Sindhi (1876), Punjabi (1870), Gujarati (1879), Tamil (1884) and Bengali (1886), also began to appear. Beginning a new trend, a printed Turkish translation appeared in Cairo in 1842, and the first printed Persian translation was produced in 1855, in Tehran.[17]

In the first half of the twentieth century, printed translations of the Qur'an began to appear in other parts of Asia and Africa. An African translation into Yoruba appeared in 1906 and into the Zanzibar dialect of Swahili, in 1923. In East and North Asia, the Qur'an was translated into languages such as Japanese (1920), Malay (1923), Chinese (1927) and Indonesian (1928).[18] During this period, Muslim converts in Europe also began contributing to the growing collection of translations. The first English example of this kind was the 1930 publication by the British author Marmaduke Pickthall (d.1936), entitled *The Meaning of the Glorious Koran* (London, 1930).

Efforts to translate the Qur'an into different languages increased significantly after the Second World War, particularly among Muslim scholars.

A number of prominent English translations were produced in this period, including Abdullah Yusuf Ali's 1934 translation, which remained the most popular translation among Muslims until recently; Abdul Majid Daryabadi's 1957 translation, published in Lahore; the translation by Muhammad Zafrullah Khan (London, 1971), which is still preferred today by members of the Ahmadiyya movement;[19] and *The Message of the Qur'an* (Gibraltar, 1980), by the prominent Austrian Muslim convert and journalist, Muhammad Asad (d.1992).[20]

Further European-language translations also appeared, including German translations in the 1990s by Muslim scholars and, earlier, French translations by Indian scholar Muhammad Hamidullah (1959) and North African scholar Sheikh Si Hamza Boubakeur (1972). Both French translations included detailed commentaries based on traditional sources; Boubakeur's translation is still popular among North African migrants in France today.[21] It was not until 1985 that the first North American English translation was produced by T.B. Irving.

As the above suggests, the twentieth century saw a proliferation of translations of the Qur'an by both Muslims and non-Muslims.

Key translations of the Qur'an

7th century CE onwards
- First translation of some Qur'anic verses into Persian by Salman al-Farisi
- Translation of parts of the Qur'an or commentary into local Muslim languages continued
- 961–976 – Translation of Tabari's monumental Qur'anic commentary, *Jami' al-bayan*, into Persian and later into Turkish; included first major translation of the Qur'an

12th century
- 1143 – First Latin translation of the Qur'an by Robert of Ketton

16th century
- 1547 – First Italian translation of the Qur'an. Paraphrase of Ketton's Latin translation by Andrea Arrivabene

17th century
- 1616 – German translation by Salomon Schweigger

- 1641 – Dutch translation by unknown translator, based on Schweigger's German translation
- 1647 – First French translation by André du Ryer
- 1649 – First English translation by Scottish author Alexander Ross; based on du Ryer's French translation
- First Malay translation by Abd al-Ra'uf al-Fansuri

18th century
- 1716 – Russian translation by Piotr Vasilyevich Postnikov; based on du Ryer's French translation
- 1734 – English translation, directly from Arabic, by George Sale
- 1773 – German translation by Friedrich E. Boysen
- 1776 – Urdu translation by Shah Rafi al-Din
- 1786 – French translation by Claude E. Savary

19th century
- 1843 – Swedish translation from Arabic by Fredrik Crusenstolpe
- 1844 – Spanish translation by De Jose Garber de Robles
- 1877–1879 – Russian translation from Arabic by Gordii Semyonovich Sablukov
- 1881–1886 – Bengali translation by Girish Chandra Sen
- 1879 – Gujarati translation by Abd al-Qadir ibn Luqman

20th century
- 1906 – First translation into Yoruba; first printed translation in an African language
- 1915 – First complete modern Hindi translation by Ahmad Shah Masihi
- 1917 – English translation by Muhammad Ali
- 1920 – First Japanese translation by Ken-ichi Sakamoto; from an English translation
- 1923 – First Swahili translation by Godfrey Dale
- 1927 – First complete Chinese translation by Li Tiezheng; from Sakamoto's Japanese translation
- 1930 – English translation by Marmaduke Pickthall
- 1934 – English translation by Abdullah Yusuf Ali
- 1955 – English translation by Arthur J. Arberry
- 1955 – English translation by Sher Ali
- 1956 – English translation by N.J. Dawood

- 1967 – English publication of Abul A'la Mawdudi's Urdu commentary *Tafhim al-Qur'an*
- 1972 – First translation by a North African scholar, Sheikh Si Hamza Boubakeur
- 1977 – Saudi-sponsored English translation by Muhammad Muhsin Khan and Taqiuddin al-Hilali
- 1980 – English translation by Muhammad Asad
- 1988 – English translation by Syed Mir Ahmed Ali, reflecting Shi'i doctrines
- 2004 – English translation by M.A.S. Abdel Haleem

Muslim discourse on translation

Given the large number of non-Arabic-speaking Muslims today (approximately 80 per cent of all Muslims) the level of debate concerning the translation of the Qur'an has increased. Muslim opinions vary widely on this issue, ranging from the extremely conservative view that translation of the Qur'an is impossible or illegitimate to much more accommodating perspectives.

Muslims who argue that the Qur'an cannot be translated provide a number of reasons for their viewpoint. For instance, a theological argument is that the Qur'an is the Word of God and, hence, has a unique style that cannot be matched, even in Arabic. They argue that if a piece of writing like the Qur'an cannot be imitated in Arabic, it follows that it can never be replicated in an entirely different language.

A linguistic argument is that translation from one language to another is always laden with difficulties. The meaning of a word in one language may not fully be conveyed in translation, resulting in the loss of part of the original meaning. This problem is amplified in the case of words whose meanings are associated with the cultural and linguistic context of a particular language and its community. In Arabic there are some words with no direct equivalent in other languages. Any attempt to convey their meaning is therefore approximate. For instance, words such as *salat* (usually translated as prayer) and *zakat* (usually translated as almsgiving) are unique to the Arab and Islamic contexts. Like a number of Islamic ethical-legal terms, they have technical meanings, which are difficult to convey through an English translation. Similarly, some words in Arabic may have more than one meaning. For instance, the verb *daraba* may have meanings as diverse as 'to travel', 'to condemn', 'to give' or 'to strike', depending on the context.[22] Such multiplicity of meaning is impossible to reflect in a translation where a translator is forced to choose a single word in the target language, and is only able to partially reflect this complexity in accompanying commentary.

Many translators therefore specify that their works represent a translation of the Qur'an's 'meanings', rather than of the Qur'an itself. The latter, if it were possible, would be equivalent to the Arabic Qur'an, whereas the former is simply an interpretation of the text. The following *fatwa* illustrates this view:

Question:
Is translating the Holy Qur'an or some of its verses into a foreign language with the aim of disseminating the Islamic Call [preaching of Islam] in non-Muslim countries an act that does not conform to Islamic law?

Answer:
Praise be to God alone, and prayers and peace be upon the last Prophet Muhammad.

Translating the Holy Qur'an or some of its verses and all the meanings implied in them is impossible. Literal translation is not permissible as it distorts the meanings.

As for translating the meanings of a verse or more and pointing out its legal rulings and teachings into other languages such as English, French or Persian languages with the aim of disseminating the meanings of the Holy Qur'an and calling others to believe in it, [it] is a permissible act. It is similar to explaining the meanings of Qur'anic verses in Arabic. Yet, it is stipulated that the translator should have the ability to give the meanings of the Holy Qur'an accurately and explain its rulings and teachings.

If he does not have the means that may help him in fully under-standing the Holy Qur'an, or if he does not have the ability to accurately convey such meanings in other languages, he should not translate the meanings of the Holy Qur'an. He may distort the meanings and he will be punished [by God] instead of being rewarded.[23]

In line with the idea that only the meanings of the Qur'an can be trans-lated, the twentieth-century British Muslim Marmaduke Pickthall argued in the introduction to his translation:

The Koran [Qur'an] cannot be translated. That is the belief of old-fashioned Shaykhs [Islamic scholars] and the view of the present writer. The Book [Qur'an] is here rendered almost literally and every effort has been made to choose befitting language. But the result is not the Glorious Koran, that inimitable symphony, the very sounds of which move men to tears and ecstasy. It is only an attempt to present the meaning of the Koran – and peradventure something of the charm – in English. It can never take the place of the Koran in Arabic, nor is it meant to do so.[24]

Another argument is that even if it were possible to translate individual words into another language, other stylistic, linguistic and rhetorical features of the Qur'an which are essential to its meaning would be lost. This is the case with literary texts of any language, as each language has its own unique features and forms of expression. In response to a question on this issue, the scholar and former head of the Azhar Fatwa Committee of Egypt, Atiyya Saqr, issued a *fatwa* which reflects the thinking of many Muslims on the subject. While including points similar to those already listed above, Saqr also stated that:

> [T]ranslation of the Qur'an can never be considered as a Qur'an in itself, in its rulings and sacredness. The reason for this is that translation is not the word of Allah which was revealed to the Prophet (peace and blessings be upon him); but it is human words offered to explain the Divine revelation [the Qur'an].
> [. . .]
> [T]he translated copy of the Qur'an does not enjoy the same lofty standard of the original one; it does not bear the sense of miracles initiated by Allah Almighty.
> [. . .]
> It is worth mentioning that no matter how a translation has effect [*sic*] on one, it can never have the same grandiloquent effect and beauty of the Qur'an itself.[25]

Some Muslims argue that since direct translation is not possible, any attempt at translation is in fact a form of interpretation and paraphrase and will, to some extent, be affected by the translator's theological and ideological orientation. Whether conscious or not, this 'bias' is likely to result in inaccuracies or misrepresentations, regardless of the translator's attempts to be faithful to the original text and meaning of the Qur'an.

Thus, most Muslims would argue that there is one version of the Qur'an – the Arabic version – along with many interpretations, which represent translations of the Qur'an's 'meanings'. Also, Muslims do not generally refer to 'versions' of the Qur'an (such as the French or American version) as this can imply that there are different 'versions' of the original Qur'an that are accepted as authentic. Most would argue that there is only one version of the Qur'an – the Arabic version – although there are many interpretations.

Thus, in summary, while many Muslims have engaged in translation of the Qur'anic text with varying degrees of interest and emphasis from the very beginning of Islam, there have always been Muslim voices against the translation of the Qur'an, for the reasons set out above.

Translation: a case study

To illustrate the difficulties involved in attempting to translate the meanings of the Qur'an, we will look at a current debate among Muslims today, regarding the translation of the Qur'anic verse 4:34. This is a well-known verse dealing with the area of gender relations, and its interpretation is highly contested.

Before looking at some actual translations of this verse, it is useful to examine some general approaches to translation of the Qur'an. In most cases, a translator may take one of three possible approaches. Some translators attempt to convey the meaning of the Qur'an as they understand it. Although they may perceive themselves to be objective, their choice of words will still be influenced by their worldview. For instance, many traditionalist translators may not be particularly concerned with issues of gender equality, and often provide interpretations of the text that emphasize patriarchal understandings and gender inequality.

In contrast, some translators attempt to remain aware of the influence their views may have by providing a translation that is as literal as possible, expressing their own understanding of the text in separate commentaries. Although their final choice of words will, to some extent, be influenced by their own understandings, these translators tend to be more conscious of this.

The third approach of some translators is to include phrases and words in the translation that reflect their own opinions but may have very little connection to the text's actual meaning. This is perhaps best described as claiming to translate the text, but actually providing a translation which includes a commentary in the body of the translation itself.

Thus, to varying degrees, translators express their particular orientation to issues such as gender equality and, in some cases, when not conscious of their own bias, may provide a misrepresentation of the Qur'anic text. The following examples of translations of a Qur'anic verse reflect the different approaches to translation and the ways in which a translator's own views become apparent through their choice of words.

Pickthall's early twentieth-century reading of this verse (Q.4:34) is representative of many available translations into English, and he translates it as:

> Men are in charge of women, because Allah hath made the one of them to excel the other, and because they spend of their property (for the support of women). So good women are the obedient, guarding in secret that which Allah hath guarded. As for those from whom ye fear rebellion, admonish them and banish them to beds apart, and scourge them. Then if they obey you, seek not a way against them. Lo! Allah is ever High, Exalted, Great.[26]

Similarly, Muhsin Khan and Taqiuddin al-Hilali provide an example of a more conservative translation. Their reading emphasizes protection of women by men, but also adds that righteous women should be devoutly obedient to their husbands and that women should be beaten lightly if necessary:

> Men are the protectors and maintainers of women, because Allah has made one of them to excel the other, and because they spend (to support them) from their means. Therefore the righteous women are devoutly obedient (to Allah and to their husbands), and guard in the husband's absence what Allah orders them to guard (e.g. their chastity, their husband's property, etc). As to those women on whose part you see ill conduct, admonish them (first), (next) refuse to share their beds, (and last) beat them (lightly, if it is useful), but if they return to obedience, seek not against them means (of annoyance). Surely, Allah is ever Most High, Most Great.[27]

Muhammad Asad, a modernist scholar, provides a carefully considered and almost literal translation of the verse. He also gives extensive explanatory notes to highlight his concerns about the literal reading of the key word '*idribuhunna*', translated below as 'beat them'. Asad emphasizes that in this case, a literal reading may not be the most appropriate.

> Men shall take full care of women with the bounties which God has bestowed more abundantly on the former than on the latter, and with what they may spend out of their possessions. And the righteous women are the truly devout ones, who guard the intimacy which God has

[ordained to be] guarded. And as for those women whose ill-will you
have reason to fear, admonish them [first]; then leave them alone in bed;
then beat them; and if thereupon they pay you heed, do not seek to harm
them. Behold, God is indeed most high, great![28]

In relation to his rendering of the phrase 'then beat them', Asad explains in
a lengthy footnote that the verse should not be taken literally, as the
apparent command to beat one's wife is contradicted by the practice of the
Prophet himself. He cites several prominent scholars in support of his view:

> It is evident from many authentic Traditions that the Prophet himself
> intensely detested the idea of beating one's wife, and said on more than
> one occasion, 'Could any of you beat his wife as he would beat a slave,
> and then lie with her in the evening?' (Bukhari and Muslim) . . . All the
> authorities stress that this 'beating', if resorted to at all, should be more
> or less symbolic – 'with a toothbrush, or some such thing' (Tabari,
> quoting the views of scholars of the earliest times), or even 'with a folded
> handkerchief' (Razi); and some of the greatest Muslim scholars (e.g.,
> Ash-Shafi'i) are of the opinion that it is just barely permissible, and
> should preferably be avoided: and they justify this opinion by the
> Prophet's personal feelings with regard to this problem.[29]

Another modernist scholar, Ahmed Ali (d.1994), translates the word
'*idribuhunna*' very differently. He goes against the general understanding of
this word in the exegetical tradition, where its meaning is usually understood
as 'to beat', rendering it instead as, '[to] have intercourse (with them)'. Ali
justifies his translation in an explanatory note, which includes both linguistic
and textual evidence in support of his reading.[30] He suggests that the phrase
is in fact closely related to another meaning of the word '*daraba*'. Thus, his
translation is in line with some of the contemporary Muslim feminist
thinking on this issue:

> Men are the support of women as God gives some more means than
> others, and because they spend of their wealth (to provide for them). So
> women who are virtuous are obedient to God and guard the hidden
> as God has guarded it. As for women you feel are averse, talk to them
> persuasively; then leave them alone in bed (without molesting them) and
> go to bed with them (when they are willing). If they open out to you, do
> not seek an excuse for blaming them. Surely God is sublime and great.[31]

Interpretation of this verse has been the focus of much attention among feminist scholars of the Qur'an. Although we have briefly discussed interpretation

of the phrase often translated as 'beat them', the scholarship of contemporary Muslim feminists such as Amina Wadud, Riffat Hassan and Aziza al-Hibri has also addressed the interpretation of other aspects of this verse.[32] For instance, all three of these scholars argue that based on a holistic reading of the Qu'ran, the notion of 'providing for', as it is expressed here, refers to the responsibility of men to provide for women in the specific context of raising a child. They further suggest that, contrary to the traditional understanding of this verse, it does not imply that men have unconditional control over women. Similarly, it does not necessarily suggest that women are not permitted to provide for themselves while raising a child, if they have the means to do so.[33]

In relation to the phrase 'beat them', Amina Wadud highlights a number of issues in regards to its interpretation. First, she argues that interpretations of this verse that in any way encourage violence towards women must be rejected, as such interpretations contradict basic Islamic teachings which emphasize the importance of mutual consultation and harmony between spouses.[34] Secondly, she highlights the fact that this word does not necessarily indicate the use of force and argues that it does not represent permission, but rather 'a severe restriction of existing practices'.[35]

A recent translation by Laleh Bakhtiar, an Iranian-American scholar, has also interpreted the verse in a new light. Bakhtiar relied on other translations and several years of classical Arabic study to produce her work. In a useful innovation, she indicates the feminine form of Arabic words that are gender-neutral in English by adding '(f)'. Bakhtiar translates verse 4:34 as follows:

> Men are supporters of wives because God has given some of them an advantage over others and because they spend of their wealth. So the ones (f) who are in accord with morality are the ones (f) who are morally obligated, the ones (f) who guard the unseen of what God has kept safe. But those (f) whose resistance you fear, then admonish them (f) and abandon them (f) in their sleeping place, then go away from them (f); and if they (f) obey you, surely look not for any way against them (f); truly God is Lofty, Great.[36]

Bakhtiar translates the word *idribuhunna* as 'go away from them', which she found to be the most likely translation out of the six pages of possible translations of the word *daraba* found in Edward Lane's highly respected *Arabic-English Lexicon*.[37] Bakhtiar argues that the Prophet himself never beat his wives, and hence the word, which is in the imperative form, could not be a command as the Prophet did not obey it. Further, she cites verse 2:231, which forbids husbands from holding back wives from divorce by harming or committing aggression towards them. Bakhtiar argues that, if 4:34 is interpreted as meaning 'beat them', it would contradict verse 2:231.[38]

In summary, this section has demonstrated the difficulty involved in conveying the sense of certain Qur'anic terms in English. In particular, the translation of a single Arabic word as 'beat', 'scourge', 'go to bed with them' or 'go away from them' has highlighted the fact that it is sometimes impossible to avoid the use of loaded words in translation. A sample of feminist interpretations of this verse, in particular Wadud's interpretation, has also touched on the fact that, even once an appropriate translation is decided upon, the implications of a verse may still be interpreted in different ways.

Some commonly available translations of the Qur'an in English

In this section, we provide a rough guide to some commonly available translations of the Qur'an in English, with some comments to help readers in choosing an appropriate translation for their use. If a translation is generally considered to reflect views that are specifically attributable to a particular stream or sect of Islam, this is indicated where possible. However, such labelling is often fraught with difficulties. Students are encouraged to make their own comparisons between the translations, which are listed in chronological order.

Ali, Muhammad. *The Holy Qur'an: English Translation* (Lahore, 1917).

Written by a key figure in the Ahmadiyya sect, this translation is criticized by many for its sectarian slant.[39] Ali considerably departs from a traditional rendering in several areas, including verses referring to a 'messiah' and to the Prophet Muhammad as the seal of the prophets. Ali also puts forward rationalist interpretations of verses referring to miracles and appears to have negative views of Judaism and Christianity; for example, he appears to deny Qur'anic support for Jesus' virgin birth. Interestingly, this translation came to be adopted as the standard translation of the Nation of Islam[40] in the United States. It has also apparently formed the basis of other mainstream translations, though this is usually unacknowledged.[41]

Pickthall, Muhammad Marmaduke William. *The Meaning of the Glorious Koran* (London, 1930).[42]

One of the earliest English translations by a Muslim convert, and still widely used. Pickthall was an English Muslim convert, and was fluent in Arabic, Turkish and Urdu. He tried to remedy the problems found in Christian missionaries' translations. The language is elegant, though archaic, and there is little or no commentary. The lack of the annotation could limit its usefulness to the uninitiated reader. Pickthall may have been influenced by figures like Muhammad Ali, particularly in his bias against miracles.[43]

Ali, Abdullah Yusuf. *The Holy Qur'an: Translation and Commentary* (Lahore, 1934).

Until recently, one of the most popular translations among Muslims. Ali was an Indian civil servant educated in India and Europe and his translation was informed by a modernist emphasis on rationalism. It includes extensive comments to explain particular words or phrases and his poetic style seeks to convey the richness of the original. However, the copious footnotes often reproduce material from medieval texts without contextualization.[44] It has now lost some of its influence due to its dated language.

Daryabadi, Abdul Majid. *The Holy Qur'an: With English Translation and Commentary* (Lahore, 1943).

Written by a well-known Indian writer and scholar, this translation is closely in line with traditional Muslim positions and is considered a faithful rendering, with useful notes.

Ali, Sher. *The Holy Qur'an* (Lahore, 1955).

This translation is described as the official (Ahmadi) translation of the Qur'an.[45] Perhaps even more so than in other Ahmadi translations, Ali interpolates his view that Mirza Ghulam Ahmad is the 'promised messiah' into his translation.

Arberry, Arthur J. *The Koran Interpreted* (London, 1955).

This well-known translation by the late Cambridge professor of Arabic is considered by many as the first English translation by a genuine scholar of Arabic and Islam. It stands out from many other English translations in its readability and the quality of its style. The title acknowledges the orthodox view that the Qur'an cannot be translated. Though some have commented on a few mistranslations,[46] this translation is still considered one of the best available, and is well respected by academics.[47]

Dawood, N.J. *The Koran* (London, 1956).

This translation by a Jewish scholar of Iraqi descent is one of the most widely available print editions, and it is published by Penguin Classics. The original edition arranged chapters in a non-standard, chronological order, though this was changed in a later edition. Several Muslim writers have criticized it for inaccuracies and for showing a systematic bias against Islam.[48]

Mawdudi, Abul A'la. *The Meaning of the Qur'an* (Lahore, 1967), English translation of Mawdudi's Urdu commentary *Tafhim al-Qur'an*.

This was written by the noted Indo-Pakistani scholar and political activist, the founder of Pakistan's Jamaat-e-Islami, a major religio-political organization. It emphasizes Islam as a way of life. Mawdudi provides a commentary on the classical Islamic scholarship of the Qur'an and attempts throughout to relate the Qur'an's message to contemporary concerns.

Khan, Zafrullah. *The Qur'an: Arabic Text and English Translation* (London, 1970).

This translation, like others from Ahmadi translators, is considered by mainstream Muslims to be flawed by its sectarian approach. In particular, the Ahmadi belief that Muhammad was not the last Prophet is evident.[49]

al-Hilali, Taqiuddin and Khan, Muhammad Muhsin. *Explanatory English Translation of the Meaning of the Holy Qur'an* (Chicago, 1977).

This translation is widely available in Sunni mosques and Islamic bookstores in the United States and in Europe, due to its free distribution by some conservative Muslim states and philanthropists. It is drawn largely from the work of the early exegetes, namely Tabari, Qurtubi and Ibn Kathir, with comments from *Sahih al-Bukhari* (a major collection of hadith).[50] Numerous interpolations in the text reflect strongly negative views of Jews and Christians, as does a polemical appendix comparing Jesus and Muhammad.

Asad, Muhammad. *The Message of the Qur'an* (Gibraltar, 1980).

Written by a Jewish convert to Islam; a 'simple and straightforward' rendering that seeks to exercise independent thought rather than relying solely on traditional scholarship.[51] It is written in more modern English than the popular translations of Marmaduke Pickthall and Yusuf Ali, and has extensive footnotes and commentary. Since it departs from traditional Muslim viewpoints on a number of issues, particularly some theological positions, some would consider it rationalist in orientation.

Shakir, M.H. *Holy Qur'an* (New York, 1982).

This translation has attracted some controversy; it is written from a Shi'i perspective. This is most clearly seen in the subject index, where Shi'i doctrines are linked to particular passages in the Qur'an that are said to support them. Many have criticized it for apparently plagiarizing the Ahmadi translation of Muhammad Ali.[52] There is also confusion surrounding the identity of the author; some even suggest that Shakir may have been an alias of an Indian financier who commissioned the translation by a group of scholars.[53]

Ali, Ahmad. *Al-Qur'an: A Contemporary Translation* (Karachi, 1984).

A clear rendering in fluent, contemporary English, written by a Pakistani poet and diplomat. Although certain words seem archaic, it is clear and readable. Some have criticized it for adopting unorthodox interpretations of certain passages.[54] It provides some notes, but lacks extensive commentary.

Irving, T.B. (Ta'lim Ali). *The Quran: The First American Version* (Vermont, 1985).

Written by an American convert to Islam in modern American English, this translation is considered to have some problems with basic linguistic accuracy. The subtitle is also considered problematic by many Muslims because it seems to imply that there are different 'versions' of the Qur'an.

Khatib, M.M. *The Bounteous Qur'an: A Translation of Meaning and Commentary* (London, 1986).

Considered a reasonably faithful translation in readable, modern English, its introduction discusses Islam, the Qur'an and the life of the Prophet. It includes brief notes on the circumstances of revelation of particular verses and the meanings of certain Qur'anic allusions and expressions.[55]

Ali, Syed V. Mir Ahmed. *The Holy Qur'an: Arabic Text with English Translation and Commentary* (New York, 1988).

This is considered a standard Shi'i translation, and includes extensive instructions on Shi'i doctrine and rituals. It is considered to have a strong Shi'i bias. The Shi'a respect it, partially because it includes commentary by Ayatollah Mirza Mahdi Pooya Yazdi, one of the highest-ranking authorities of contemporary Shi'ism.[56]

Bewley, Abdalhaqq and Bewley, Aisha. *The Noble Qur'an: A New Rendering of Its Meaning in English* (Norwich, 1999).

This translation is considered highly readable and accurate. Although the authors are Sufi followers of Sunni Islam, the translation itself does not show an obvious bias.[57] The authors' intent appears to have been to allow the meaning of the original to 'come straight through',[58] and they are largely successful. However, due to a lack of funding support, it is not widely available.

Fakhry, Majid. *An Interpretation of the Qur'an* (New York, 2002).

This translation has been criticized by some academic reviewers for linguistic deficiencies, which fail to convey adequately the style of the original Arabic rhetoric.[59] It does not appear to be widely popular.

Abdel Haleem, M.A.S. *The Qur'an: A New Translation* (New York, 2005).

This is a recent translation by Abdel Haleem, professor of Islamic Studies at the University of London. A highly accessible and accurate translation, it contains the minimum number of footnotes and commentary necessary to explain the context, and has brief chapter summaries. Abdel Haleem's translation has been criticized due to what some consider to be his orthodox reading.[60] The English is smooth and free from archaic language, though some argue the beauty of the original is not always conveyed.

Bakhtiar, Laleh. *The Sublime Quran* (Chicago, 2007).

This recently published translation is the first to be completed by an American woman. It differs from other Muslim translations in that verses are arranged in chronological order, rather than the standard Muslim ordering, and the controversial 'wife-beating' verse (4:34) is given a new, non-standard translation. Also potentially controversial is Bakhtiar's adoption of a method of translation which is largely the same as that used for the King James Version of the Bible.[61] Initial responses to this translation have varied.

Translations of the Qur'an on the Internet

The following section provides a guide to different translations of the Qur'an on the Internet. Readers are recommended to use online copies of translations only as a guide. They should not be used as a replacement for the published originals. In some online copies, terminology may have been changed slightly or texts may have accidentally been copied incorrectly.

Qur'an: www.quranm.multicom.ba

- 22 English translations available. Most can be viewed online or downloaded as Microsoft Word documents.
- Translations available in 55 other languages. Some languages such as Italian, Dutch, Russian and Turkish have multiple translations.
- Audio recordings, videos and commentaries in English, Arabic, Bosnian and Urdu also available.

The University of Southern California Muslim Student Association, Compendium of Muslim Texts: http://www.usc.edu/dept/MSA/quran/

- A transliteration of the Qur'an and complete English translations by Yusuf Ali, Pickthall and Shakir (however, a small number of 'corrections' to the original translations have been made by the South African Majlis of Ulema, and by readers of the website).[62]
- Can also search by verse, words or phrases.
- Introduction to each chapter by the Indo-Pakistani scholar, Abul A'la Mawdudi, and links to general articles about the Qur'an. Also includes general articles about Islam and a hadith search mechanism.

IslamiCity.com – The Holy Qur'an Centre:
http://www.islamicity.com/mosque/quran/

- English translations of the Qur'an by Yusuf Ali, Pickthall and Muhammad Asad, as well as Turkish, Malay, French, German and Chinese translations.
- A mechanism to search by topic, words and Arabic transliterations in the above languages. Results include translations, Arabic script and transliteration, a list of topics discussed in the verse and a link to audio recordings.
- Audio recitations in Arabic, English, Urdu and Bangla. External links are also available to written translations. Seventeen languages had valid links at the time of writing, including Albanian, Thai, Italian and Japanese.

King Fahd Complex for the Printing of the Holy Qur'an: www.quran complex.com

- Translation available in Hausa, Indonesian, Spanish, French and English.
- Also includes general information about the Qur'an and Islam, and a database of *fatwas*.

Summary

Some of the important points we have discussed in this chapter include:

- Since the beginning of Islam, Muslims have accepted the need for translation of the Qur'an into languages other than Arabic, though somewhat reluctantly in many cases, even for prayers.
- Muslims do not consider a translation of the Qur'an to be equivalent to the Qur'an itself; rather, they refer to a 'translation of the meanings of the Qur'an'.
- Reasons for this include the impossibility of replicating the Qur'an's original style, the richness of the Arabic language, the existence of certain untranslatable terms, and the fact that a translation can never be completely exact or neutral.
- The first significant non-Muslim translations of the Qur'an began in the twelfth century CE, and have until relatively recently been mainly polemical.
- The twentieth century has seen some highly accurate translations by Western scholars as well as by Muslims themselves, and there are now hundreds of different translations available in over 65 languages.

There is a range of commonly available translations of the Qur'an in English, and some of these have been outlined here.

NOTES

1 Hdayet Aydar and Necmettn Gökkir, 'Discussions on the Language of Prayer in Turkey: A Modern Version of the Classical Debate', pp. 123–124, *Turkish Studies*, vol. 8, no. 1, 2007, pp. 121–136.
2 Aydar and Gökkir, 'Discussions on the Language of Prayer in Turkey', p. 125.

3 Reciting or memorizing the Holy Qur'an in a language other than Arabic. Fatwa No. 89. *Fatwas Delivered by Shaikhul-Islam Ahmad Ibn Taimiah.* Published 13 February 2005. Accessed 12 February 2007: http://www. qurancomplex.org/qfatwa/display.asp?f=89&l=eng&ps=subFtwa.

4 Hartmut Bobzin, 'Translations of the Qur'an', in J.D. McAuliffe (ed.), *Encyclopaedia of the Qur'an*, vol. 5, p. 341.

5 Bobzin, 'Translations of the Qur'an', p. 344. See Chapter 6 (this volume) for further discussions of early translations from Arabic.

6 Bobzin, 'Translations of the Qur'an', p. 346.

7 Bobzin, 'Translations of the Qur'an', p. 347.

8 S.M. Zwemer, *Muslim World*, 5, 1915, p. 250. Cited in A.R. Kidwai, 'English Translations of the Holy Qur'an – An Annotated Bibliography', *Anti-Ahmadiyya Movement in Islam*, October 2000. Accessed 12 February 2007: http://alhafeez.org/rashid/qtranslate.html.

9 Kidwai, 'English Translations of the Holy Qur'an'.

10 Bobzin, 'Translations of the Qur'an', pp. 348–349.

11 Bobzin, 'Translations of the Qur'an', p. 348.

12 Kidwai, 'English Translations of the Holy Qur'an'.

13 Khaleel Mohammed, 'Assessing English Translations of the Qur'an', *Middle East Quarterly*, Spring 2005. Accessed 12 February 2007: http://www. meforum.org/article/717.

14 Bobzin, 'Translations of the Qur'an', pp. 352–354.

15 Bobzin, 'Translations of the Qur'an', p. 341.

16 This work was titled: *Fath al-Rahman bitarjamat al-Quran* and was published in 1737.

17 Bobzin, 'Translations of the Qur'an', p. 342.

18 Bobzin, 'Translations of the Qur'an', p. 342.

19 Followers of the teachings of Mirza Ghulam Ahmad (d.1908), who proclaimed to be the promised Messiah or *Mahdi*. Ahmadis belong to one of two distinct sub-groups – the Ahmadiyya Muslim Community, which has branches in 182 countries and claims to have tens of millions of followers; or the Lahore Ahmadiyya Movement, which has branches in 17 countries and an unknown number of followers. Ahmadis consider themselves Muslim but are not recognized as Muslim by most Sunnis or Shi'a.

20 Bobzin, 'Translations of the Qur'an', p. 343.

21 Bobzin, 'Translations of the Qur'an' p. 343.

22 Edip Yuksel, 'Beating Women, or Beating Around the Bush, or...'. Accessed 2 February 2007: http://www.yuksel.org/e/religion/unorthodox.htm.

23 The legal ruling on translating the Holy Qur'an. Fatwa No. 42. *Fatwas Issued by the Permanent Committee for Scholarly Research and Ifta', Saudi Arabia.* Reference: Fatwa No. 833, Volume IV, Page 132. 13 February 2005. Accessed 12 February 2007: http://www.qurancomplex.org/qfatwa/ display.asp?f=42&l=eng&ps=subFtwa.

24 Marmaduke Pickthall, *The Meaning of the Glorious Koran*, London: George Allen & Unwin, 1930; repr. 1957, p. vii.

25 Shaykh Atiyya Saqr, former Head of Azhar Fatwa Committee (of Egypt). Translating the Glorious Qur'an. Fatwa. 15 November 2006. Accessed 12 February 2007: http://www.islamonline.net/servlet/Satellite?pagename=

IslamOnline-English-Ask_Scholar/FatwaE/FatwaE&cid=1119503544404.

26 Pickthall, *The Meaning of the Glorious Koran*, p. 97.

27 Muhsin Khan and Muhammad Al-Hilali (trans.), '4: The Women'. Accessed 2 February 2007: http://en.quran.nu/.

28 Muhammad Asad (trans.), 'The Fourth Surah: An-Nisa (Women) Medina Period', *The Message of The Quran by Muhammad Asad*. Accessed 2 February 2007: http://www.geocities.com/masad02/004.

29 Asad, *The Message of the Quran*.

30 'Raghib points out that *daraba* metaphorically means to have intercourse, and quotes the expression *darab al-fahl an-naqah*, "the stud camel covered the she-camel", which is also quoted by *Lisan al-Arab*. It cannot be taken here to mean "to strike them (women)". This view is strengthened by the Prophet's authentic hadith found in a number of authorities, including Bukhari and Muslim: "Could any of you beat your wife as he would a slave, and then lie with her in the evening?" There are other traditions in Abu Da'ud, Nasa'i, Ibn Majah, Ahmad bin Hanbal and others, to the effect that he forbade the beating of any woman, saying: "Never beat God's handmaidens."' Kecia Ali, 'Muslim Sexual Ethics: Understanding a Difficult Verse, Qur'an 4:34'. Accessed 30 August 2007: http://www.brandeis.edu/projects/fse/muslim/mus-essays/mus-ess-diffverse-transl.html. The original book version of the translation was published in 1988.

31 Ahmed Ali, *Al-Qur'an: A Contemporary Translation*, Princeton: Princeton University Press, 1988, pp. 78–79.

32 See, for example, Amina Wadud, *Qur'an and Women: Rereading the Sacred Text from a Woman's Perspective*, New York; Oxford: Oxford University Press, 1999, pp. 70–78 for further discussions specifically related to this verse.

33 Margot Badran, 'Feminism and the Qur'an', p. 203, in McAuliffe (ed.), *Encyclopaedia of the Qur'an*, vol. 2, pp. 199–203.

34 Wadud, *Qur'an and Women*, p. 75.

35 Wadud, *Qur'an and Women*, p. 76.

36 Laleh Bakhtiar, *The Sublime Qur'an*, Chicago: Kazi Publications, 2007. Accessed 30 August 2007: http://www.sublimequran.org/index.php.

37 New York: Ungar Pub. Co., 1955–1956.

38 See Bakhtiar, *The Sublime Qur'an*.

39 See Mohammed, 'Assessing English Translations of the Qur'an'; A.R. Kidwai, 'Translating the Untranslatable: A Survey of English Translations of the Qur'an', *The Muslim World Book Review*, vol. 7, no. 4, Summer 1987. Accessed 30 August 2007: http://www.iiie.net/node/47.

40 A sect which developed among African Americans in the USA in the early twentieth century and held its founder, Wallace Fard Muhammad, to be a new prophet. At least in its formative years, the sect was known for promoting black supremacy and until today, it is generally not accepted as a valid stream of Islam by most Muslims.

41 Mohammed, 'Assessing English Translations of the Qur'an'.

42 Available electronically at http://www.usc.edu/dept/MSA/quran/qmtintro.html and http://www.quranm.multicom.ba/translations/Pickthall%20Mohammed%20Marmaduke.htm. Accessed 9 August 2004.

43 Mohammed. 'Assessing English Translations of the Qur'an'.
44 Mohammed. 'Assessing English Translations of the Qur'an'.
45 Kidwai, 'Translating the Untranslatable'.
46 Kidwai, 'Translating the Untranslatable'.
47 Mohammed, 'Assessing English Translations of the Qur'an'.
48 See Kidwai, 'Translating the Untranslatable' and Ziauddin Sardar, 'Lost in Translation: The Qur'an', review of *The Qur'an*, translated by M.A.S. Abdel Haleem, *The New Statesman*, 9 August 2004. Accessed 16 September 2007: http://www.newstatesman.com/200408090035.
49 Kidwai, 'Translating the Untranslatable'.
50 Mohammed, 'Assessing English Translations of the Qur'an'.
51 Mohammed, 'Assessing English Translations of the Qur'an'.
52 See Kidwai, 'English Translations of the Holy Qur'an'; Zahid Aziz, 'Shakir's Quran Translation – Blatant Plagiarism of the First Edition of Maulana Muhammad Ali's translation', *Lahore Ahmadiyya Movement*. Accessed 30 August 2007: http://www.ahmadiyya.org/movement/shakir.htm.
      Mohammed is of the opinion that it also draws heavily, without acknowledgement, from Pickthall's translation: Mohammed, 'Assessing English Translations of the Qur'an'.
53 See, for example, Zahid Aziz, 'Shakir identified', *Lahore Ahmadiyya Movement*. Accessed 30 August 2007: http://www.ahmadiyya.org/movement/shakir-2.htm.
54 Kidwai, 'English Translations of the Holy Qur'an'.
55 Mohammed, 'Assessing English Translations of the Qur'an'.
56 Mohammed, 'Assessing English Translations of the Qur'an'.
57 Mohammed, 'Assessing English Translations of the Qur'an'.
58 Abdalhaqq Bewley and Aisha Bewley, *The Noble Qur'an: A New Rendering of Its Meaning in English*, Norwich: Bookwork, 1999, p. iii.
59 See Mohammed, 'Assessing English Translations', and A.H. Johns, 'Review of *An Interpretation of the Qur'an*', *Middle East Studies Association Bulletin*, June 2004, pp. 83–84.
60 See Mohammed, 'Assessing English Translations'.
61 *The Sublime Qur'an*. Accessed 3 September 2007: http://www.kazi.org/product_info.php?manufacturers_id=154&products_id=2232&osCsid=fe493be0fa9874081270aaa2b277726e
62 The South African Majlis of Ulema are a council of traditionalist Muslim scholars based in South Africa. Examples of their views can be seen in *The Majlis* (http://themajlis.net/).

8 The Qur'an and other scriptures

THE THREE ABRAHAMIC RELIGIONS, JUDAISM, Christianity and Islam, are linked both by their belief in the One God and also by their scriptures. As the following Qur'anic verses show, the Qur'an recognizes the Torah of Moses (*Tawrat*) and the Gospel of Jesus (*Injil*) as being revelations from God:

> Step by step, He [God] has sent the Scripture down to you [Prophet] with the Truth, confirming what went before: He sent down the Torah and the Gospel earlier as a guide for people and He has sent down the distinction [between right and wrong].[1]

Despite the differences between the Qur'an, the Torah and the Gospel, a number of verses show that the Qur'an recognizes the authenticity of earlier revelations. In fact, Muslim theologians placed belief in prior revelation, including the Jewish and Christian scriptures, among Islam's 'six pillars of faith' (*arkan al-iman*), on the basis of verses such as Qur'an 2:285:

> The Messenger [Muhammad] believes in what has been sent down to him from his Lord, as do the faithful. They all believe in God, His angels, His scriptures, and His messengers. 'We make no distinction between any of His messengers,' they say, 'We hear and obey. Grant us Your forgiveness, our Lord. To You we all return!'

Nonetheless, based on the interpretation of several Qur'anic verses, some early Muslims came to think that the scriptures of the Jews and Christians as they existed at the time of the Prophet (the first/seventh century) had been 'distorted' by human beings. Therefore, they could no longer be considered the same as the authentic revelations described above, which the biblical prophets had received from God. Over time, these conflicting ideas of authenticity and distortion have been the source of much debate regarding the Qur'anic view of other religious traditions and scriptures. Today, views among Muslims range from those who believe that much of the Jewish and Christian scriptures can still be considered authoritative, through to those who argue that those scriptures are distorted and corrupted and therefore cannot be relied upon as valid scriptures.

In this chapter we will discuss:

- the tension between the standard Muslim understanding of scripture and several texts on this issue presented in the Qur'an;
- Qur'anic views of Jewish and Christian scriptures;
- different interpretations of the Qur'anic concept of 'distortion';

- Muslim scholarly engagement with Jewish and Christian sources; and
- some modern views regarding Jewish and Christian scriptures.

Muslim understandings of scripture

As discussed in Chapter 3, the Muslim concept of 'scripture' is closely connected with the idea of the written record of revelations that God has sent to His prophets. Based on the Muslim experience with the Qur'an, this written scripture is understood to represent the exact Words of God. According to this understanding, revelation and scripture are identical. Thus, any 'texts' included in a written scripture must only be direct revelations from God, and nothing else; the Words of God and the words of human beings must be kept separate. This understanding of scripture is not clearly described in the Qur'an or hadith; rather, it was developed by early Muslim theologians based on their understanding of the Qur'an's revelation and documentation. Over time, this concept developed into a theological statement and was eventually adopted as an important point of belief.

An important factor in the dominance of this conception of scripture among Muslims was the perceived need during the early centuries of Islam to demonstrate the authenticity and authority of the Qur'an vis-à-vis the scriptures of other religions. This need increased as greater contact took place between the established Christian empires in particular and the emerging Muslim caliphate. In Christianity, Muslims encountered a religious tradition that was already theologically highly sophisticated, and was able to draw upon a long tradition of philosophy, logic and theology in its claims to authenticity and in support of its basic dogma. Lacking such a tradition, Muslims relied on the argument that their holy scripture, the Qur'an, was 'purer' in its divine origin than the scriptures of the Christians and the Jews. It followed that if the scripture was purer and more authentic, then Islam, the religion based on it, must therefore also be purer and more authentic than Judaism or Christianity.[2]

Examination of what the Qur'an has to say on this, however, suggests that the Qur'an itself takes a broad view of the concept of a valid scripture. For instance, it accepts the validity and authenticity of earlier scriptures. This is despite the possibility that those scriptures may not have been documented during the lifetime or immediately after the death of the prophet to whom the revelation was given, or that they may not even have been written down in the language of that prophet. This acceptance of their authenticity is reflected, in part, in the following Qur'anic commandment: 'So let the followers of the Gospel judge according to what God has sent down in it.

Those who do not judge according to what God has revealed are law-breakers.'[3] From the context of the verse, this is clearly an instruction given to Christians at the time of the Prophet, rather than a reference to earlier times. Thus, although it is possible that, since the time of Jesus, the process of narration and translation may have resulted in some 'Words of God' becoming mingled with 'words of human beings', this does not seem to detract from the text's strong connection to the original revelation and the authority vested in that revelation.

The Qur'an's focus here appears to be on preservation of the essential message, rather than the language or narrative of the original revelation. Understood in this sense, even translations of the revelation could be considered scripture. The Qur'an does not enter into a debate about the overall 'authenticity' of earlier scriptures. Rather, with some exceptions it seems to accept the authenticity and validity of the scriptures of Jews and Christians as they existed at the time of the Prophet Muhammad.

Jewish and Christian scriptures in the Qur'an

As mentioned above, the Qur'an shows the utmost respect and reverence towards those scriptures it describes as previous revelations: in particular, the Torah of the Jews revealed to Moses, and the Gospel (*Injil*) of the Christians revealed to Jesus. It never makes disparaging statements about these 'books', which are referred to as coming from God. However, the Qur'an does criticize the People of the Book[4] (*ahl al-kitab*), Jews and Christians in particular, as individuals or groups, in instances where it alleges they have not remained faithful to the message of their prophets.

According to the Qur'an, the 'books' – the Torah and the Gospel – are said to contain wisdom, guidance and light:

> We revealed the Torah with guidance and light, and the prophets, who had submitted to God, judged according to it for the Jews. So did the rabbis and the scholars in accordance with that part of God's Scripture which they were entrusted to preserve, and to which they were witnesses.[5]

And:

> We sent Jesus, son of Mary, in their footsteps, to confirm the Torah that had been sent before him: We gave him the Gospel with guidance, light, and confirmation of the Torah already revealed – a guide and lesson for those who take heed of God.[6]

The Qur'an makes many references to the existence of these scriptures and the fact that they contain guidance from God. In fact, it repeatedly confirms the existence of Christianity and Judaism as valid religious traditions.

In the Qur'anic view, the key message of all the prophets, and what links the Qur'an, the Torah and the Gospel, is the belief in, and submission to, the One God. Consequently, in the Qur'an, both Jews and Christians are collectively given the honorific title of People of the Book. The Qur'an describes the People of the Book as reciting 'God's revelations',[7] and, in several instances, refers to them as those to whom God 'gave the scripture'.[8] They are further asked to 'uphold the Torah [and] the Gospel'.[9] The following well-known verse seems to suggest that, if they are sincere in their faith, then their good deeds too will be accepted by God: 'The [Muslim] believers, the Jews, the Sabians, and the Christians – those who believe in God and the Last Day and do good deeds – will have nothing to fear or regret.'[10]

The Qur'an's positive view of the Torah and the Gospel is perhaps not a surprising one; as it claims to be the Word of God, it seems natural that the Qur'an would honour previous divine scriptures. However, as mentioned earlier, although the Qur'an explicitly acknowledges these Christian and Jewish scriptures, some verses of the Qur'an seem to suggest the possibility of their 'distortion'. The presence of these seemingly conflicting messages has led to extensive debate among Muslim scholars and laity regarding the way in which these scriptures should be recognized and the extent to which they can be considered authentic and reliable in their current forms. In the following section, we will explore some of the arguments in this debate, along with a number of interpretations that Muslims have made of the concept of 'distortion' over time.

Muslim views on 'distortion' of Jewish and Christian scriptures

As we have seen, the Qur'an clearly recognizes and respects the scriptures revealed to Jews and Christians. Despite these references, there is a widely held view among Muslims that the Jewish and Christian scriptures as they exist today have been significantly 'distorted'. In the modern era, this view has to a great extent become a standard part of accepted Muslim beliefs. Because of this perceived 'distortion', it is believed that Jewish and Christian scriptures can no longer be relied on as the 'Word of God' in any matters of religion, faith or law.[11]

Although the scholarly views on this issue are more nuanced,[12] this popular view maintains that: (1) the scriptures the Qur'an approves of and praises are those that were actually revealed to Moses and Jesus; and either

(2) significant parts of the scriptures that exist today are 'distorted' or 'corrupted' and it is difficult to know which these parts are; or (3) the scriptures which the Qur'an refers to as the Torah or Gospel have been lost entirely, and accurate records of them no longer exist. This last appears to be the most common, particularly among more conservative Muslims. Although this is a popular view of scripture, most Muslims appear to believe that the People of the Book themselves must still be respected as part of a valid religious tradition, regardless of whether their scriptures are considered to be 'distorted'.

There are a number of Qur'anic texts that appear to support the view that there was some 'distortion' of parts of the Jewish and Christian scriptures. One of the more common terms used in the Qur'an in this respect is *tahrif*, defined as 'corruption of a document, whereby the original sense or text is altered'.[13] For example, the Qur'an states: 'They distort [*yuharrifun*] the meaning of [revealed] words and have forgotten some of what they were told to remember.'[14] Another word used by the Qur'an is *baddala*, which means 'to change, exchange or substitute'. The Qur'an says: 'But the wrongdoers substituted [*baddala*] a different word from the one they had been given.'[15]

Many scholars of Qur'anic interpretation have explored the meaning of those verses in which *tahrif* and other related terms are used. It is notable that most of these scholars have been far more cautious in their assessment of 'distortions' than might be expected from the popular view held among Muslims today. Among the pre-modern scholars whose ideas about distortion were influential were the great exegetes Tabari (d.310/923), Razi (d.606/1209) and Qurtubi (d.671/1273).

Distortion in meaning or wording?

One of the areas in which pre-modern scholarly opinion of distortion varied was on the issue of how distortion had actually occurred. While some scholars argued that distortion had taken place in the meaning or interpretation of a text, others suggested that the actual words of the text had been changed. For example, Razi argued that the meanings of the texts were distorted. In his interpretation of two verses that refer to *tahrif*, namely Qur'an 5:13, cited above, and Qur'an 5:41, which includes the phrase '[the Jews] who distort the meanings of [revealed] words', Razi thought that these texts referred to misleading interpretation of instructions from God, rather than changes to the actual scripture. He believed that changes to the words of a scripture which had already been transmitted by a large number of people were not likely to have occurred.[16] Razi seemed to believe that distortions in the text of a scripture could only arise at the very early stage of a community's history, when the number of followers of a revelation, and hence those to whom the text was known, were very few.[17]

Tabari, a prominent scholar of the Qur'an, also favoured the view that distortions occurred in the meanings of texts, not the actual texts themselves.[18] In commenting on Qur'an 5:13, Tabari said that the text of the revelation had been changed through false interpretations, which were then written down and attributed to God.[19] In interpreting the following verse, Tabari understood the term 'yuharrifunahu' to mean 'they alter its meaning':[20] 'So can you [believers] hope that such people will believe you, when some of them used to hear the Words of God and then deliberately twist them [yuharrifunahu], even when they understood them?'[21]

Another Qur'anic scholar, Qurtubi, also in his commentary on Q.5:13, was of the view that this reference to 'distortion' could be related to the alteration of either words or meaning. According to him, the verse meant that 'they [the Jews] interpret [texts] wrongly and provide the common people with these false interpretations'. He also observed that 'it is said that [alteration of] its [the verse's] meaning is changing of the letters [of the text]'.[22]

Based on the following verse, some scholars also suggested that distortion of scripture may have occurred 'by the tongue', referring to distortions in verbal narration:

> There are some who twist the Scripture with their tongues to make you [people] think that what they say is part of the Scripture when it is not; they say it is from God when it is not; they attribute lies to God and they know it.[23]

Qurtubi, in his interpretation of this verse, understood it to mean changing of what is intended by the text.[24] The verse clearly refers to distortion of the text or its meaning through speech; thus, the Qur'an seems to suggest that this process may have involved either narrating something and attributing it falsely to scripture, or giving a false or distorted impression of what these earlier scriptures say on a particular issue to the Prophet Muhammad.

Distortion by concealing the text

Some scholars also suggested the possibility that distortion occurred through concealment of a text. In this scenario, the text itself existed and was authentic, but was 'concealed' by Jewish or Christian scholars. The best-known instance of this type of alleged distortion relates to the theory that the Prophet Muhammad and his mission were foretold in the Torah and

Gospel. According to this theory, Jewish and Christian scholars of the Prophet's time 'concealed' these texts in order to deny his prophethood. For instance, Tabari saw some Qur'anic verses as supporting the allegation that Jewish scholars of Medina had concealed references to the Prophet in the Torah.[25] One of these includes the phrase 'As for those who conceal the Scripture that God sent down and sell it for a small price, they only fill their bellies with Fire.'[26] Similarly, he interpreted the verse below as referring to both Jewish and Christian scholars who had concealed what was written in their scriptures about Muhammad's prophethood:[27]

> As for those who hide the proofs and guidance We [God] send down, after We have made them clear to people in the scripture, God rejects them, and so do others, unless they repent, make amends, and declare the truth.[28]

Tabari's interpretation appears to be based on evidence contained in other verses which assert that Muhammad is described in the Torah and the Gospel as the 'gentile' Prophet. For instance:

> I [God] shall ordain My mercy for those who are conscious of God and pay the prescribed alms; who believe in Our Revelations; who follow the Messenger – the unlettered [*ummiy*] prophet they find described in the Torah that is with them, and in the Gospel.[29]

As Muhammad Abdel Haleem notes in his translation of this verse, *ummiy* can mean both 'unlettered' and 'gentile'.[30]

Tabari also refers to other verses which suggest that Jesus foretold the coming of Muhammad, referring to him as Ahmad, or 'the praised one', a name that has approximately the same meaning as Muhammad:[31] 'Jesus, son of Mary, said, "Children of Israel, I am sent to you by God, confirming the Torah that came before me and bringing good news of a messenger to follow me whose name will be Ahmad."'[32] Thus, the form of 'concealment' referred to here by Tabari appears to mean not recognizing either Muhammad or the 'signs' that point to him which are apparently found in both the Jewish and Christian scriptures.[33]

Scholarly engagement with Jewish and Christian sources

A significant number of Qur'anic verses refer to biblical prophets of the past, who had been sent by God before the Prophet Muhammad. Although the

Prophet and many of his followers would have had some knowledge of the existing traditions of Judaism and Christianity, their knowledge of these figures, who were often only alluded to in the Qur'an, was incomplete. Thus, Islamic tradition tells us that many early Muslims, including some of the Prophet's Companions, would often seek clarification from early Jewish converts to Islam such as Ka'b al-Ahbar (d. ca.32/652). Some sources suggest that Ka'b al-Ahbar would read and explain the Torah in the mosque in Medina.[34] The Prophet's own cousin, Abd Allah ibn Abbas, is reported to have been an avid collector and transmitter of biblical legends.

As Islam began to expand after the Prophet's death, an increasing number of Muslims wanted to learn more about prophets who were often only alluded to in the Qur'an. While some sought this knowledge purely for pious purposes, others were known to have incorporated it into popular story-telling of the time. Regardless of their reasons, many of these early Muslims would have relied on the traditions of the People of the Book to fill in the missing details.

In the following centuries, Muslim scholars often debated with People of the Book or referred to Jewish and Christian sources in the development of areas such as Qur'anic theology and law.[35] Beginning with Wahb ibn Munabbih's (d. ca.113/732) *Stories of the Prophets* in the second/eighth century, a number of Muslim historians also began to produce historical works which drew on Muslim, Jewish and Christian sources.[36] Among these early works was Mas'udi's (d.344/956) world history, titled *The Meadows of Gold and Mines of Gems*. The excerpt below illustrates the way in which Mas'udi moved freely between references to the Qur'an or Torah, and information received orally from People of the Book:

> Now the People of the Torah and the First Books say that Moses, son of Manasseh, son of Joseph, son of Jacob, was a prophet before Moses the son of Amram, and that it was he who went in search of al-Khidr . . . Some among the People of the Book say that al-Khidr is Khidrun.
>
> Now Pharaoh's soothsayers, astrologers, and sorcerers informed him that a child would be born that would put an end to his reign and would cause terrible things to happen in Egypt, and this worried Pharaoh very much. He ordered [their] children to be slain. But God revealed to [Moses'] mother that she was to cast him into the water, as God has reported and explained with regard to him through his Prophet Muhammad [cf. Sura 20:38, 28:7].
>
> And God spoke to Moses directly [Sura 4:164], and He strengthened the support of this brother Aaron, and He sent both of them to Pharaoh. He, however, opposed them, and God drowned him [cf. Exodus 3:10].

Then God ordered Moses to lead the Israelites out into the desert. They were 600,000 mature men, besides the ones not yet grown up [cf. Exodus 12:37].[37]

Around the same time, a trend which would later be labelled 'Muhammadan' Bible exegesis (referring both to the Christian Bible and Jewish Torah) also began to develop. An example of this was Ibn Qutayba's (d.275/889) *Dala'il al-nubuwwa* (*The Proofs of Prophethood*), which cites a number of biblical passages in support of Muhammad's prophethood.[38] In the following centuries, as a stronger and more independent sense of Muslim identity and scholarship developed, Muslim scholars came to view Jewish and Christian sources with increasing suspicion. Not only was reliance on these sources increasingly discouraged, but also references in earlier works were apparently reviewed and often censored. It was in this environment that scholars such as the Muslim jurist and theologian Ibn Hazm (d.456/1064) engaged in scriptural criticisms of the Jewish and Christian scriptures. His works were highly critical and rational in nature, and have been referred to by some as the forerunner of today's biblical criticism.[39]

Muslim attitudes to Jewish and Christian scriptures

A view from the pre-modern period

Referring to the divergent views on this issue, Ibn Taymiyya (d.728/1328), a scholar usually known for his conservative views, says:

It is said that in the world there is no single copy that corresponds to what God revealed in the Torah and Gospel. All that exist are changed. As for the Torah, its transmission from a large number of people to a [subsequent] large number of people has stopped and the Gospel is taken from four [people].

Then, among these people [Muslims] there are those who allege that much of what is in the Torah and Gospels [today] is false, not of God's word. Some of them said: [what is false] is not much. It is [also said]: No one has changed any text of the Scriptures. Rather they [Jews and Christians] have falsified their meanings by [false] interpretations. Many Muslims have held both of these views.

The correct [view] is the third view, which is that in the world there are true copies [versions], and these remained until the time of the

Prophet (peace be upon him), and many copies [versions] which are corrupted. Whoever says that nothing in [these] copies [versions] was corrupted he has denied what cannot be denied. Whoever says that after the Prophet [Muhammad] (peace be upon him) all copies [versions] have been distorted, he has said what is manifestly false. The Qur'an commands them to judge with what God revealed in the Torah and Gospels. [God] informs that in both there is wisdom. There is nothing in the Qur'an to indicate that they altered all copies [versions].[40]

However, Ibn Taymiyya also provides a basis for understanding what should be considered the 'Word of God', suggesting that the Word of God is represented by 'what the messengers report from God', not what scribes have written after the death of the messenger; for instance, about the life and times of a prophet.[41] His student, Ibn Kathir (d.774/1373), further suggested that the narratives found in the Gospel and Torah can be divided into three categories:

1) that which we know is authentic because we have [in Islam] what testifies to its truth; 2) that which we know to be false based on what we have that contradicts it; and 3) that which is neutral, neither from the first or second type; we neither affirm nor deny it, and we are allowed to narrate it.[42]

Two opposing views in the modern period

The following two modern-day opinions on 'distortion' illustrate two very different approaches to the issue. The first is that of Muhammed Salih al-Munajjid, a Salafi scholar in Saudi Arabia.[43] The second example shows the opinions of Ulil Abshar-Abdalla, co-founder of the Liberal Islam Network (*Jaringan Islam Liberal*) of Indonesia, which has attracted much criticism from conservative Muslim circles.

Based on Qur'an 5:48, which states 'We sent to you [Muhammad] the Scripture with the truth, confirming the Scriptures that came before it, and with final authority over them', al-Munajjid argues that the Qur'an abrogates all previous scriptures, including the psalms of David, the Torah and the Gospel; the only remaining authentic revealed scripture is the Qur'an. Citing a number of other verses,[44] he claims all Muslims are obliged to believe in this complete 'abrogation' of past scriptures, as well as the alleged textual distortion of the Torah and the Gospel.[45] Al-Munajjid concludes that any truth contained in the previous scriptures has also been abrogated by Islam. He uses the following hadith as textual proof of his position:

It was reported that the Prophet (peace and blessings of God be upon him) became angry when he saw that Umar had a page with something from the Torah written on it, and he (peace and blessings of God be upon him) said: 'Are you in doubt, O son of al-Khattab [Umar]? Have I not brought you something shining and pure? If my brother Musa [Moses] were alive, he would have no choice but to follow me.'[46]

Al-Munajjid's views regarding distortion seem to be underpinned by his strict and exclusivist notions regarding inter-religious relations more generally. He says:

One of the basic principles of belief in Islam is that we must believe that every Jew, Christian or other person who does not enter Islam is a *kafir* [unbeliever] against whom proof is established [and or who] must be named as unbelievers and regarded as enemies of Allah, His Messenger and the believers, and that they are the people of Hell.[47]

Al-Munajjid explains his understanding of distortion as follows:

When the previous books were distorted and altered because of men's desires and division among the Jews and Christians, it was no longer possible to rely on them. Allah abrogated all previous laws (*shari'as*) when Islam came, and all previous Books when the Qur'an was revealed. When He sent Muhammad (peace and blessings of Allah be upon him) as the final Messenger and Seal of the prophets, it became obligatory to believe in and follow the Qur'an which was revealed to him, especially since Allah has guaranteed to preserve the Qur'an and protect it from alteration and distortion.[48]

Al-Munajjid also cites the following *fatwa*, issued by the Saudi Arabian Permanent Committee for Islamic Research and Fatwa:

A great deal of distortion, addition and subtraction has befallen the previous divinely-revealed scriptures, as Allah has stated, so it is not permissible for a Muslim to read them and study them, unless he is one who has deep knowledge and is seeking to explain the distortions and contradictions therein.[49]

In stark contrast, the Indonesian thinker, Ulil Abshar-Abdalla, states that Muslims need to re-evaluate their understanding of the authenticity of scripture. He says:

To me, all scriptures are authentic and genuine. But we have to remember that scripture grows like plants. It means that there is no scripture born in the world and fully grown. Scripture is like a human; it experiences an infant, teenage, adult and elder phase. I don't find a ready-made human history. When we see Al-Qur'an, Torah, Vedas, Bible, and Upanishads, all are growing scriptures. All are genuine and authentic scriptures according to their religious teaching, but they change or grow according to the phases they pass through.

There was a view within the Muslim community that scriptures outside of Islam are distorted. But we have to revisit what is meant. Is it a distortion of content or substance . . . or of its implementation? Even Qur'anic implementation itself is distorted.[50]

Ulil Abshar-Abdalla believes that many Muslims have misunderstood the concept of distortion due to an erroneous belief that the Torah and Gospel were revealed in a manner similar to the Qur'an. He argues that Jesus, for instance, did not receive revelation in the same manner as Muhammad and, hence, the notion of revelation for the Bible is different to that of the Qur'an. He argues for a contextual approach to revelation:

I want to emphasize that Muslims should understand the revelation concept in a different context. Revelation in Islam, in Christianity, in Judaism etc. all are revelations, with different contexts, and should be appraised in those contexts. So one should not appraise other revelations based on [an] Islamic criterion. It is unfair.[51]

According to Ulil Abshar-Abdalla's pluralistic approach, good can be found in all scriptures and this good should be shared among people of all faiths. Each scripture was revealed and preserved in its own way.

The two examples shown above are not meant to be representative of the views held by most Muslims, or Muslim scholars, in regards to distortion; rather, they illustrate the diversity of opinions on this matter, and the ongoing debate and constantly evolving understandings of Muslim views of other scriptures.

Summary

Some of the important points we have discussed in this chapter include:

- Belief in the Jewish and Christian scriptures (the Torah and Gospel in particular) is one of the six pillars of faith in Islam, and their followers are referred to as 'People of the Book'.
- Muslims understand the concept of 'distortion' as referring to written distortion of words, verbal distortion of meaning or intentional concealment of the text.
- In the early centuries of Islam, reference to Jewish and Christian sources in Muslim scholarship was common, although it later came to be marginalized.
- Muslim views of other scriptures today range from the belief that they are completely inauthentic in their current form, to the belief that all scriptures are protected by God.

Recommended reading

Camilla Adang, *Muslim Writers on Judaism and the Hebrew Bible From Ibn Rabban to Ibn Hazm*, Leiden: Brill Academic Publishers, 1996.

- In this book, Adang examines the views of nine medieval scholars on Judaism and its holy scriptures. She examines their knowledge of the Torah and also explores issues such as the claim that the Torah contains references to Muhammad and that it has been abrogated and changed.

Kenneth Cragg, *A Certain Sympathy of Scriptures: Biblical and Quranic*, Brighton: Sussex Academic Press, 2004.

- In this book, Cragg looks at the common ground found in the holy scriptures of Islam and Christianity. In particular, he looks at the relevance to the twenty-first century of issues such as the divine will for a created order and the entrustment of this order in human hands.

F.E. Peters, *Judaism, Christianity and Islam: The Classical Texts and Their Interpretation – Volume I: From Covenant to Community, Volume II: The Word and the Law and the People of God, Volume III: The Works of the Spirit*, Princeton: Princeton University Press, 1990.

- In these three volumes, Peters compares the basic texts of Judaism, Christianity and Islam, focusing on issues of concern to all these 'children of Abraham'. Each volume includes references from a range of sources including scripture, theologians, priests, rulers and the ruled. Among the array of topics covered are prophethood, the notions of church and state, scriptural interpretation and law, and spirituality and worship.

Abdullah Saeed, 'The Charge of Distortion of Jewish and Christian Scriptures', *The Muslim World*, Fall 2002, 92(3/4), pages 419–436.

- In this article, Saeed examines accusations that the scriptures of the Jews and Christians have, over time, been corrupted and changed and hence can no longer be relied on as the Word of God. The author discusses the issue of distortion and the difficulties that have been experienced by Muslim scholars in this area.

Jacques Waardenburg (ed.), *Muslim Perceptions of Other Religions – A Historical Survey*, New York and Oxford: Oxford University Press, 1999.

- In this book, Waardenburg brings together a collection of essays that examine the historical writings of Muslim travellers, historians, theologians and jurists. Each of these essays examines Muslim writings about different cultures and their religions, ranging from different forms of Judaism and Christianity to Hinduism and Buddhism, as well as some of the tribal religions of Africa, Russia and Central Asia.

NOTES

1 Qur'an: 3:3–4.
2 Abdullah Saeed, 'The Charge of Distortion of Jewish and Christian Scriptures', *The Muslim World*, Fall 2002, vol. 92, nos. 3/4, pp. 431–433.
3 Qur'an: 5:47.
4 Throughout Muslim history, other religions, such as certain streams of Hinduism, Buddhism, Zoroastrianism and Mazdeism, have also at times been referred to as People of the Book, or *shibh kitab*, people who have the 'semblance' of a Book. Jacques Waardenburg, 'The Medieval Period: 650–1500', in *Muslim Perceptions of Other Religions*, New York; Oxford: Oxford University Press, 1999. See pp. 28–29 for Hinduism and pp. 56–57 for 'semblance' of a Book.
5 Qur'an: 5:44.
6 Qur'an: 5:46.
7 Qur'an: 3:113.
8 See, for example, Qur'an: 3:187; 4:131; 5:5; 74:31; 98:4.
9 Qur'an: 5:68.
10 Qur'an: 5:69.

11 This problem is discussed by Seyyed Hossein Nasr as one of the obstacles for Christian–Muslim dialogue. Seyyed Hossein Nasr, 'Islamic-Christian Dialogue – Problems and Obstacles to be Pondered and Overcome', *The Muslim World*, vol. 88, nos. 3–4, July–October, 1998.

12 See, for example, Taqiyy al-Din Ibn Taymiyya, *al-Tafsir al-Kabir*, ed. Abd al-Rahman Umayra, Beirut: Dar al-Kutub al-Ilmiyya, n.d., I, pp. 207–209.

13 'Tahrif' in H.A.R. Gibb and J.H. Kramers (eds), *Shorter Encyclopaedia of Islam*, Leiden: E.J. Brill, 1991, p. 560.

14 Qur'an: 5:13.

15 Qur'an: 2:59.

16 Al-Fakhr al-Razi, *al-Tafsir al-kabir*, Beirut: Dar Ihya' al-Turath al-Arabi, third edition, n.d., VI, part 11, p. 187.

17 Razi, *al-Tafsir*, II, part 3, p. 134.

18 Tabari, *Jami'*, I, p. 367.

19 Tabari, *Jami'*, IV, part 6, p. 155.

20 Tabari, *Jami'*, I, p. 368.

21 Qur'an: 2:75.

22 Abu Abd Allah Muhammad ibn Ahmad al-Ansari al-Qurtubi, *Al-Jami' li ahkam al-Qur'an*, Beirut: Dar al-Kutub al-Ilmiyya, 1993, III, part 6, p. 77.

23 Qur'an: 3:78.

24 Qurtubi, *Al-Jami'*, II, part 4, 78.

25 Tabari, *Jami'*, II, 89.

26 Qur'an: 2:174.

27 Tabari, *Jami'*, II, 52.

28 Qur'an: 2:159.

29 Qur'an: 7:157.

30 Muhammad Abdel Haleem (trans.), *The Qur'an: A New Translation*, New York: Oxford University Press, 2005, p. 105.

31 Qur'an: 61:6.

32 Qur'an: 61:6.

33 Tabari, *Jami'*, II, 53.

34 M.J. Kister, '*Haddithu an bani isra'ila wa-la haraja*. A Study of an early tradition', p. 232, *Israel Oriental Studies*, vol. 2, 1972, pp. 215–239, cited in Camilla Adang, *Muslim Writers on Judaism and the Hebrew Bible From Ibn Rabban to Ibn Hazm*, Leiden: Brill Academic Publishers, 1996, p. 8.

35 See Waardenburg, *Muslim Perceptions of Other Religions*, p. 55.

36 Wahb ibn Munabbih, *Qisas al-Anbiya* ('Stories of the Prophets'). For modern English translations which refer to Ibn Munabbih's work see: Muhammad Ibn Abd Allah Kisai, *Tales of the Prophets (Qisas Al-Anbiya)*, trans. Wheeler Thackston, Chicago: Kazi Publications, 1997.

37 Al-Mas'udi, *Muruj al-dhahab*, I, pp. 53–55, cited in Adang, *Muslim Writers on Judaism and the Hebrew Bible*, pp. 122–123 (square brackets in original).

38 Adang, *Muslim Writers on Judaism and the Hebrew Bible*, p. 35.

39 Waardenburg, *Muslim Perceptions of Other Religions*, pp. 27–28.

40 Ibn Taymiyya, *al-Tafsir al-Kabir*, I, p. 209.

41 Ibn Taymiyya, *al-Tafsir al-Kabir*, I, p. 210.

42 Imad al-Din Abu al-Fida' Isma'il Ibn Kathir, *Tafsir al-Qur'an al-'Azim*, Beirut: Dar al-Jil, n.d., I, p. 4.
43 Al-Munajjid's 'Islam Q & A' website – www.islamqa.com (accessed 16 September 2007).
44 Including Qur'an: 5:13; 2:79; and 3:78.
45 The term 'abrogation' is more generally used in Islam to refer to the 'cancellation' of earlier Qur'anic rulings by later ones. For discussion of this issue, see Chapter 9.
46 Narrated by Ahmad, al-Darimi and others. Al-Munajjid also quotes Permanent Committee for Scholarly Research and Legal Rulings of Saudi Arabia. See 'Ruling on the Call to Unite all Religions', Question No. 10,213, *Islam Question & Answer*. Accessed 30 August 2007: http://www.islam-qa.com/index.php?ref=10213&ln=eng&txt=distortion.
47 Sheikh Muhammed Salih Al-Munajjid, 'Ruling on the Call to Unite all Religions', *Fatwa, Islam Question & Answer*. Accessed 31 August 2007: http://www.islam-qa.com/index.php?ref=10213&ln=eng&txt=distortion.
48 Sheikh Muhammed Salih Al-Munajjid, 'Muslim View of Ibrahim (upon whom be peace) and the Tawrat (Torah)', Question No. 1,400. *Islam Question & Answer*. Accessed 31 August 2007: http://www.islam-qa.com/index.php?ref=1400&ln=eng&txt=distortion.
49 Sheikh Muhammed Salih Al-Munajjid, 'Ruling on Reading the Books of Ahl al-Kitaab and Debating with them on the Internet', *Fatwa, Islam Question & Answer*. Accessed 31 August 2007: http://www.islam-qa.com/index.php?ref=22029&ln=eng&txt=distortion.
50 Ulil Abshar-Abdalla, 'I Try to be like At-Tahtawi', Liberal Islam Network. Accessed 31 August 2007: http://islamlib.com/en/page.php?page=article&id=599.
51 Abshar-Abdalla, 'I Try to be like At-Tahtawi'.

Ethico-legal teachings

ONE OF THE MOST EXTENSIVELY STUDIED AREAS of the Qur'an are the texts that are of an ethical or legal nature. These are intended to guide Muslims towards leading moral lives, underpinned by a belief in the One God. The Qur'an's ethical and legal texts address both ritual worship and also more worldly affairs, such as marriage and inheritance. These texts have been studied over the centuries by Muslim scholars, who have attempted to understand how they affect the lives of ordinary Muslims in each time and place. Well-known scholars, such as Malik ibn Anas (d.179/795), Abu Hanifa (d.150/767), al-Shafi'i (d.204/820) and Ahmad ibn Hanbal (d.241/855) founded schools of legal thought or jurisprudence (*fiqh*), which now bear their names. Today, Muslims living in the modern world attempt to apply these teachings to a greater or lesser extent in their daily lives. Understanding some basic concepts around the Qur'an's ethical and legal prescriptions helps us to analyse the relevance of the Qur'an's teachings to Muslims today.

In this chapter we will discuss:

- the relationship between scripture and religious law;
- the ways in which the ethico-legal teachings of the Qur'an can be categorized;
- the concept of 'abrogation' and its relationship to the adaptability of the Qur'anic text; and
- the Qur'an's general approach to ethico-legal issues.

Scripture and religious law

The concept of religious law refers to the idea that the Word of God (or scripture) is the ultimate and most authoritative legal source. Religious law is thus understood to be revealed by God and designed to govern human affairs. In this framework, law also includes codes of ethics and morality.

Religious laws can be found in all three of the monotheistic religions that trace their roots to Abraham: Judaism, Christianity and Islam. Such laws are known as *halakha* in Judaism, *shari'a* in Islam and canon law in some forms of Christianity. The purpose of these laws may range from providing purely individual moral guidance, to forming the basis of a nation's legal system. However, being laws of divine origin, there is an implicit assumption that they are static and unalterable. Hence amendments through legislative acts of government, or developments through judicial precedent, may not be permitted, although changes through evolving interpretations may be possible.

The *halakha* is followed by some Orthodox Jews in both religious and civil relations. While it may not be the basis for any national legal system, in some countries Jews may choose to have a dispute heard by a Jewish court, and to be bound by its rulings. Among Muslim majority countries, some, including Saudi Arabia and Iran, claim to be governed by *shari'a* (Islamic law). Most, however, have at least a dual legal system and use *shari'a* only for certain civil matters, such as family law, property rights and sometimes contracts or public law. In some countries, *shari'a* is also referred to in criminal cases. In the Christian context, the Roman Catholic Church, for instance, is still governed by canon law.

Types of ethico-legal texts in the Qur'an

There are a number of different types of ethico-legal teachings found in the Qur'an. These range from obligatory teachings (which Muslims are obliged to follow) to non-obligatory teachings. While one can look at these teachings from a number of perspectives, our interest here is related to how Muslims are expected to abide by them.

Traditionally, Muslim scholars have been interested in such classifications. The most common way that the Qur'an's ethico-legal teachings have been classified is according to the well-known 'five categories of Islamic law': obligatory, prohibited, recommended, reprehensible or permissible. In Islamic law, the entire range of possible human actions falls into one of these five categories. For example, performing the five daily prayers is obligatory, while performing additional prayers is merely recommended. Stealing is prohibited, while most scholars would consider being greedy or covetous only to be reprehensible. Of course, the categories only apply to adult Muslims of sound mind.

While this classification is useful, in order to explore the nature and relevance of the Qur'an's ethico-legal teachings to the contemporary concerns and needs of today, it is necessary to go beyond these strictly legal categories. In the following section, we will provide a summary of categories of Qur'anic ethico-legal teachings from the perspective of the applicability of the teaching. Some teachings may be universally applicable, while others may be specific to particular circumstances. Others may have some degree of ambiguity and require further investigation to determine their applicability. We will look at five categories of ethico-legal teaching: obligatory, fundamental, protectional, implementational and instructional. These categories go beyond the traditional classification of human actions mentioned above, and allow us to consider the framework of values within which the Qur'an's ethical prescriptions are located.

Obligatory teachings

Obligatory teachings represent those teachings of the Qur'an which a Muslim must follow. Such teachings are considered to be universally applicable to all Muslims, in all times, places and circumstances. Adopting them is seen to be one of the most important and obvious markers of being Muslim. They are found in a variety of forms in the Qur'an and can be divided into a number of sub-categories.

First, teachings related to the system of belief (*iman*); for instance, belief in God, the prophets, the scriptures, the Day of Judgement, accountability and life after death. These teachings are described in the Qur'an as follows:

> You who believe, believe in God and His Messenger and in the Scripture He sent down to His Messenger, as well as what He sent down before. Anyone who does not believe in God, His angels, His Scriptures, His messengers, and the Last Day has gone far, far astray.[1]

Second, teachings related to devotional practices, generally referred to as *ibadat* (forms of worship). Examples of *ibadat* are prayer, fasting, pilgrimage and remembrance of God. All these are emphasized frequently in the Qur'an. Third, teachings about what is permissible (*halal*) and what is prohibited (*haram*). For such teachings to fall into the category of obligatory teachings, they need to be unambiguously and clearly stated in the Qur'an. If something is made categorically lawful and is intended to remain so forever, this is indicated by the Qur'an's use of terms such as 'God made it lawful or permissible' (*ahalla*), as in the following verses:

> It is permitted for you to catch and eat seafood.[2]

> Today all good things have been made lawful for you. The food of the People of the Book is lawful for you as your food is lawful for them.[3]

On the other hand, what is categorically prohibited is indicated by terms such as 'God has prohibited' (*harrama*). Examples of such prohibitions include eating carrion, blood or the meat of swine,[4] the practice of usury (*riba*)[5] or marrying certain close relatives.[6]

It seems that what the Qur'an categorically prohibits or unambiguously declares lawful is intended to remain so forever. The following verses illustrate the Qur'an's unequivocal position regarding those who attempt to change what God has determined:

> You who believe, do not forbid the good things God has made lawful for you – do not exceed the limits: God does not love those who exceed the limits.[7]

> Do not say falsely, 'This is lawful and this is forbidden', inventing a lie about God: those who invent lies about God will not prosper.[8]

The importance of this last verse has been noted by Qur'anic commentators such as Muhammad Asad, who states:

> In accordance with the doctrine that everything which has not been expressly forbidden by the Qur'an or the explicit teachings of the Prophet is *eo ipso* lawful, this verse takes a clear-cut stand against all arbitrary prohibitions invented by man or artificially 'deduced' from the Qur'an or the Prophet's Sunnah [his words and actions].[9]

Similarly, the Qur'an reminds us of the ease with which we may accidentally forget this instruction by reprimanding even the Prophet Muhammad for apparently 'forbidding' for himself that which God had made lawful. Although traditional explanations of this verse vary, it is generally accepted that it refers to a case where the Prophet, in an emotional reaction to a situation of mutual jealousy and bickering among his wives, declared that he would not have marital relations with them for one month. In response to this, the following verse was revealed: 'O Prophet, why do you forbid what God has made lawful to you in your desire to please your wives?'[10] Qur'anic commentators have generally agreed that this verse serves to remind us that we are not permitted to make unlawful that which God has permitted, even if we think it may please someone. Based on this, and other similar verses, those things that are clearly and unambiguously permissible (*halal*) or prohibited (*haram*) appear to be fundamental to Islam and are generally considered immutable.

However, it is important to distinguish between this basic category, and the extensive lists of *halal* and *haram* that are found in standard Islamic legal texts. The rulings listed in such texts are often derived mainly from direct interpretation of the Qur'an and sunna, or are arrived at on the basis of other tools of interpretation, known as analogical reasoning (*qiyas*) and consensus (*ijma*). These rulings are relevant to a discussion of *shari'a*, but opinions vary as to whether they should be considered obligatory.

Fundamental teachings

A survey of the Qur'an shows that it repeatedly emphasizes certain basic 'human' values, referred to here as fundamental teachings. Such teachings were often discussed by classical scholars of Islamic jurisprudence. Ghazali (d.505/1111), for instance, discusses what he calls the 'five universal values'.[11] These are the protection of life, intellect, property, honour (or lineage) and religion, and have come to constitute the 'key objectives of *shari'a*'.[12]

These five universal values were arrived at by a process of 'inductive corroboration'[13] by a number of eminent scholars. Although limited to five by well-known scholars such as Ghazali, Izz ibn Abd al-Salam (d.678/1279) and Shatibi (d.790/1388), these fundamental values could be elaborated on to develop additional values. Such values may include freedom of speech, equality before the law, freedom from torture or inhumane punishment, freedom from arbitrary arrest, detention or exile, and the presumption of innocence. Many such values were in fact discussed and adopted by classical Muslim thinkers, but they were not considered 'fundamental' values, as was the case with the five universal values.

Although the Qur'an itself does not change, the fundamental values derived from it are likely to be expressed in different ways over time. Such expressions are likely to reflect our knowledge and understanding of the text, along with the issues and concerns of our own generations. For instance, today we are now increasingly conscious of issues concerning human rights in a way that is quite unique to our times, although many of the basic ideas of human rights exist in the Islamic tradition.

Protectional teachings

Protectional teachings provide legislative support to the fundamental teachings mentioned above. For instance, the fundamental teaching of protection of property remains theoretical unless it is put into practice. The Qur'an provides us with teachings which serve to 'protect' this value, such as the prohibition of theft. While a fundamental teaching may be emphasized throughout the Qur'an, protectional teachings often appear to depend on only one or a few texts. This does not reduce their importance; rather, the strength of a protectional teaching is derived from the fundamental teaching which it supports. Since protectional teachings are essential to the maintenance of fundamental teachings, we could consider them to be universal.

Implementational teachings

Just as fundamental teachings are put into practice through protectional teachings, implementational teachings provide specific measures to implement these protectional teachings. For instance, the prohibition of theft is to be implemented in a society by taking specific measures against those who go against this norm, as stated in the Qur'an: 'Cut off the hands of thieves, whether they are male or female, as punishment for what they have done – a deterrent from God: God is almighty and wise.'[14]

Examples of other implementational teachings include: the law of like for like retribution (*qisas*) or payment of blood money (*diya*) for murder;[15] the punishment of 100 lashes for unmarried men and women who commit unlawful sexual intercourse (*zina*);[16] and the punishment of 80 lashes for a person who provides false testimony to a case involving accusation of unlawful sexual intercourse (*qadhf*).[17]

Unlike obligatory, fundamental and protectional teachings, implementational teachings do not always appear to be universally applicable. For instance, there are heated debates among Muslims today about whether these teachings should be implemented in Muslim societies as punishments for the crimes specified. Those who argue they are universally applicable call for their implementation, at least in Muslim majority societies, as a marker of being Muslim today and as a means of restoring an idealized, perfect Muslim social order. However, others who do not see them as universally applicable argue that such implementation is not necessary. Those who take the latter position argue that, in determining the relevance of implementational teachings in the modern period, it is necessary to consider the cultural context of the Qur'anic revelation in the first/seventh century. For instance, in Arabia during that period, capital and corporal punishment were entrenched in the society; hence, measures that would be effective in that context were required and thus the Qur'an stipulated such measures.

Proponents of the view that certain implementational teachings are not universally applicable would argue that the measures themselves do not appear to be the fundamental objective of the Qur'an. Instead, the Qur'an appears to indicate that its primary objective is to prevent unacceptable behaviour. Hence, proponents of this view see such measures as a means to an end.

Numerous Qur'anic passages suggest that once someone has committed an offence, what is important is that they repent and refrain from further offences. In practice, classical Muslim jurists did not fully consider this teaching and, generally speaking, emphasized punishment. The examples below illustrate the Qur'an's general approach of following an implementational measure with a suggestion that repentance may lead to a waiving of the measure. For instance, having stated that the punishment for theft is the amputation of a hand, the Qur'an goes on to say: 'But if anyone repents after his wrong-doing and makes amends, God will accept his repentance: God is most forgiving, most merciful.'[18] Similarly, having stated that those who engage in unlawful sexual intercourse (*zina*) must receive 100 lashes, and those who make false accusations of unlawful sexual relations should be given 80 lashes, the Qur'an adds: 'Except those who repent later and make amends – God is most forgiving and merciful.'[19] Likewise, having specified the punishment for murder, the Qur'an says:

> But if the culprit is pardoned by his aggrieved brother, this shall be adhered to fairly, and the culprit shall pay what is due in a good way. This is an alleviation from your Lord and an act of mercy.[20]

We can see, therefore, that while some implementational teachings may appear to be harsh, many Qur'anic verses allow for repentance, 'remission' and 'following what is right'. It may be argued that if punishment were the key objective and must be applied universally, further options would not have been given. Similarly, there are examples in the Islamic legal tradition which indicate that even jurists were concerned about the implications of the harsh punishments specified in the Qur'an. As a result, jurists put forward a range of conditions for implementation of such punishments. These conditions often meant that in practice it would be quite difficult to impose the punishment. According to some scholars, this made some punishments virtually obsolete for all practical purposes. This opinion is expressed succinctly by the contemporary legal scholar, Muhammad Sa'id al-Ashmawi:

> These Qur'anic punishments are so surrounded by conditions that in practice they are practically inapplicable; moreover, to these general conditions are added particular conditions for each penalty. Take for example theft: the object of theft must be marked by the seal of the owner and be in a well-guarded place, which excludes pilfering, open plundering and pick-pocketing; it must have a money value; the robber must not be in great need; finally, for the majority of jurists the Qur'anic punishment for theft cannot be applied if the robber has some 'quasi-ownership' on the goods stolen, as is notably the case with public goods.[21]

Instructional teachings

Instructional teachings appear to form the majority of ethico-legal teachings in the Qur'an. Unlike the categories mentioned earlier, these teachings refer to certain problems that were specific to circumstances at the time of the revelation. These teachings are often indicated in the text by a variety of linguistic devices: (1) in the form of a command or a prohibition; (2) a simple statement indicating the right action intended; or (3) a parable, story or reference to a particular incident. Below are a few examples of some instructional teachings, the meanings of which have been a source of some debate:

- Polygyny: The Qur'an appears to permit men to marry more than one woman in certain circumstances: 'You may marry whichever [other] women seem good to you, two, three or four. If you fear you cannot be equitable [to them], then marry only one.'[22]
- Gender relations: There is debate about the Qur'anic view on the existence of a hierarchy between men and women, on the basis of verses such as: 'Husbands should take full care of their wives with the [bounties] God has given to some more than others and with what they spend out of their own money.'[23] The first phrase of this verse is often translated as 'men are the maintainers of women'.
- Slavery: The Qur'an gives instructions to be good to specified people, including slaves: 'Be good to parents, to relatives, to orphans, to the needy, to neighbors near and far, to travelers in need, and to your slaves.'[24] This suggests that the Qur'an allows slavery.
- Relations with non-Muslims: In the following verse, the Qur'an appears to order Muslims not to take unbelievers as friends or allies, saying: 'They would dearly like you to reject faith, as they themselves have done, to be like them. So do not take them as allies until they migrate [to Medina] for God's cause.'[25]

As indicated by the above examples, instructional teachings often provide the greatest challenges in relating the Qur'anic text to the life of the believer today. Do these teachings transcend cultural specificity and apply to all Muslims regardless of time, place and circumstances? Are Muslims obliged to try and 'recreate' the circumstances of the revelation in order to put such teachings into practice? For instance, when the Qur'an tells Muslims how they should treat slaves,[26] should Muslims insist on reviving the social structure in which slaves formed a part of the Muslim community? More importantly, if this is not the case, then how should a believer respond to these instructional teachings in the modern period?

Given the ambiguities and difficulties associated with interpreting instructional teachings, it follows that they should be closely analysed before they are accepted as universally applicable and binding. Such analysis will also assist us in determining the extent to which these teachings should be applied.

The Qur'anic texts from which many instructional teachings are derived often appear to relate to a specific cultural setting. For instance, in the phrase often translated as 'men are maintainers of women', the Qur'an seems to be taking into account the situation of women and men at the time in Arabia. The social structure of pre-Islamic and early Islamic Hijaz meant that, with some exceptions, women were generally excluded from important public decision-making and were often financially dependent on men. They also did not, generally speaking, take active part in raids or battles, which was a key public role, although there were some well-known exceptions. It was believed that women needed to be 'protected' by men. Without such protection, most women would have found it difficult to survive in the harsh conditions of Hijaz. Hence, the instructional teaching, 'men are maintainers of women', reflects an idea and practice that was appropriate at the time.

Under similar circumstances, it seems reasonable to expect that this instructional teaching would remain operative. However, the question arises as to whether it would still be applicable were the circumstances of women and society to change dramatically. If we consider the frequency of Qur'anic references to this teaching, we discover that it is not emphasized elsewhere in the Qur'an, and is never phrased in a way that indicates that it should be applied in all contexts. It is possible to conclude that the teaching may be culturally specific and that its applicability should be considered in light of newly emerging circumstances.

In the next section we will explore two aspects of ethico-legal texts of the Qur'an: their adaptability and the 'minimalist' approach of the Qur'an to ethico-legal matters.

Adaptability of ethico-legal teachings

Muslims early on developed the idea that certain Qur'anic rulings were 'abrogated' by later rulings. While there are relatively few clear cases of abrogation, the theory of abrogation remains an important point of debate and discussion in the principles of Islamic jurisprudence. The Arabic word for abrogation is *naskh*. In the Qur'anic context, it refers to the process by which some of the Qur'an's earlier verses are said to have been annulled by later revelations. Some Muslims reject the idea of abrogation as they understand it to imply that there may be inconsistency within the Qur'an. This idea of inconsistency is rejected by most Muslims. Other Muslims, however, see abrogation as evidence that the Qur'an is adaptable and was not revealed as a self-contained document divorced from its socio-historical context.

A number of Qur'anic verses appear to support the concept of abrogation. For example, the Qur'an says: 'Any revelation We cause to be superseded or forgotten, We replace with something better or similar. Do you [Prophet] not know that God has power over everything?'[27] Some scholars understand Qur'anic references to the prohibition of wine, for example, to be an instance of abrogation. The Qur'an first considered consumption of wine 'a great sin', but did not forbid it. Then, it was forbidden to be intoxicated during prayer. Finally, at a later time, it was totally forbidden.[28]

The concept of abrogation has a number of implications for interpreting the Qur'an's ethico-legal texts. First, it highlights the problematic assertion of some Muslims that once a ruling is present in the Qur'an, it cannot be reinterpreted and remains an ideal for all times and places. This view ignores the fact that a number of Qur'anic rulings were changed, through abrogation, up to two or three times during the Prophet's 22-year mission.

This change in a ruling does not mean that the moral purpose behind that ruling also changes. For instance, the punishment initially prescribed for a woman who committed unlawful sexual intercourse was that she be confined to her home until death, but this punishment was later changed to flogging. The moral purpose in this case remained, that is, deterring a person from engaging in unlawful sexual intercourse, but the method of achieving that aim was changed.

The importance of abrogation is that it challenges the view that all of the Qur'an's ethico-legal texts are set rules, fixed for all times and places. While some theologians argue that the 'law' of the Qur'an should be maintained regardless of context, and that it is the community's responsibility to adapt and change in accordance with that law, abrogation provides a historical example of the Qur'an as a dynamic text, aware of the complexities faced by the society in which it was revealed.

The Qur'an's general approach to ethico-legal matters

In general, the Qur'an is 'minimalist' in its approach to ethico-legal matters. It does not set out a detailed regulation of daily life; rather, it emphasizes God's relationship to His creation, and all its teachings, legal or otherwise, must be viewed from the perspective of this relationship. Thus, only that which is directly related to this relationship is dealt with in the Qur'an in detail. Other issues, which appear to be related specifically to the social and cultural context of Hijaz, are usually mentioned very briefly.

This aspect of the Qur'an's approach to socially and culturally specific issues appears to have been overshadowed by the approach of the early jurists, who developed Islamic law and its principles. One of the key objectives of these jurists was to bring all aspects of a Muslim's life under the Islamic law, including those areas not discussed directly by the Qur'an or the Prophet. With this aim in mind, many Muslim jurists significantly expanded the rulings provided in the Qur'an and sunna to cover a vast range of areas.

In their quest to develop detailed regulations for all areas of life, the jurists even drew on sources that were foreign to Islam, including classical Greek thought. For instance, Aristotelian logic was used to develop a set of principles to facilitate the construction of rulings and regulations from the Qur'an and sunna. In fact, an examination of many regulations said to be derived from the Qur'an reveals many that cannot be described as having a Qur'anic basis. In many cases, the Qur'an may have made a passing comment, or provided a general instruction to a particular person or group; these comments were then extended to a wide range of areas of human activity in the quest to construct a system of law that would cover all aspects of human life. Evidence of the Qur'an's minimalist approach is shown in the following verse:

> You who believe, do not ask about matters which, if made known to you, might make things difficult for you – if you ask them while the Qur'an is being revealed, they will be made known to you – God has kept silent about them: God is most forgiving and forbearing.[29]

Thus, historically, if a particular regulation or revelation was not specified by the Qur'an, Muslims had the freedom to follow the social and cultural norms of their society. This seems to have been the Prophet's own practice, given that he was functioning in a society that had its own customs, values and regulations, and did not want to interfere with them unless necessary.

Summary

Some of the important points we have discussed in this chapter include:

*   Muslims understand law based on scripture as the most authoritative ordering principle of reality.

- The process of determining whether an ethico-legal teaching is universal or not is highly complex.
- *Implementational* teachings of the Qur'an provide the specific measures by which *protectional* teachings are implemented, whereas *protectional* teachings provide legislative support for *fundamental* Qur'anic teachings and values.
- The bulk of the Qur'an's ethico-legal texts are *instructional*, and determining their relevance in the modern era is a highly complex endeavour.
- The Qur'an's main emphasis is on the relationship of God with His creation, rather than on providing detailed regulation for daily life.

Recommended reading

Khaled Abou El Fadl, *Speaking in God's Name: Islamic Law, Authority and Women*, Oxford: Oneworld, 2001.

- In this book Abou El Fadl argues that much of Islamic legal tradition does not reflect the intended ethico-legal message of the Qur'an. This tradition appears to emphasize the legal message of Islam and the role of law. Additionally, elements of the classical Islamic legal tradition are male-dominated and seem prejudiced against women.

Michael Cook, 'Koran and Koranic Exegesis', in *Commanding Right and Forbidding Wrong in Islamic Thought*, Cambridge: Cambridge University Press, 2000, pages 13–31.

- In this chapter Cook examines the core ethico-legal issue of commanding right and forbidding wrong in Islam from the perspective of the Qur'an and its exegetical tradition.

Yasin Dutton, *The Origins of Islamic Law: The Qur'an, The Muwatta' and Madinan Amal*, Richmond, Surrey: Curzon, 1999.

- In this book Dutton looks at the origins of Islamic law. In certain sections of the book he focuses specifically on the issues of authority and the role and significance of the Qur'an in the early development of Islamic law.

Wael B. Hallaq, *A History of Islamic Legal Theories: An Introduction to Sunni Usul al-Fiqh*, Cambridge: Cambridge University Press, 1997; *Authority, Continuity and Change in Islamic Law*, Cambridge: Cambridge University Press, 2001; (ed.), *The Formation of Islamic Law*, Aldershot:

Ashgate, 2004; *The Origins and Evolution of Islamic Law*, Cambridge: Cambridge University Press, 2005.

- In these books Hallaq provides a number of insights into the Qur'an's role and position in the development of Islamic law, both past and present.

S. Mahmassani, 'Shari'ah Sources', 'The Book', in *Falsafat al-Tashri Fi al-Islam: The Philosophy of Jurisprudence in Islam*, translated by Farhat J. Ziadeh, Leiden: E.J. Brill, 1961, pages 63–70.

- In these chapters Mahmassani provides a brief overview of the authority of the Qur'an in relation to law and its role in the development of Islamic law.

Yvonne Yazbeck Haddad and Barbara Freyer Stowasser (eds), *Islamic Law and the Challenges of Modernity*, Lanham, MD: Rowman & Littlefield Publishers, 2004.

- This book contains a collection of academic articles which discuss how Islamic law is being re-examined in the face of modernity. A common theme throughout the articles is the role of Qur'anic reinterpretation in relation to Islamic legal issues.

NOTES

1 Qur'an: 4:136.
2 Qur'an: 5:96.
3 Qur'an: 5:5.
4 Qur'an: 2:173.
5 Qur'an: 2:275.
6 Qur'an: 4:23.
7 Qur'an: 5:87.
8 Qur'an: 16:116.
9 Muhammad Asad, *The Message of the Qur'an*, Gibraltar: Dar-al-Andalus, 1980, p. 300.
10 Qur'an: 66:1.
11 Wael B. Hallaq, *A History of Islamic Legal Theories*, Cambridge: Cambridge University Press, 1997, p. 166.
12 Hallaq, *A History*, pp. 88ff; Isma'il al-Hasani, *Nazariyyat al-Maqasid ind al-Imam Muhammad al-Tahir bin Ashur*, Virginia: IIIT, 1995, p. 46.
13 This process means that a wide variety of pieces of evidence, which in their totality support a particular position and lead to certitude, do not rise above the level of probability when taken individually. Hallaq, *A History*, p. 166.
14 Qur'an: 5:38.

15 Qur'an: 2:178.
16 Qur'an: 24:2.
17 Qur'an: 24:4.
18 Qur'an: 5:39.
19 Qur'an: 24:5.
20 Qur'an: 2:178.
21 Muhammad Sa'id Al-Ashmawi, 'Shari'a: The Codification of Islamic Law',
    in Charles Kurzman (ed.), *Liberal Islam*, New York: Oxford University
    Press, pp. 49–56, 1998, p. 53.
22 Qur'an: 4:3.
23 Qur'an: 4:34.
24 Qur'an: 4:36.
25 Qur'an: 4:89.
26 See Qur'an: 2:177; 4:36; 24:33; 90:12–17.
27 Qur'an: 2:106.
28 Qur'an: 5:90–91.
29 Qur'an: 5:101.

10

Selected exegetical principles and ideas

Q UR'ANIC EXEGESIS (INTERPRETATION), OR *TAFSIR*, HAS been central to the intellectual development and practical application of Islam as a religion since the very beginning of Islam in the seventh century CE. Over time, Muslim scholars have developed a range of principles and methods for approaching the Qur'an, all of which have been designed to assist in interpreting and understanding its meaning. These intellectual approaches have varied; some scholars have focused more on interpreting the Qur'an according to the Qur'an itself, or as it was interpreted by the Prophet and the earliest Muslims; others have focused on the use of independent reasoning and the ability of individual scholars to deduce meaning from the text. Other developments have related to classification of the text itself; for example, whether a given verse is ambiguous or clear and whether its meaning can be best understood literally or as a metaphor. As with all areas of intellectual endeavour in Islam, the development of these classifications and approaches has been accompanied by a rich history of debate and discussion.

In this chapter we will discuss:

- the differences between tradition- and reason-based exegesis;
- the early history of exegesis, including how the distinction between tradition- and reason-based exegesis arose; and
- the significance of different types of classification of the Qur'anic text, including:

  – clear and ambiguous texts;
  – literal and metaphorical texts
  – general and specific texts;
  – immediate and secondary meanings of a text;
  – early and late texts; and
  – mutable and immutable texts.

Tradition- or reason-based exegesis

Qur'anic exegesis can be divided into two broad categories: exegesis based on tradition or text (*tafsir bi al-ma'thur*), and exegesis based on independent reasoning or considered opinion (*tafsir bi al-ra'y*). We will refer to this first type of exegesis as 'tradition-based exegesis' and the second as 'reason-based exegesis'. Tradition-based exegesis aims to restrict the use of independent reasoning in the understanding and interpretation of the text, emphasizing instead the importance of exegesis by reference to the Qur'an itself, along with the example of the Prophet Muhammad and the earliest Muslims. In contrast, reason-based exegesis allows for interpretation of texts based on independent reasoning, albeit with certain limitations. While both of these approaches are important parts of the rich history of Qur'anic exegesis, reason-based exegesis has tended to occupy a somewhat less prominent position in the discipline.

Tradition-based exegesis

Proponents of tradition-based exegesis argue that the Prophet explicitly prohibited anyone from engaging in exegesis that was not based on tradition. For instance, Abd Allah ibn Abbas (d.68/687), a cousin of the Prophet and a well-known interpreter of the Qur'an, reported: 'The messenger of God said: "He who interprets the Qur'an according to his opinions (ra'y) should have his place prepared in the fire of hell."' Similarly, another hadith states: 'He who says something concerning the Qur'an according to his opinion [even if it] is correct has erred.'[1]

Based on their reading of such texts, proponents of tradition-based exegesis argue that only the following forms of exegesis are acceptable: interpretation of one text of the Qur'an by reference to another text or texts of the Qur'an; interpretation of a text of the Qur'an by reference to hadith; and, according to some, interpretation of a text of the Qur'an by reference to the religious authorities of the first and second generations of Muslims, commonly referred to respectively as the Companions and the Successors.

Interpretation of the Qur'an by reference to the Qur'an itself refers to instances when a difficult or ambiguous verse is elaborated on or explained in another verse. This form of interpretation is considered by many exegetes to be the best and most authoritative;[2] for instance, in the case of the 'words' (*kalimat*) which Adam is said to have received from God, the Qur'an says: 'Then Adam received words from his Lord, and He accepted his repentance: He is the Ever Relenting, the Most Merciful.'[3] These 'words' appear to be elaborated on in a number of other Qur'anic verses.

An interpretation by the Prophet is considered the next most authoritative form of exegesis. As the transmitter of God's Word, the Prophet was deeply involved with the Qur'an emotionally, spiritually and intellectually. This unique and intimate connection, together with what certain verses of the Qur'an appear to say on this issue, supports the Prophet's authority in interpreting the Qur'anic message.[4]

Although the followers of the Prophet were already familiar with the language and social context of the Qur'an, there were times when further explanation was needed. For instance, the Prophet would often provide a practical example of the way in which a Qur'anic commandment should be put into practice. Less frequently, the Companions would ask the Prophet to clarify the implied meaning of specific words, phrases or verses which appeared to contain metaphorical expressions or references to unknown historical figures. In such cases, the Prophet would sometimes offer an expository or direct interpretation. For instance, it is reported that on one occasion, the Prophet was asked by the Companion, Adiy ibn Hatim (d.68/ 687–688), to explain the meaning of a metaphorical reference to the 'black thread' and the 'white thread' in a verse related to fasting.[5] The Prophet reportedly replied by explaining, 'It is the darkness of night and light of the day',[6] – which indicate the times to end and begin fasting each day.

The next most authoritative interpreters of the Qur'an according to tradition-based exegesis are the Companions. Since they lived during the time of the Prophet, Muslims in general, particularly the Sunnis, regard them as having an elevated status in Islam, such that their practices and example are seen as being in accord with, and second only to, the Prophet's example (*sunna*). The interpretations of the Companions often appear to have been highly personal and based on their own independent judgement (*ijtihad*). In general, the Companions did not use a particular systematic approach to interpretation, nor did they feel bound to provide evidence to support their understandings. Instead, they often relied on their own under-standings of what was appropriate presumably based on their familiarity with the 'spirit' of the Qur'an.

In the first/seventh century, as the Muslim state established itself and its influence grew, an increasing number of people began to convert to Islam. New Muslims, being from diverse religious, cultural and linguistic back-grounds, often relied heavily on the Companions to interpret the Qur'an. Thus, leading Companions in places such as Syria, Egypt and Yemen became authoritative exponents of the Qur'anic text. It was the students of these Companions, the 'Successors', who were to become the third most important group of exponents of the Qur'an. Like the Companions, the Successors had a rather personal and unsystematic approach to interpretation, which was often based on the insights and understanding of their teachers and also reflected their own considered opinions.

After the time of the earliest generations, the interpretation of the Qur'an began to take on a more systematic character and differing schools of thought began to emerge. One of the major trends to emerge was reason-based exegesis, which will be discussed below.

Reason-based exegesis

Reason-based exegetes, in contrast to their tradition-based counterparts, came to consider not only the Qur'an, hadith and views of the Companions and Successors in their interpretations, but also the views of later scholars, as well as legal rulings and principles of jurisprudence, historical texts and theological writings.

Proponents of reason-based exegesis, such as the rationalist theologians known as Mu'tazilis, argued that verses related to God's attributes, for example, needed to be interpreted using a metaphorical, reason-based reading in order to avoid attributing human characteristics to God. For instance, they argued that the phrase, 'the Most Gracious [God] ascended the Throne',[7] should be interpreted as, 'the Most Gracious [God] [was] established on the Throne of His Almightiness'. However, this approach was strongly rejected by scholars who advocated a more tradition-based understanding of the Qur'an, such as Ibn Taymiyya (d.728/1328), who regarded such an approach as an unacceptable innovation.

Despite later opposition, Mu'tazili theologians as well as Arabic linguists produced a number of specialist works on exegesis and its methodology which supported reason-based interpretation.[8] Such works provided important intellectual contributions to the debate surrounding the methods of exegesis.[9]

Scholars, such as the exegete, Qurtubi (d.671/1273), believed that independent reasoning (*ijtihad*) was essential for developing an adequate interpretation of the Qur'an.[10] However, Qurtubi also argued that such *ijtihad* should be based on tradition, and that interpreters should have expert knowledge of the Islamic religious disciplines before attempting such a process.[11] Thus, in a sense, Qurtubi's thinking can be seen as supporting both reason- and tradition-based exegesis.

One of the foremost proponents of reason-based exegesis was the Spanish Muslim philosopher, Ibn Rushd (d.595/1198). He argued that Islam addresses people of different intellectual and psychological capabilities, necessitating that the Qur'an be dealt with at different levels. Just as one person's comprehension may differ from another's, it is also possible that one person may be more comfortable with simple explanations while another may prefer to rely on complex, rational evidence. Ibn Rushd believed that while certain texts of the Qur'an and hadith do not clearly contradict what reason demands, others, at face value, may appear to present a contradiction between text and reason. Such texts should therefore be subjected to *ta'wil* (allegorical interpretation, a form of exegesis based on reason).[12] Reason-based interpretation, Ibn Rushd argued, is essential for effectively communicating the message of the Qur'an.

Other arguments advanced in favour of a reason-based approach to interpretation highlight, for instance, the complexities associated with 'meaning' and the need to interpret legal texts in line with the changing circumstances of society by using *ijtihad*. Given the significant differences between modern society and that of the Prophet, the argument goes, a simple reliance on tradition is no longer sufficient for understanding and interpreting the sacred text.

Despite this apparent divide between tradition-based and reason-based interpretation, historically, the tendency of Qur'anic exegesis was to be as inclusive as possible, accommodating both tradition- and reason-based exegesis.

Tradition-based and reason-based exegesis

Tradition-based exegesis restricts the scope for independent reasoning in the interpretation of the Qur'an, relying instead on the primary sources of Islam. Such exegesis includes:

- interpretation of the Qur'an by another Qur'anic text;
- interpretation of the Qur'an by a hadith of the Prophet; or
- interpretation of the Qur'an by reference to a reported opinion of one of the first or second generations of Muslims and other early Muslims.

Reason-based exegesis allows greater scope for independent reasoning, within certain limitations. Some features of reason-based exegesis include:

- heavy reliance on linguistic analysis and exploring the implications of different language uses on meaning;
- a metaphorical reading of certain types of verses;
- an allegorical interpretation of texts that, if taken literally, appear to contradict reason; and
- use of *ijtihad* (independent reasoning).

Selected principles in Qur'anic exegesis

One of the key concepts in exegesis is the division of Qur'anic verses into different categories. In this section we will explore a number of the key categories developed in exegetical methodology.

Clear and ambiguous verses

Two of the most important categories of Qur'anic verses are those related to the distinction between 'clear' and 'ambiguous' verses.[13] The basis for this division of Qur'anic verses can be found in the following verse:

> It is He who has sent this Scripture [Qur'an] down to you [Prophet]. Some of its verses are definite in meaning – these are the cornerstone of the Scripture – and others are ambiguous. The perverse at heart eagerly pursue the ambiguities in their attempt to make trouble and to pin down a specific meaning of their own: only God knows the true meaning. Those firmly grounded in knowledge say, 'We believe in it: it is all from our Lord' – only those with real perception will take heed.[14]

The first type of verse described above is called *muhkam* (clear), while the second type is referred to as *mutashabih* (ambiguous). The definitions of these words have long been debated in Islamic scholarship and are still contentious. Some understand *muhkam* as referring to those verses that can be understood without additional interpretation or reflection, while *mutashabih* are those that require interpretation. Others argue that *muhkam* verses have only one possible meaning whereas *mutashabih* verses have many possible meanings, from which the most 'appropriate' meaning must be deduced.

Some scholars argue that *muhkam* verses do not require any interpretation, as their meanings are obvious to anyone who is fluent in Arabic. For example, verses that appear to be clear include 'Praise belongs to God, Lord of the Worlds',[15] or 'Perform the prayer [*salat*]'.[16] However, on further examination, verses that are said to be *muhkam* do not always have meanings which are entirely clear. In some cases, what may initially appear to be 'clear' may turn out to be more complex when considered from another perspective. Take for instance the first verse mentioned above. On the surface, this verse seems to be clear in its meaning. However, there are ambiguities associated with terms like 'worlds' and 'praise', which lead to debates in the literature as to their proper interpretation. Other verses considered to be in this category appear to be clearer, such as the Qur'anic command to 'perform the prayer'. However, even in this case, although the command is clear, the nature of what is meant by 'prayer' is not. The details of what counts as 'prayer' need to be worked out.

The second category, *mutashabih*, is considered to include verses whose meanings are ambiguous and must generally be interpreted in order to be understood. Scholars of exegesis have identified several types of these verses.

Among the most important *mutashabih* verses are those using terms such as 'the Everlasting' and 'the Omnipotent'. These can also describe God using anthropomorphic terms, including references to Him being on, or ascending, 'the Throne', or having 'Hands' and a 'Face'. In the early centuries of Islam, there was extensive debate about the theological issues arising from these references, and this debate still continues to this day. For instance, some scholars, such as Ahmad ibn Hanbal (d.241/855), believed that these attributes should be interpreted literally, a view that was diametrically opposed to that of the rationalist Mu'tazilis, who argued that they require interpretation and should be read metaphorically. Similarly, scholars such as Baghawi (d.515/1122), Ibn Taymiyya and Ibn Kathir also preferred a more literal reading of such verses. Other well-known exegetes, such as Razi (d.606/1209), Zamakhshari (d.539/1144), Baydawi (d.685/1286) and Ibn Arabi (d.638/1240), had views more similar to that of the Mu'tazilis and considered verses related to God's attributes to be 'ambiguous' and requiring some form of interpretation.

Literal and metaphorical

Another categorization that is used in interpreting the Qur'an is literal (*haqiqi*) and metaphorical (*majazi*).[17] A more literalist approach to reading the text is one which argues that the literal meaning of the text is always clear. In contrast, scholars who prefer a more rational approach take into account the linguistic meaning of the text, but also consider whether a metaphorical meaning may sometimes be more appropriate.

A commonly held view is that when interpreting the Qur'anic text, priority should be given to the literal meaning of the text in attempting to understand God's intent. However, others argue that some texts cannot be understood if one reads them literally, in which case a metaphorical meaning should be given preference. For instance, in reference to God's 'hands' mentioned in the Qur'an, most theologians would argue that the literal meaning of 'hand' is clearly inappropriate for God, as it is a human attribute. Thus, in this case, the metaphorical reading of this term as referring to God's 'power' is generally preferred.

Nonetheless, some scholars, such as Ibn Taymiyya and the modern Sunni exegete, Muhammad al-Shinqiti, have rejected the idea of any metaphorical meaning in the Qur'an. They have vehemently argued that the Qur'an's 'metaphorical' texts, particularly those that are related to God's attributes and the like, should all be read literally, and that issues of metaphor and metaphorical meaning need not be discussed.

General and specific

Scholars have also differentiated between texts which are general (*amm*) and those that are specific (*khass*).[18]

General texts are defined as those which use certain words to indicate that they apply to a broad category of things, such as 'human being'. For instance, if the Qur'an instructs human beings to do something, this implies that the instruction is for all people. Other words that have a similarly broad sense include 'men', 'women' and 'Muslims'. Identification of such texts was very important both for interpreters of the Qur'an and Muslim jurists who were developing Islamic law. However, once these texts were identified and agreed upon, there were still considerable differences of opinion among jurists in relation to the details of their interpretation, and how they should be applied in the development of Islamic law.

There are certain words in the Qur'an that may be more specific, such as 'Pharaoh', 'Prophet Muhammad' or 'People of the Book', in which case the text in which any of these occur is said to apply to a particular person or group of people. Texts classified as 'specific' tend to be clearer than general texts in that the person or thing to which they refer is clearly stated. For instance, the Qur'an specifies that thieves should be punished by amputation of a hand, and that unlawful sexual intercourse is punishable by 100 lashes. In both instances, the punishment is described in very specific, definite terms.

Although general texts may also be quite clear, there are often exceptions to the applicability of the rulings of such texts. For instance, a text which says that 'Muslims' should perform the pilgrimage may seem clear, but it does not necessarily apply to all Muslims; some people may be exempted from this requirement, such as those who are ill, cannot afford it, or are not in a position to travel to Mecca for other reasons. Similarly, because such verses apply to a very broad category of people, the instructions are often general. For instance, if a verse instructs people to 'glorify God', how and when this is to be done is unclear and thus considered more difficult to implement.

When dealing with the area of legal exegesis, classical scholars described specific texts as having more 'weight' than general verses. That is, a specific text outweighs a general text when dealing with a particular circumstance but should not be taken as a general rule.

Immediate and secondary meanings

In interpreting verses of the Qur'an, scholars have established a hierarchy of meanings which generally categorizes an understanding of a verse as being either immediate or secondary. For instance, verse 2:233 says in relation to who is responsible for the expenses of a child, 'clothing and maintenance must be borne by the father in a fair manner'. The immediate meaning of the verse is that a father is responsible for his child's welfare. This level of meaning is known as *mantuq* or 'pronounced'. Such meanings are defined as being immediately apprehended on hearing the text, without any analysis or reference to other sources.[19]

The secondary meaning of this verse is related to the idea that a father should publicly acknowledge his offspring. This is described as the 'implied' meaning. Such additional meanings must be derived by a process of deduction or induction, through reference to other sources, or by what we might call 'reading into' the text additional layers of meaning. This process allows for more than one meaning to be derived from a verse. However, generally speaking, immediate meanings are considered to have more weight than secondary meanings, since they are less susceptible to errors in reasoning and analysis.[20]

Early texts and late texts

In compiling the Qur'an as a single text, the early Muslims, reportedly under instructions given by the Prophet Muhammad himself, generally assembled it according to the length of its chapters, rather than in chronological order. Thus, generally speaking, the longest chapters were placed at the beginning of the Qur'an and the shortest at the end. Because of this arrangement of chapters according to their length, many chapters that were revealed earlier in the Prophet's mission, referred to as the Meccan period (610–622 CE), appear at the end of the Qur'an. In contrast, many of those revealed in the later part of his mission, referred to as the Medinan period (622–632 CE), appear at the beginning.

In relation to ethico-legal issues, the chronology of Qur'anic texts is important because several instructions given to the Muslim community earlier in the Prophet's mission were modified by later revelations. Consequently, if we read some of the Qur'an's instructions on the same issue without being aware of their chronology, they may appear to be in conflict. For instance, in the case of the consumption of wine, the Qur'an seems to give three different instructions: first, there is some benefit and some sin in its consumption;[21] second, if one is intoxicated one should avoid prayer;[22] and third, a believer must not consume wine at all.[23] Unless one is aware of the chronological order of these instructions it is difficult to determine which should be given priority over, or should supersede, the others. Such considerations led early Muslims to discuss the chronology of the Qur'anic texts and the impact it had on their interpretation.

In general, a broad distinction was drawn between those verses revealed earlier, in Mecca, and those revealed later, in Medina. However, the distinction did not consider the exact time of revelation, nor did it take into consideration some chapters that had verses from both the Meccan and Medinan periods. Early Muslims overcame this problem by generally considering any chapter which began to be revealed in Mecca to be Meccan and, similarly, if a chapter's revelation began in Medina, it was generally labelled Medinan. According to this convention, there are 85 Meccan and 29 Medinan chapters.[24] In the modern period, a chapter which is predominantly Meccan is usually considered Meccan and, similarly, if a chapter is predominantly Medinan it is deemed Medinan. In recent editions of the Qur'an, this information is usually provided at the beginning of each chapter. However, such descriptions rarely identify chapters that are a composite of Meccan and Medinan verses.

The general practice of classifying entire chapters as either Meccan or Medinan has caused some difficulties in determining when a particular verse was revealed. Some Muslim scholars have suggested that verses can be identified by considering certain stylistic features as well as their content. Elements for consideration include the length of the verse, the nature of the issues dealt with, the language used to address people, the type of people mentioned (such as Jews, Christians, religious hypocrites or pagans), and the events referred to.

Thus, some common features of Meccan texts of the Qur'an are: verses are generally brief, assertive, forceful, and/or alliterative; references are made to previous prophets such as Noah, Abraham, Jesus and Jonah, and their struggles with their communities; people are generally addressed by saying 'O humankind' or 'O people'; certain phrases called 'oaths' are used, such as 'By the enshrouding night'[25] and 'By the morning brightness';[26] references are made to Adam and Iblis (Satan); there is the use of texts mainly concerning Paradise, Hell and the Day of Judgement; and, chapters begin with a series of letters of the Arabic alphabet, with no apparent meaning, such as *ya' sin* and *alif lam mim* (except for the two chapters *al-Baqara* (the Cow) and *Al Imran* (the Family of Imran)).

The following is an example of one of the earliest complete Meccan chapters, which reminds the reader of the consequences of the paths people choose in their lives, and stresses God's guidance and warning:

By the enshrouding night, by the radiant day, by the creation of male and female! The ways you take differ greatly. There is the one who gives, who is mindful of God, who testifies to goodness – We shall smooth his way towards ease. There is the one who is miserly, who is self-satisfied, who denies goodness – We shall smooth his way towards hardship and his wealth will not help him as he falls. Our part is to provide guidance – this world and the next belong to Us – so I warn you about the raging Fire, in which none but the most wicked will burn, who denied [the truth], and turned away. The most pious will be spared this – who gives his wealth away as self-purification, not to return a favour to anyone but for the sake of his Lord the Most High – and he will be well pleased.[27]

Some common features of Medinan texts are: verses are generally longer, free flowing and non-alliterative; references are made to specifically Medinan phenomena, for instance, the religious hypocrites, struggles between Muslims and Jews in Medina, battles between Muslims and non-Muslims, and regulations about warfare; references are made to a variety of specific rules, regulations and punishments, such as the prohibition of adultery, theft and slander; rules relating to battle gains, blood money and social etiquette; rules about marriage, divorce and custody; and rules about war and peace; and, people are generally addressed by saying 'You who believe' or 'O People of the Book'.

An example of a typically Medinan text is as follows:

You who believe, fasting is prescribed for you, as it was prescribed for those before you, so that you may be mindful of God. Fast for a specific number of days, but if one of you is ill, or on a journey, on other days later. For those who can fast only with extreme difficulty, there is a way to compensate – feed a needy person. But if anyone does good of his own accord, it is better for him, and fasting is better for you, if only you knew. It was in the month of Ramadan that the Qur'an was revealed as guidance for humankind, clear messages giving guidance and distinguishing between right and wrong. So any one of you who is present that month should fast, and anyone who is ill or on a journey should make up for the lost days by fasting on other days later. God wants ease for you, not hardship. He wants you to complete the prescribed period and to glorify Him for having guided you, so that you may be thankful.[28]

Mutable and immutable

An important issue that is related to exegesis is what is mutable and what is immutable in Qur'anic instructions.

Although the general tendency in the interpretation of ethico-legal texts of the Qur'an has been to emphasize the view that instructions that are provided in the Qur'an should be followed regardless of time, place or circumstances, there has been some debate on whether one can make a distinction between two domains of instructions: those that are related to rituals and worship (*ibadat*), and those that are related to 'transactions' (*mu'amalat*). In general, the former are considered immutable whereas the latter are mutable.

The idea that texts related to ritual and worship should be regarded as immutable is based on the view that the rules of ritual and worship come from God and the Prophet; no one else can provide such rules, and no human being, other than the Prophet, has the authority to change them. Hence, they are non-negotiable and not open to reinterpretation, unlike texts relating to human interactions (*mu'amalat*). The details of such teachings, such as those that are related to protocols of buying and selling, are often based on local custom or practice and thus are regarded as mutable and open to reinterpretation. Discussions regarding the distinctions between these types of texts and the way in which they should be treated are evident in early scholarly works. For example, in the early legal texts of the Hanafi school there is evidence for the permissibility of changing of laws according to local customs. As with most areas of Islamic law and Qur'anic interpretation, such issues tend to be hotly debated and contested.

Summary

Some of the important points we have discussed in this chapter include:

- Tradition-based approaches to the Qur'an emphasize interpretation by the Qur'an, the Prophet and the first generation of Muslims, and restrict the use of independent reasoning by later Muslims.
- Reason-based approaches to the Qur'an allow for more use of independent reasoning while taking into account key aspects of tradition-based interpretation.
- Verses related to God's attributes are often considered to be ambiguous and metaphorical.
- Verses directed towards specific groups or individuals often contain clearer details than those directed towards humanity at large, which are often expressed more generally.
- Interpretations related to areas such as worship are generally accepted as immutable; however, there is ongoing debate about whether verses related to transactions should be considered mutable or immutable.

Recommended reading

G.R. Hawting and Abdul-Kader A. Shareef (eds), *Approaches to the Qur'an*, London: Routledge, 1993.

- This work is a collection of scholarly articles that provide insight into various aspects of Qur'anic interpretation. The articles cover: (1) aspects of the style and content of the Qur'an; (2) aspects of traditional and modern exegesis of the Qur'an; and (3) the Qur'an and its exegesis in a wider context.

Andrew Rippin (ed.), *Approaches to the History of the Interpretation of the Qur'an*, Oxford: Oxford University Press; New York: Oxford University Press, 1988; *The Qur'an: Formative Interpretation*, Aldershot: Ashgate/Variorum, 1999.

- These books by Rippin provide an insight into the history and development of the various types and methods of interpretation of the Qur'an, as well as the factors affecting this development.

Abdullah Saeed, *Interpreting the Qur'an: Towards a Contemporary Approach*, London and New York: Routledge, 2006.

- In this book Saeed argues for a contemporary methodology for interpreting the Qur'an. He surveys classical discourses on Qur'anic interpretation, citing precedents for his suggestions from early Islam, evaluating classical and later Islamic exegesis and discussing the role of context in interpreting and applying the teachings of the Qur'an in the modern world.

Ahmad von Denffer, *Ulum al-Qur'an: An Introduction to the Sciences of the Qur'an*, Leicester: The Islamic Foundation, 1985, reprint 1994.

- In this book von Denffer provides an introduction to the sciences of the Qur'an (*ulum al-qur'an*). He discusses methodologies of Qur'anic interpretation, exegetical literature and key ideas that affect methods of Qur'anic interpretation. First published in 1983, it was the first book in English on this topic.

NOTES

1 Cited in Norman Calder, '*Tafsir* from Tabari to Ibn Kathir: Problems in the Description of a Genre, Illustrated with References to the Story of

Abraham', pp. 101–40, in G.R. Hawting and Abdul-Kader A. Shareef (eds), *Approaches to the Qur'an*, London: Routledge, 1993, p. 133.

2 Sayyid Muhammad Husayn Tabataba'i, *The Qur'an in Islam*, London: Zahra Publications, 1987, pp. 130–134.

3 Qur'an: 2:37.

4 See, for instance, Qur'an: 16:44: 'We have sent down the message to you too [Prophet], so that you can explain to people what was sent for them, so that they may reflect.'

5 Qur'an: 2:187.

6 Ibn Hajar Al-Asqalani, *Fath al-bari*, vol. IV, Beirut: Dar al-Fikr li al-Tiba'a wa al-Nashr wa al-Tawzi', 1411–1414/1990–1993, p. 629.

7 Qur'an: 20:5.

8 For example see Abu Ubayda Ma'mar Ibn al-Muthanna, *Majaz al-Qur'an*, ed. F. Sezgin, 2 vols, Cairo: Dar al-Ma'arif, 1954–1962, which focused on questions of metaphor.

9 Abdullah Saeed, *Interpreting the Qur'an: Towards a Contemporary Approach*, London and New York: Routledge, 2006, p. 60.

10 Calder, '*Tafsir* from Tabari to Ibn Kathir', p. 133.

11 Saeed, *Interpreting the Qur'an*, p. 64.

12 Ibn Rushd, *Fasl al-maqal*, Beirut: Markaz Dirasat al-Wihda al-'Arabiyya, 1999, pp. 39ff.

13 Mohammad Hashim Kamali, *Principles of Islamic Jurisprudence*, Selangor: Pelanduk Publications, 1995.

14 Qur'an: 3:7.

15 Qur'an: 1:2.

16 Qur'an: 2:110.

17 Kamali, *Principles of Islamic Jurisprudence*.

18 Kamali, *Principles of Islamic Jurisprudence*.

19 Kamali, *Principles of Islamic Jurisprudence*.

20 Kamali, *Principles of Islamic Jurisprudence*.

21 Qur'an: 2:219.

22 Qur'an: 4:43.

23 Qur'an: 5:90–91.

24 Kamali, *Principles of Islamic Jurisprudence*, p. 22.

25 Qur'an: 92:1.

26 Qur'an: 93:1.

27 Qur'an: 92:1–21.

28 Qur'an: 2:183–185.

11

Approaches to Qur'anic exegesis

E VER SINCE THE QUR'AN WAS REVEALED IN the seventh century CE, Muslims have sought to understand its meaning. The great importance placed on this endeavour arose from the Muslim belief that the Qur'an is God's Word as revealed to the Prophet Muhammad, in the Arabic language. Muslim laity and scholars have always used their knowledge of Arabic for formal and informal interpretation of the Qur'an. By drawing on the Qur'an, the example of the Prophet and interpretations of earlier generations as well as knowledge of Arabic language, each generation of Muslims has sought to understand the Qur'an as it applies to their own context. This remains true of Muslims today.

In this chapter we will discuss:

• the development of early religio-political groups in Islam and their emergent exegetical traditions;
• early approaches to exegesis, for example, theological, legal, mystical and philosophical approaches;
• exegetical developments in the modern era; and
• the work of some of the major exegetes from these traditions.

Early exegesis

Beginning with the first recipients of the Qur'an, the Companions of the Prophet, Muslims recognized that the Qur'an introduced new ideas and terms and also adapted a range of pre-Islamic concepts. This meant that some interpretation was needed to clarify the Qur'an's teachings. It was the Prophet who first undertook this task.

Indeed, the Qur'an states that part of the Prophet's mission was to assist in explaining the meanings of the Qur'an.[1] The Prophet did this using both words and actions, but mainly through his actions. History suggests that he only verbally interpreted particular parts of the Qur'an to his followers. Since most of the Companions were Arabic-speaking and were generally familiar with the broader context and meanings of the Qur'an, an in-depth explanation of the entire text would not have been necessary. However, there was a need for some explanation of verses that expressed new concepts or used certain pre-Islamic terms in new ways, or where there were linguistic difficulties, particularly for people who were not familiar with the Arabic dialect of Mecca.

Of the few verbal explanations provided by the Prophet, even fewer were actually recorded. Most of the Prophet's interpretation existed in the form of 'practical exegesis': that is, the Prophet's practical illustration of a particular Qur'anic term or concept. Fortunately, much of this 'practical exegesis' survived in the memory of the Companions and the practice of the community. A significant amount of this was later recorded in the hadith literature. An example of this is the Prophet's detailed demonstration of how the five daily prayers were to be performed.

After the death of the Prophet, only a small number of his immediate Companions are reported to have contributed to the area of Qur'anic exegesis. Those Companions who engaged in exegesis drew on several sources for understanding and interpreting the Qur'an, including relevant sections of the Qur'an itself, oral and praxis information received from the Prophet, and their own understanding of the language of the text. They also relied on the traditions of the People of the Book (Jews and Christians), particularly in relation to narratives in the Qur'an about past prophets, peoples and events. Their exegesis remained largely oral and was transmitted through their students.

The first/seventh century saw the expansion of Islam into what we call today the Middle East and North Africa. It was in the middle of this century that the second generation of Muslims began to grow in number and make significant contributions to the emerging body of Islamic knowledge. This second generation, known as the Successors, included the children of the first generation as well as a large number of converts to Islam, mainly from Christian and Zoroastrian backgrounds. The Successors were a much more heterogeneous group than the Companions. Given their different cultural and linguistic backgrounds, and the wider gap between themselves and the time of the Prophet, the community's need for interpretation of the Qur'an increased. Thus exegesis, though still informal, began to develop on a larger scale, mainly in key centres of learning in Mecca, Medina, Damascus, Yemen and Iraq. Muslims also began to find themselves interacting with the cultural, political and legal practices of the former Byzantine and Sassanid empires, whose lands they had by then conquered. Thus, many began to look to the Qur'an and its interpretation in search of guidance in the face of these new social contexts.

The expansion of Islam also resulted in greater interaction between Islam and other religious traditions of the region. Popular preachers and story-tellers among Muslims began to fill in details of the stories of past prophets – usually only alluded to in the Qur'an – by drawing on Jewish and Christian sources. Other Qur'anic narratives related to early Islamic events such as the battles between Muslims and their opponents were also elaborated on, based on accounts that were circulating at the time. Much of this information became part of early Qur'anic exegesis and was also used in popular storytelling.

As the Muslim community grew in the first/seventh century, interpretation and understanding of the Qur'an also became increasingly diverse. During this time, significant divisions among Muslims along religio-political and theological lines began to emerge. These led to heated debates about questions such as the extent to which human action is free or predetermined, who should be considered a Muslim, and who the rightful ruler of the growing Muslim community should be after the Prophet's death. The competing parties often used passages from the Qur'an to argue points. At the same time, Islamic disciplines such as hadith, law, the study of the Prophet's life and Arabic linguistics were also emerging. A rudimentary form of the discipline of Qur'anic exegesis was also beginning to develop. As all these disciplines emerged together, they were each influenced to varying degrees by the social and political environment of the time.

Although most of the earliest forms of Qur'anic exegesis were transmitted orally, recent research has confirmed that written exegesis had emerged by at least the early part of the second/eighth century.[2] The exegetical writings from this period did not consist of complete commentaries of the Qur'an; rather, they represented the beginnings of a process of documentation of Qur'anic exegesis. Initially, these works comprised brief explanatory comments regarding unclear, difficult or ambiguous words and phrases. They also discussed legal and ritual matters, such as how to perform prayer, calculate *zakat* (alms) or perform the pilgrimage, and dealt with certain commandments and prohibitions found in the Qur'an. In matters where the Qur'an only provided a general instruction, such as to perform daily prayers, these early exegetical writings attempted to provide explanations and fill in the gaps based on the example of the Prophet and the practice of the earliest Muslims.

By the end of the second/eighth century, exegetical works dealing with the entire Qur'an were beginning to emerge and by the early third/ninth century, Qur'anic exegesis was a fully established discipline. From this period onwards, the body of exegetical works became increasingly large and varied, and came to include theological, legal, religio-political and mystical works.

Three broad trends of exegesis

The third/ninth century saw the maturation of distinct schools of thought within Islam. Although the origins of these schools date back to the middle of the first/seventh century, it took several decades of debate and scholarship before they became established as independent schools of thought. By the third/ninth century, major religio-political groupings such as Sunni, Shi'a and Khariji had developed distinct approaches to legal and theological matters as well as Qur'anic exegesis. The vast majority of Muslims came to be known as Sunnis, and the Shi'a became a smaller minority, while the Kharijis were even fewer in number. Thus, the terms Sunni, Shi'i or Khariji exegesis, which had been meaningless in the first/seventh century, were firmly established by the third/ninth century.

Sunni exegesis

Sunni exegesis represents the dominant exegetical tradition. Sunnism emerged out of the many competing streams of thought that existed in the first/seventh and second/eighth centuries. Sunni exegesis was influenced heavily by all the key intellectual currents of the period, and its theological and exegetical positions represent a refining of the positions debated among the Muslims of the time.

Key characteristics of Sunni exegesis include an emphasis on a literal, rather than allegorical reading of the Qur'an, supported by linguistic evidence wherever possible. Generally, many Sunni exegetes have preferred to rely on hadith and exegetical traditions from the earliest Muslims (the Companions) rather than adopt a reason-based approach to interpretation. They argue that one has to rely on the earliest authorities to determine what is acceptable and what is not in matters of exegesis. This preference reflects the high degree of respect bestowed on all Companions, who Sunnis consider to be the most important source of religious authority after the Prophet. In contrast, the Shi'a and Kharijis believe that many Companions were simply sinners and even apostates.

In general, Sunni exegetes have rejected esoteric or hidden meanings of the Qur'an, as they are considered to represent unjustifiable speculation. This may also be contrasted with Shi'i exegesis, which tends to emphasize such hidden meanings. Sunnis also adopt theological positions regarding God's attributes, life after death, prophecy and revelation. Similarly, Sunni theologians share a particular definition of a 'believer' (*mu'min*) and 'un-believer' (*kafir*) and they reject a number of key theological positions held by their opponents (such as the Kharijis).

Tabari, a Sunni exegete

One of the best-known Sunni exegetes was Abu Ja'far Muhammad ibn Jarir al-Tabari (d.310/923), from the Persian province of Tabaristan. Tabari had memorized the Qur'an by the age of seven, and mastered a range of other Islamic disciplines at an early age. As a youth, Tabari left home in the pursuit of knowledge and studied in Persia, Syria and Egypt. He wrote major works in Qur'anic exegesis and Islamic history and law, and established his own school of Islamic jurisprudence, which is now extinct.

Tabari's major exegetical work, known as *Jami' al-bayan*, was a monumental 30-volume work. It was immediately regarded very highly and is generally considered to be Tabari's most outstanding achievement. It has certainly retained its importance for scholars to the present day. In this work, Tabari generally approached the verses of the Qur'an from a grammatical and lexicographical standpoint, but also made some theological and legal deductions from the text.[3] One of the distinguishing features of the work is that it deals with each verse of the Qur'an separately. As a scholar of hadith, law and history, Tabari attempted to collect and refer to as many relevant hadith of the Prophet as possible. He also cited the views of many early Muslim authorities in relation to each Qur'anic verse. His work is regarded as an example of exegesis based on tradition; however, it also adopts some elements of reason-based interpretation.[4] The following excerpt from Tabari illustrates his approach. He first quotes Qur'an 98:1: 'The unbelievers of the People of the Book and the idolaters would not leave off until the clear sign comes to them.' He then goes on to state the different opinions of exegetes regarding its meaning, and provides supporting reports from the earliest Muslims:

> The interpreters differ in the interpretation of [the verse] 'The un-believers of the People of the Book and the idolaters would not leave off until the clear sign comes to them'. Some of them [interpreters] say the meaning is that those unbelievers from the people of the Torah and the Gospel and the idolaters who worship idols will not leave off, that is to say, will not renounce their disbelief until this Qur'an comes to them. The interpreters who support what we have said about that say the following . . .

> *[Tabari then quotes three reports from various sources supporting this interpretation. He specifies his source for each report; for example, 'Yunus told me that Ibn Wahb informed him that Ibn Zayd said . . .'. He then goes on to say:]*

> The others [interpreters] say that, instead, the meaning of that statement [the verse above] is that the People of the Book are those who are the idolaters, and they will not ignore the description of Muhammad as found in their book until he is sent to them. When he is sent, however, they will split up into groups over him.

Finally, Tabari indicates his preferred interpretation of the verse:

> The first of these interpretations concerning that verse which is sound is the one which says that the meaning is those who disbelieve among the People of the Book and the idolaters will break into groups concerning the matter of Muhammad until the clear sign comes to them, which is God's sending of him to His creation as a messenger from God.[5]

Shi'i exegesis

Shi'i exegesis also emerged in the first three centuries of Islam. Shi'i exegetes on the whole have tended to adopt a reason-based approach to Qur'anic exegesis. Similarly, Shi'i exegesis is often influenced by Shi'i theological beliefs, which differ from Sunni beliefs in a number of ways. A major difference between the two approaches to exegesis is that Shi'i exegesis generally attempts to find explicit references in the Qur'an to themes such as the 'imams' and other specifically Shi'i doctrines,[6] whereas Sunnis generally reject such readings as speculative.

Imams and major Shi'i schools of thought

In Shi'ism, the imams are male descendants of the Prophet Muhammad, through his cousin and son-in-law Ali and one of Ali's sons, Husayn or Hasan. The people who are recognized as imams vary between schools. The imam is regarded as the religious and political leader of Shi'i Muslims and is also seen as a guide for the human race more generally. In the majority stream of Imami Shi'i Islam, the imam is believed to be infallible, divinely inspired and, because of his close relationship to God, the only one who truly understands Islam and is able to interpret the Qur'an and hadith. Although he is not seen as a prophet, his sayings, writings and deeds are considered to be authoritative religious texts of similar standing to prophetic texts.[7]

11/632:	The Prophet Muhammad dies; Ali ibn Abi Talib, the Prophet's cousin and son-in-law, becomes the first imam.
41/661:	Ali is assassinated; Ali's oldest son Hasan becomes the second imam.
48/669:	Hasan dies; Husayn, the second son of Ali, becomes the third imam.
61/680:	Husayn is martyred; Ali Zayn al-Abidin, the only son of Husayn to survive at Kerbala, becomes the fourth imam.

Separation of the Zaydi tradition

94/713:   Ali Zayn al-Abidin dies; his son, Muhammad al-Baqir, becomes the fifth imam in Isma'ili and Imami traditions; Ali's second son, Zayd, becomes the fifth imam in the Zaydi tradition.

125/743:   Muhammad al-Baqir dies; Jafar al-Sadiq becomes the sixth imam in Isma'ili and Imami traditions.

Separation of the Isma'ili tradition

144/762:   Jafar al-Sadiq's eldest son Isma'il dies before his father; Isma'il is recognized as the seventh imam in the Isma'ili tradition and his son, Muhammad, becomes the eighth Isma'ili imam. (The Isma'ili imamate continues from here.)

Imami tradition

147/765:   Jafar dies; his son Musa al-Kazim becomes the seventh imam in the Imami tradition.

182/799:   Musa is killed; his son Ali al-Rida becomes the eighth imam.

202/818:   Ali al-Rida dies; his seven-year-old son Muhammad al-Taqi becomes the ninth imam.

219/835:   Muhammad al-Taqi dies; his son, seven-year-old Ali al-Hadi, becomes the tenth imam.

254/868:   Ali al-Hadi dies; his son Hasan al-Askari becomes the eleventh imam.

259/873:   Hasan dies; his son Muhammad al-Mahdi, who had been hidden since birth, reappears to claim the imamate and then disappears again.

329/941:   Communication with the Mahdi (the twelfth imam) through intermediaries ceases; it is believed that the Mahdi will reappear leading up to the Day of Judgement.

While all traditions of Shi'i exegesis share common characteristics, there are also significant differences. The Zaydi sub-sect of Shi'ism is the closest to the Sunnis to the extent that some Zaydi exegetical works are widely used by Sunnis. For example, *Fath al-Qadir*,[8] by the Yemeni Zaydi scholar Shawkani (d.1834), is now commonly used in Sunni circles. Apart from some emphasis on imams and the family of the Prophet, this Zaydi work differs little from Sunni work.

Another Shi'a sub-group is that of the Isma'ilis. In contrast to Zaydis, Isma'ilis are the most distant Shi'i sub-group to Sunnis. Isma'ili exegesis is heavily influenced by their theological positions, including that God is unknowable and nameless and that He does not intervene in human life. Isma'ilis also recognize two kinds of religious knowledge: the *zahir* (exoteric), which is obligatory for all Isma'ilis to know, and the *batin* (esoteric), which can only be understood through secret learning and reflection on Isma'ili esoteric values.[9] They believe that it is only through this second, esoteric form of knowledge that the meaning of the Qur'an can be understood.[10] Unlike other Shi'i groups, Isma'ilis do not seem to have produced many exegetical works.

The largest Shi'a sub-group is Imami, or 'Twelver Imam' Shi'ism. Imami theological positions are heavily influenced by the strongly rationalist Mu'tazili school. Although Imami Shi'a believe that the only person capable of truly understanding the meaning of the Qur'an is the imam, this does not mean that Imami Shi'i scholars have not engaged in Qur'anic exegesis. In fact, Imami scholars have produced a great number of exegetical works throughout the history of Islam. In general, Imami scholars of the Qur'an also believe it has different 'inner' and 'outer' meanings. Some Sunnis argue that this belief allows them to read into the Qur'anic text their own theological and religio-political views, although it could be argued that this is a practice shared by all groups in Islam.

Ja'far al-Sadiq, a Shi'i exegete

Ja'far al-Sadiq (d.148/765) is one of the most important figures of Shi'ism. He is the sixth imam of Imami and Isma'ili Shi'ism, and the main Shi'i school of law (the Ja'fari school) is named after him. Most of his exegetical writings available today are known for being generally mystical, rather than specifically Shi'i in character.[11] There are, however, some passages where a specifically Shi'i interpretation is evident.

In the text below, Ja'far al-Sadiq comments on Qur'an 2:31, 'He taught Adam all the names', a verse usually understood as referring to the names of 'all things'. As we shall see, Ja'far understands this as having an inner (esoteric) meaning relating to the Prophet's family, who are accorded special status in Shi'i cosmology. He writes:

> Before any of his creation existed, God was. He created five creatures from the light of his glory, and attributed to each one of them, one of his names. As the Glorified (*mahmud*), he called his Prophet Muhammad ['Muhammad' also means 'the praised' or the 'deserving-of-praise'].

Being the Sublime (*ali*) he called the Emir of the believers Ali. Being the Creator (*fatir*) of the heavens and the earth, he fashioned the name Fatima [the Prophet's daughter, Ali's wife]. Because he had names that were called [in the Qur'an] the most beautiful (*husna*), he fashioned two names [from the same Arabic root] for Hasan and Husayn [the Prophet's grandsons, the second and third imams of Shi'ism]. Then he placed them to the right of the throne.[12]

Khariji exegesis

Among the first religio-political groupings that emerged in the second half of the first/seventh century were the Kharijis. The key issue on which they differed from the mainstream Muslim community was that of legitimate political leadership of the community as well as several, mainly theological, issues. Khariji beliefs, which underlie their approach to Qur'anic exegesis, have often been characterized as 'puritanical'. For instance, Kharijis argued that a Muslim who committed a grave sin (such as unlawfully killing another Muslim) was no longer a Muslim and would go to Hell. They were uncompromising about the application of the Qur'an's commandments and prohibitions, and believed that Muslims who did not support their position were unbelievers or religious hypocrites and could be killed with impunity. As for leadership, they believed that the most God-conscious and pious Muslim among them should be the leader of the community, and that the position should not be based on tribal kinship. Furthermore, they held that a leader who was not considered righteous – one who did not strictly follow the sacred law – could be deposed.[13]

Khariji exegesis, which often draws on these ideas, is based primarily on a literal reading of the text and does not often consider any deeper meanings. In the current era, a small percentage of Muslims, most of whom are descendants of early Kharijis, still maintain some of these ideas. Most of these descendants now live in Oman and North Africa and are known as 'Ibadis'. They do not refer to themselves as Kharijis as they regard it as a pejorative term, only used by their opponents.

Other key trends

In addition to the broad religio-political developments discussed above, a number of other important forms of exegesis also emerged in the first three centuries of Islam. Exegetes who were associated with these forms (theological, legal, mystical and philosophical exegesis) were usually also associated with one of the main religio-political groupings (Sunni, Shi'a or Khariji). However, labels such as 'theological', 'legal', 'mystical' or 'philosophical' indicate the emphasis of particular exegetical works and should not be confused with the distinction between Sunni, Shi'i or Khariji exegesis.

Theological exegesis

Scholars of theological exegesis were often associated with one of the two major theological schools of early Islam: Mu'tazilis and Ash'aris. Smaller theological schools, such as the Maturidis, also existed, although their theology did not differ significantly from that of the larger schools. The Mu'tazili school emerged first. It is best known for its uncompromising interpretation of God's unity[14] and consequent belief that the Qur'an is created as it could not possibly be co-eternal with God.[15] Other issues which were addressed in Mu'tazili theology include the definition of a true believer and free will; the status of human beings in the Hereafter and the nature of Paradise and Hell; and God's attributes.

In their exegesis, the Mu'tazilis relied heavily on linguistic and literary analysis of texts, particularly when literal readings contradicted Mu'tazili theological positions. They emphasized rationalist interpretations and the metaphorical nature of Qur'anic language, particularly when it speaks about God. They used philosophical arguments in defence of their theological positions and rejected any hadith that conflicted with them.

Although most early Mu'tazili works are now lost, commentaries of the Qur'an are believed to have been compiled by scholars such as Abu Bakr al-Asamm (d.201/816) and Abu Ali al-Jubba'i (d.303/915). From surviving fragments of Asamm's work, it appears that he attempted to produce a comprehensive Qur'anic theology that dealt with issues of abrogation, and also suggested that both clear and ambiguous verses of the Qur'an could be understood rationally, the latter merely requiring deeper reflection.[16]

In the early fourth/tenth century, the Ash'ari theological school emerged out of the Mu'tazili tradition. Towards the end of the third/ninth century, Abu al-Hasan al-Ash'ari (d. ca.324/935–936), the theologian after whom the Ash'ari school of theology is named, had produced works based on Mu'tazili theology. Ash'ari later came to doubt key Mu'tazili beliefs. He broke away from them, and began teaching doctrines that denied his Mu'tazili past.

In addition to strongly questioning the original Mu'tazili understandings of God's essence and attributes, the Ash'aris also attacked Mu'tazili beliefs regarding free will, the nature of divine law, the definition of evil and the role of reason. In time, Ash'ari theology became the dominant theological school for Sunnis, while Mu'tazili theology remained the dominant school in Shi'ism.[17]

Imam al-Haramayn al-Juwayni, an Ash'ari theologian

The following is an interpretation of the notion of the 'Oneness' of God by the great Ash'ari theologian, Imam al-Haramayn al-Juwayni (d.478/1085):

> The Creator – hallowed and exalted is He – is one. One, in the idiom of the Metaphysicians, is the thing that is indivisible. If one says that the one is the thing, this should be a sufficient stipulation. The Lord – hallowed and exalted is He – is a unique existent, transcending all possibility of division and difference. Speaking of Him as one means that He has not like or peer. A clear consequence of the reality of the doctrine of absolute Oneness is the proof that God is not a composition, because, if that were the case – exalted is He and glorified above that – each separate portion of Him would subsist as knowing, living and powerful in and of itself. And that is an admission of belief in two gods.[18]

Legal exegesis

Immediately after the death of the Prophet, there was a pressing need to understand the rulings, commandments, prohibitions and instructions of the Qur'an as they related to a Muslim's daily life. Thus, legal exegesis was among the first forms of exegesis to emerge. Approaches to legal exegesis varied considerably among early Muslims, and disagreements often arose about the intended meaning of concepts that were addressed in two or more seemingly contradictory verses of the Qur'an. If such disagreements could not be resolved by a close examination of the text and the context of its revelation, rulings based on later revelations were generally given precedence over earlier ones.

In the second/eighth and third/ninth centuries, as the discipline of hadith began to develop, an increasing number of reports of the Prophet's sayings and actions were collected. As the volume of these reports increased, differences in scholarly opinions about which hadith had more weight also emerged. Thus, the Qur'an became one of the most important aids in determining the authenticity or weight of a given hadith. Despite the use of the Qur'an, differences in opinions continued to exist and eventually developed into the different classical schools of law, described in Chapter 1. Because of their primary focus on matters of law, these schools are also known as the Islamic legal schools, or *madhhabs*.

Jurists from each of these schools produced a large number of works of legal exegesis, many of which are still in circulation today. Scholars of legal exegesis often focused on what appeared to be legal texts of the Qur'an at the expense of other verses and provided exegesis in the form of legal opinions.

Ibn Rushd on the interpretation of covering

In the following passage, Ibn Rushd (d.595/1198), a leading legal scholar from the Maliki school of law, discusses the different interpretations of *awra* (the parts of the body that should be covered, for example, for prayer). One of the instructions of the Qur'an and the Prophet is that when a Muslim intends to perform the daily prayer, they should cover certain parts of their body. Ibn Rushd says:

> The third issue relates to the limits of the *awra* [area of the body that should be covered] in the case of a woman. Most of the jurists maintained that her entire body constitutes *awra*, except for the face and the hands. Abu Hanifa maintained that her feet are not a part of the *awra*. Abu Bakr ibn Abd al-Rahman and Ahmad said that her entire body is *awra*.
>
> The reason for their disagreement is based on the possible interpretations of the words of the Exalted [God], 'And to display of their adornment only that which is apparent', that is whether the exemption relates to defined parts or to those parts that she cannot [help but] display. Those who maintained that the intended exemption is only for those parts that she cannot help but display while moving, said that her entire body is *awra*, even her back. They argued for this on the basis of the general implication of the words of the Exalted, 'O Prophet! Tell thy wives and thy daughters and the women of the believers to draw their cloaks close round them. That will make them recognizable and they will not be exposed to harm'.[19] Those who held that the intended exemption is for what is customarily not covered, that is, the face and the hands, said that these are not included in the *awra*. They (further) argued for this on the grounds that a woman does not cover her face during *hajj* [the pilgrimage to Mecca].[20]

Mystical exegesis

This type of exegesis is based on ideas that developed among Muslim mystics or Sufis around the second/eighth century. Islamic mysticism or Sufism is thought to have emerged as a distinct movement around this time in reaction to the wider Muslim community's increasing emphasis on material aspects of life and the growing number of political and factional struggles. Proponents of mystical exegesis emphasized the spiritual aspects of Islam, rather than the political, legal and worldly dimensions. Sufi scholars often preferred to explore questions regarding knowledge of God or the nature of human existence and its relation to the divine. They believed that the mystical allusions in the Qur'anic text were related most closely to the human spiritual condition and were impossible to understand through superficial readings or arguments over points of law and theology. Thus, in mystical exegesis, the spiritual and inner meanings of the Qur'an were considered paramount.

Major scholars from the early period of mystical exegesis include Hasan al-Basri (d.110/728), Ja'far al-Sadiq, Tustari (d.283/896) and Sulami (d.412/1021). The focus on spirituality in mystical exegesis is evident in the titles of many exegetical works, for example *The Spiritual Realities of Exegesis*, written by Sulami, and *The Divine Openings and the Secret Keys*, by the Ottoman scholar Nakhjuwani (d.920/1514).[21]

Another well-known mystical exegete was Ibn Arabi (d.638/1240), who came from Muslim Spain. Known to Sufis simply as the *Shaykh al-Akbar*, the Greatest Master, Ibn Arabi is widely considered one of the most significant, if not the most significant, Sufi sages, and he contributed greatly to the tradition of mystical exegesis.[22] An example of mystical exegesis is Ibn Arabi's discussion of the Qur'anic account of when Moses asked God to show Himself to him. The Qur'an states:

> When Moses came at the time We appointed, and his Lord spoke to him, he said, 'My Lord, show Yourself to me: let me see You!' He said, 'You will never see Me, but look at that mountain: if it remains standing firm, you will see Me.' When his Lord revealed Himself to the mountain, He made it crumble: Moses fell down unconscious. When he recovered, he said, 'Glory be to You! To You I turn in repentance! I am the first to believe!'[23]

Ibn Arabi interprets the difference between the mountain's crumbling and Moses' losing consciousness as follows:

> *When his Lord disclosed Himself to the mountain*, that self-disclosure *made it crumble to dust*, but it did not make it non-existent. Rather, it caused its loftiness and highness to disappear. Moses had looked upon it in the state of its loftiness, and the self-disclosure had occurred from the direction not adjacent to Moses. When the mountain crumbled,

what made it crumble became manifest to Moses, so *Moses fell down thunderstruck*. For Moses possessed a spirit, which has the property of maintaining the form as it is. The spirit of everything other than animals is identical with its life, nothing else. So Moses' being thunderstruck was like the mountain's crumbling, because of the diversity of the preparedness, since the mountain has no spirit to maintain its form for it. Thus the name *mountain* disappeared from the mountain, but neither the name *Moses* nor the name *human being* disappeared from Moses through his being thunderstruck. Moses regained consciousness, but the mountain did not return as a mountain after crumbling, since it had no spirit to make it abide.

After all, the property of spirits in things is not like the property of life in them, because life is perpetual in all things, while spirits are like rulers: Sometimes they are described as dismissed, sometimes as possessing rulership, and sometimes as absent while rulership remains. Rulership belongs to the spirit as long as it governs this animal body, death is its dismissal, and sleep is its absence while its rulership remains.[24]

Philosophical exegesis

As Muslim interest in Greek philosophical works began to develop in the early centuries of Islam, so too did arguments over the acceptability of philosophy and its place in Islam. While many Muslims argued against the use of philosophy in exegesis, those of a more rationalist orientation wholeheartedly adopted philosophy as a valuable part of the exegetical process. Such scholars preferred an allegorical interpretation of the Qur'an, as it enabled them to harmonize philosophical ideas more easily with those of the Qur'an. As such, philosophical interpretations of the Qur'an, particularly verses related to God, His nature and relationship to creation, and the concepts of Paradise and Hell, tended to differ greatly from more literal readings of Qur'anic verses.

The renowned philosopher and scientist Farabi (d.399/950) had such an influence on knowledge and science that he was known to many as the 'second teacher', the first being Aristotle. Although we do not know whether he produced a full commentary of the Qur'an, his views had a significant influence on philosophical exegesis. Farabi believed that while philosophy had come to an end elsewhere, it had found its place again in the world of Islam. A similarly influential philosopher, Ibn Sina (d.428/1037), who was also a physician, produced a number of works, including a minor work of exegesis.[25]

Ibn Rushd on philosophical exegesis

The use of allegorical interpretation is a distinctive feature of philosophical exegesis of the Qur'an. In the following extract from the philosopher Ibn Rushd's *The Decisive Treatise Determining the Nature of the Connection between Religion and Philosophy*, we see how he first argues that the Qur'an and philosophical reasoning do not contradict each other, as both are paths to 'the Truth'. He goes on to suggest circumstances when an allegorical interpretation of a verse in the Qur'an would be called for.

> Now since this religion [Islam] is true and summons to the study which leads to the knowledge of the Truth, we the Muslim community know definitively that demonstrative study [that is, philosophy] does not lead to [conclusions] conflicting with what Scripture has given us; for truth does not oppose truth but accords with it and bears witness to it.
>
> This being so, whenever demonstrative study leads to any manner of knowledge about any being, that being is inevitably either unmentioned or mentioned in Scripture. If it is unmentioned, there is no contradiction, and it is the same case as an act whose category is unmentioned so that the (Muslim) lawyer has to infer it by reasoning from Scripture. If Scripture does speak about it, the apparent meaning of the words inevitably either accords or conflicts with the conclusions of (philosophical) demonstration about it. If this apparent meaning accords, there is no conflict. If it conflicts, there is a call for allegorical interpretation. The meaning of 'allegorical interpretation' is: the extension of the significance of an expression from real to metaphorical significance, without forsaking therein the standard metaphorical practices of Arabic, such as calling a thing by the name of something resembling it or a cause or consequence or accompaniment of it, or other such things as are enumerated in accounts of the kinds of metaphorical speech.[26]

Exegesis in the modern period

While all the above forms of exegesis continue to be studied and used in the modern period, various new forms have also emerged. In response to global developments in areas as diverse as politics, the environment and ethics, many people, including Muslims, are searching for a balance between traditional and modern views of life. It is in this environment that new forms of exegetical thinking such as modernist, scientific, socio-political, feminist, thematic and contextual exegesis have begun to emerge.

Modernist exegesis

This form of exegesis is in certain respects a continuation of Muslim reformist thought of the eighteenth century; it can also be seen as an active response by Muslims to the challenges posed by modernity while remaining faithful to the teachings of their religion. Among the first 'modernists' were Jamal al-Din al-Afghani (d.1897), Muhammad Abduh (d.1905), Sayyid Ahmad Khan (d.1898) and Muhammad Iqbal (d.1938). Since the movement began in the mid-nineteenth century, a large number of scholarly works have been written by modernist scholars. One of the best-known modernist writings is Muhammad Abduh's *Tafsir al-Manar*, which was compiled and completed after Abduh's death by Rashid Rida (d.1935), a student of Abduh.

Central to the modernist approach is the idea of reform. Figures such as Afghani argued that Muslims should have a reform movement like the ones that had taken place in Christian Europe. Put another way, Muslims needed their own Martin Luther to initiate a major reform of the Islamic heritage. According to these thinkers, the modern context demanded a reappraisal of the intellectual heritage of Muslims; this process required giving up the practice of blind imitation or *taqlid*, which modernists claimed was common among earlier scholars.

Other key ideas of modernist exegesis included the need for a flexible interpretation of Islam and its sources in order to develop ideas compatible with modern conditions. In particular, many modernists suggested the need to understand the Qur'an from a scientific worldview, which required a reinterpretation of Qur'anic ideas such as miracles.

Modernists proposed that a return to Islam as it was originally practiced would inject into Muslim societies the intellectual dynamism required to catch up with the West. For that purpose, political, legal and educational institutions in particular had to be reformed. Part of this reform involved avoiding the use of earlier exegesis that contained too much jargon and had made the Qur'anic text seem obscure. Thus, many reformers of the modern period underscored the primacy of the Qur'an and the sunna, the foundation texts of Islam. From their scriptural orientation, modernists condemned what they saw as deviations and additions not considered worthy of the early generations of Muslims.

Modernist scholars also argued that accepting the concept of revelation did not clash with the use of reason. Thus, they tried to revive Islam's rationalist philosophical tradition, and some previously discounted ideas of the rationalist Mu'tazilis came into vogue again among some modern scholars. Other popular topics to have undergone reinterpretation by proponents of modernist exegesis include the status of women, polygamy, war and peace, science, slavery and justice.

Muhammad Abduh and modernist exegesis

The following passage illustrates Muhammad Abduh's views on polygamy.

> Polygamy, although permitted in the Qur'an, is a concession to neces-
> sary social conditions which was given with the greatest reluctance, in
> as much as it is accompanied by the provision that a man may take
> more than one wife only when he is able to take equal care of all of
> them and give to each her rights with impartiality and justice. The
> *Shari'a* has, in requirement of circumstances, permitted the legality of
> four contemporaneous marriages with great reluctance. Since the pro-
> viso immediately following – if you fear that you cannot be equitable
> and just with all then (marry) only one – is given so much stress that [sic]
> the permission to contract four contemporaneous marriages becomes
> practically ineffective.[27]

Scientific exegesis

This type of exegesis has been particularly influential in the twentieth century, although its precursors can be found in the pre-modern period. For instance, the classical scholar Ghazali (d.505/1111) could be described as an early proponent of 'scientific exegesis'. This is reflected in his description of the Qur'an as being the ocean from which all sciences emerged.[28]

Similarly, early forms of scientific exegesis in the twentieth century attempted to reconcile Qur'anic teachings with scientific knowledge. Today, scientific exegesis has come to be related to the idea that the Qur'an pre-dicted many of the findings of modern science. The popular nature of this discourse is demonstrated by the large number of conferences, seminars and publications devoted to it. There are some Muslim thinkers, however, who criticize it for ignoring the open-ended nature of scientific discovery and as misreading the Qur'an. Notwithstanding these criticisms, scientific exegesis has become one of the most popular forms of exegesis in the modern period.

Maurice Bucaille and scientific exegesis

One of the most widely circulated works in this genre is by the French writer Maurice Bucaille.[29] Bucaille provided a scientific reading of a number of Qur'anic verses that appear to have some relationship to science. For instance, in his discussion of the expansion of the universe, one of the most important discoveries of modern science, he cites the verse 'We built the heavens with Our power and We are expanding it'.[30] Bucaille suggests that this verse can be linked to modern scientific understandings of the beginning of the universe. He goes on to provide an interpretation of two key phrases from this verse:

> 'Heaven' is the translation of the word *sama'* and this is exactly the extra terrestrial world that is meant.
>
> '[We] are expanding it' is the translation of the plural present participle *'musi'una'* of the verb *ausa'a* meaning 'to make wider, more spacious, and extend, to expand'.
>
> Some translators who were unable to grasp the meaning of the latter provide translations that appeared to me to be mistaken . . . there are those who armed themselves with authorized scientific opinion in the commentaries and give the meaning stated here [the expansion of the universe in totally unambiguous terms].[31]

Commenting on scientific exegesis, Mustansir Mir, a modern scholar of the Qur'an, observes that this form of exegesis has risen out of a need to counter the challenge that modern science poses for all religions. Mir states:

> The project of establishing compatibility (*muwafaqah*) between the Divine Word and scientific findings is, by definition, defensive in character. Muslim thinkers first engaged in a similar exercise in *muwafaqah* during the Abbasid period, when they felt constrained to reconcile Greek thought with Islamic religion. The arena of discussion at that time was theology; today, it is science, but the nature of the exercise is essentially the same. The challenge that modern science initially posed to Christianity has now been posed to all religions – to the very idea of religion itself. Muslims naturally feel the force of the challenge, whether or not they understand its exact nature, and some of them think that it would be an adequate defence of Islam to demonstrate that there is no conflict between the Qur'an and science or, going a step further, that the Qur'an prefigures modern science.[32]

Socio-political exegesis

Another modern approach to the Qur'an, known as 'socio-political exegesis', was developed by the Egyptian scholar, Sayyid Qutb (d.1966). Qutb was a leader of the Muslim Brotherhood, one of the political Islamic movements of the twentieth century. He was executed in 1966 by the Egyptian authorities. Despite this, Qutb is still a major source of inspiration for those who seek a closer connection between Islam and the state.

Qutb's approach to exegesis was highly political and many of his positions were controversial. Among his arguments was a suggestion that many aspects of modern society, including many modern Muslims themselves, were *jahili* (akin to pre-Islamic 'ignorance': the state of the Arabs before the emergence of Islam in the seventh century). He also uncompromisingly argued that Islam should be the guiding and dominant political force of nations with majority Muslim populations.

Sayyid Qutb on the notion of *jahili*

In his interpretation of one of the earliest Qur'anic chapters 'Say [Prophet], "Disbelievers: I do not worship what you worship, you do not worship what I worship, I will never worship what you worship, you will never worship what I worship: you have your religion and I have mine"',[33] Qutb says in his work *In the Shade of the Qur'an*:

> *Ignorance* is nothing but *Ignorance* and Islam is altogether different from it. The only way to bridge the gulf between the two is for *Ignorance* to liquidate itself completely and substitute for all its laws, values, standards and concepts their Islamic counterparts.
>
> The first step that should be taken in this field by the person calling on people to embrace Islam is to segregate himself from *Ignorance* . . . [A]ny agreement or intercourse between him and *Ignorance* is absolutely impossible unless and until the people of *Ignorance* embrace Islam completely: no intermingling, no half measures or conciliation is permissible . . . The chief basis of the personality of the person inviting others to Islam is . . . his solemn conviction of being radically different from them . . . His task is to orientate them so that they may follow his path without any fraud or pretence. Failing this, he must withdraw completely, detach himself from their life and openly declare to them: 'You have your own religion, and I have mine.'[34]

Thematic exegesis

A thematic method of enquiry emphasizes the unity of the Qur'an. It approaches interpretation as a study of the Qur'an as a whole. This method allows an interpreter to identify all verses related to a particular theme, gather them and then study and compare them. Examples of themes might be women, trade and commerce, war, tolerance, People of the Book or the poor. Proponents of this method argue that it allows for a more objective approach to the Qur'an.

Prominent scholars of thematic exegesis include Iranian Ayatullah Murtaza Mutahhari (b.1920) and the Egyptian writer Abbas Mahmud al-Aqqad (d.1964), both of whom have written on themes such as society and history, women's rights, and fundamental liberties. The Pakistani scholar Fazlur Rahman (d.1988) was also a proponent of this type of exegesis, as shown in his work *Major Themes of the Qur'an*.[35] This style of Qur'anic exegesis is particularly popular today in Egypt and Indonesia.

Feminist exegesis

Over the second half of the twentieth century, the body of Muslim feminist exegesis grew considerably. Most feminist exegetes criticize traditional male-centred interpretations of the Qur'an, arguing that the gender biases of predominantly male exegetes have, until now, largely shaped our under-standings of the Qur'an and Islam more generally. In contrast to secularist feminists, Muslim feminist scholars do not reject Islam itself. Instead, they refer to the Qur'an and the Prophet's sunna to support their claim that the Qur'an needs to be reinterpreted. Some major scholars of feminist exegesis include Fatima Mernissi, Amina Wadud and Asma Barlas. Their ventures into the once taboo field of exegesis have met with staunch opposition from traditionalist scholars, men and women alike.

One example of such work is that of Asma Barlas, who has focused much of her scholarly works on examining the ways in which Muslims 'interpret and live' the teachings of the Qur'an. In particular, she has produced a number of works examining the origins of patriarchal Qur'anic exegesis. Barlas argues that ideas of inequality and patriarchy were read into the Qur'an in order to justify existing social structures. In her book *'Believing Women' in Islam: Unreading Patriarchal Interpretations of the Qur'an*,[36] Barlas re-examines a number of these issues and suggests that the teachings of the Qur'an do not support patriarchy, but rather are highly egalitarian. She has also proposed that it is necessary to avoid 'masculinizing' God, and that it is the right of every Muslim to read and interpret the Qur'an for themselves.[37] Although Barlas' work has been referred to by some as 'Islamic feminism', Barlas herself prefers not to be referred to as a feminist; instead, she considers herself 'a believer'.

Contextualist exegesis

Contextualists are those who believe that the teachings of the Qur'an should be applied in different ways depending on the context. They tend to see the Qur'an primarily as a source of practical guidelines that should be implemented differently in different circumstances, rather than as a set of rigid laws. Advocates of this approach argue that scholars must be aware of both the social, political and cultural context of the revelation as well as the setting in which interpretation occurs today.

One of the primary figures in this movement was the Pakistani-American scholar Fazlur Rahman. He argued that *ijtihad* (independent thinking and reasoning) should play a key role in contemporary Muslim life. He also argued that contemporary Muslim scholars had largely imitated previous modes of thinking and were in need of exploring new ways of looking at the text.

The contextualist approach allows for greater scope to interpret the Qur'an and question the rulings of earlier scholars. Over the late twentieth and early twenty-first centuries, contextualist methodologies have been adopted by an increasing number of Muslim thinkers. Although many may not refer to the term 'contextualist' as such, their methods of interpretation show that they are engaging with the Qur'an in new ways that reflect this methodology. For instance, many have attempted to relate the Qur'an to contemporary concerns and needs by reference to various Qur'anic ideas and principles that are relevant to the modern period. These scholars come from a variety of backgrounds, and we should not see them as part of a single movement or school of thought. They range from the Algerian scholar Muhammad Arkoun (b.1928) and the Egyptian Nasr Hamid Abu Zayd (b.1943), to American scholars such as Amina Wadud and Khaled Abou El Fadl (b.1963). Although all these scholars can be described as contextualists, their views and understandings of the Qur'an vary significantly.

The final chapter of this book (Chapter 12) will deal with five key Muslim intellectuals, who we may broadly consider as 'Contextualist' in their approach to interpretation of the Qur'an.

Summary

Some of the important points we have discussed in this chapter include:

* The tradition of Qur'anic exegesis began with the Prophet, who often provided his followers with 'practical exegesis' of particular Qur'anic instructions.

- By the second/eighth century, exegesis had developed into an independent discipline.
- Each of the emergent religio-political groups – Sunni, Shi'a and Khariji – developed a number of their own exegetical traditions.
- The majority of Shi'i Muslims believe that the imams are infallible, and are the only people capable of truly understanding the Qur'an and hadith.
- Alongside the religio-political groups, other styles of exegesis, such as theological, legal, mystical and philosophical also developed.
- Contemporary approaches, beginning with modernist exegesis in the mid-nineteenth century, have also included scientific, socio-political, thematic and, most recently, feminist and contextualist forms of exegesis.

Recommended reading

Herbert Berg, 'Exegetical *Hadiths* and the Origins of *Tafsir*', 'Data and Analysis: The Authenticity of Ibn 'Abbas's *Hadiths* in Al-Tabari's *Tafsir*', in *The Development of Exegesis in Early Islam: The Authenticity of Muslim Literature from the Formative Period*, London: Curzon Press, 2000.

- In this book, Berg critiques the major positions on the issue of hadith authenticity. In these two chapters, he examines the authenticity of exegetical hadith in particular and then uses this analysis in order to assess the authenticity of hadith used in Tabari's classic interpretation of the Qur'an.

Norman Calder, Jawid Mojaddedi and Andrew Rippin (eds and trans.), 'Qur'anic Interpretation', *Classical Islam: A Sourcebook of Religious Literature*, London and New York: Routledge, 2003, pages 97–133.

- This book is written for introductory level students and includes more than 50 new translations of Arabic and Persian Islamic texts. This chapter begins with an explanatory preface before presenting a number of key texts on Qur'anic interpretation from the classical period of Islam.

Barbara Freyer Stowasser, *Women in the Qur'an, Traditions, and Interpretation*, New York: Oxford University Press, 1994.

- In this book, Stowasser presents an overview of the Qur'anic view of women. She tells the stories of women as they are found in the Qur'an and its interpretation. Stowasser also explores past and present understandings of women in Islamic tradition along with their political and economic implications.

Abdullah Saeed, 'Qur'an: Tradition of Scholarship and Interpretation', in Lindsey Jones (ed. in chief), *Encyclopedia of Religion*, Farmington: Thomson Gale, 2005, Volume 11, pages 7,561–7,570.

• In this article, Saeed looks at the tradition of Muslim scholarship in the discipline of Qur'anic exegesis or interpretation. He explores a number of key ideas, approaches, trends, figures, works and types of exegesis.

C.H.M. Versteegh, *Arabic Grammar and Qur'anic Exegesis in Early Islam*, Leiden: E.J. Brill, 1993.

• In this book, Versteegh examines the role and relationship of Arabic grammar to early Qur'anic interpretation. He refers to some of the earliest Qur'anic commentaries, from the first half of the second/eighth century, and analyses their exegetical methods and grammatical terminology.

NOTES

1 See Qur'an: 16:44.
2 Khan, *Die exegetischen Teile*, pp. 67–82; Neuwirth, *Die Masa'il*, cited in Claude Gilliot, 'Exegesis of the Qur'an: Classical and Medieval', in Jane D. McAuliffe (ed.), *Encyclopaedia of the Qur'an*, vol. 2, Leiden: E.J. Brill, 2001, p. 104.
3 C.E. Bosworth, 'al-Tabari, Abu Jafar Muhammad b. Jarir b. Yazid', in P. Bearman et al. (eds), *Encyclopaedia of Islam*, vol. X, Leiden: Brill, 2000, p. 14.
4 See Chapter 10 for the differences between reason- and tradition-based exegesis.
5 Cited in Norman Calder, Jawid Mohaddedi and Andrew Rippin (eds and trans.), *Classical Islam: A Sourcebook of Religious Literature*, London and New York: Routledge, 2003, p. 115.
6 Meir M. Bar-Asher, 'Shi'ism and the Qur'an', in McAuliffe (ed.), *Encyclopaedia of the Qur'an*, Vol. 4, p. 596.
7 Today, most Shi'i Muslims belong to the Imami or 'Twelver Imam' tradition. Imamis believe that there were 12 rightful imams. The second most important Shi'a group today are the Isma'ilis. They follow the first six imams of the Imami tradition, but diverged over the identity of the seventh and subsequent imams. A minority of Shi'is today also belong to the Zaydi tradition. Zaydis follow the first four imams of the Imami tradition, but diverged over the identity of the fifth and subsequent imams.

8   Muhammad ibn Ali al-Shawkani, *Fath al-qadir al-jami bayna fannay al-riwayah wa al-dirayah fi ilm al-tafsir*, 5 vols, Cairo, 1930; repr. Beirut: Dar al-Ma'rifah, 1973.

9   Tore Kjeilen (ed.), 'Isma'ilism', *Encyclopaedia of the Orient*, LexicOrient, 2007. Accessed 11 May 2007: http://lexicorient.com/e.o/ismailis.htm.

10   Bar-Asher, 'Shi'ism and the Qur'an', p. 598.

11   Michael Sells, *Early Islamic Mysticism*, New Jersey: Paulist Press, 1996, pp. 76–77.

12   Attributed to Ja'far al-Sadiq in Sulami, *Haqa'iq al-Tafsir*, trans. Paul Nwyia in *Exégèse coranique et langage mystique*, Beirut: Dar al-Machreq Editeurs, 1970, p. 159, cited in Sells, *Early Islamic Mysticism*, pp. 77–78.

13   Abdullah Saeed, *Islamic Thought: An Introduction*, London; New York: Routledge, 2006, p. 7.

14   For instance, chapter 112 of the Qur'an ('Purity [of Faith]') which says: 'Say, "He is God the One, God the eternal. He begot no one nor was He begotten. No one is comparable to Him".'

15   Sabine Schmidtke, 'Mu'tazila', in McAuliffe (ed.), *Encyclopaedia of the Qur'an*, p. 467.

16   Schmidtke, 'Mu'tazila', p. 470. See Chapter 10, 'Selected Exegetical Principles and Ideas', for further discussion of the different exegetical approaches to 'clear' and 'ambiguous' verses of the Qur'an.

17   See also Chapter 2, 'Revelation and the Qur'an', for further discussion of the differences between Ash'ari and Mu'tazili theology.

18   Imam al-Haramayn al-Juwayni, *A Guide to Conclusive Proofs for the Principles of Belief (Kitab al-Irshad ila Qawati' al-Adilla fi Usul al-i'tiqad)*, trans. Paul E. Walker, Reading: Garnet Publishing, 2000, p. 31.

19   Qur'an 33:59.

20   Ibn Rushd, 'Chapter 4, Section 1: Covering the *'awra* – Issue 3', 'The Book of Prayer (*Salah*)', in *The Distinguished Jurist's Primer*, Reading, UK: Garnet Publishing Limited, 1994, vol. I, p. 126. Words in round brackets are the translator's. Those in square brackets are mine.

21   Gilliot, 'Exegesis of the Qur'an: Classical and Medieval', pp. 118–120.

22   Gilliot, 'Exegesis of the Qur'an: Classical and Medieval', p. 119.

23   Qur'an: 7:143.

24   Muhy al-Din ibn al-Arabi, *al-Futuhat al-makiyya*, Chapter II, 540.11, cited in William C. Chittick, *The Self-Disclosure of God: Principles of Ibn al-Arabi's Cosmology*, Albany: State University of New York Press, 1998, p. 274.

25   R. Walzer, 'Al Farabi, Abu Nasr Muhammad ibn Muhammad ibn Tarkhan ibn Awzalagh', in P. Bearman et al. (eds), *Encyclopaedia of Islam*, p. 779.

26   'The Decisive Treatise, Determining the Nature of the Connection Between Religion and Philosophy', in George F. Hourani (ed. and trans.), *Averroes on the Harmony of Religion and Philosophy*, London: Luzac, 1961, pp. 46–47.

27   Muhammad Abduh, *Tarikh al-ustad al-Imam*, vol II, Egypt: Matba'at al-Manar, 1906, cited in Asghar Ali Engineer, *The Rights of Women in Islam*, London: C. Hurst & Co, 1992, p. 157.

28 Muhammad Husayn al-Dhahabi, *al-Tafsir wa al-Mufassirun*, 3 vols, Cairo: Maktabat Wahbah, 1995, vol. 2, pp. 511–521.

29 Although Maurice Bucaille's work is perhaps the most well-known in the genre of scientific exegesis, Bucaille himself is not known to have converted to Islam.

30 Qur'an 51:47.

31 Maurice Bucaille, *The Bible, The Qur'an and Science*, Indianapolis: American Trust Publications, 1979, p. 167.

32 Mustansir Mir, 'Scientific Exegesis of the Qur'an – A Viable Project?', *Islam & Science*, vol. 2, no. 1, 2004, p. 33. Accessed 10 February 2007: http://www.questia.com/PM.qst?a=o&d=5007384304.

33 Qur'an: 109:1–5.

34 Sayyid Qutb, *In the Shade of the Qur'an*, trans. M.A. Salahi and A.A. Shamis, London: Muslim Welfare House London Publishers, 1979, p. 331.

35 Fazlur Rahman, *Major Themes of the Qur'an*, Minneapolis, MN: Bibliotheca Islamica, 1994.

36 Austin, TX: University of Texas Press, 2002.

37 Novriantoni and Ramy El-Dardiry, 'Interview Asma Barlas: It is the Right for Every Muslim to Interpret the Quran for Themselves', *Liberal Islam Network*, cited at 'Dialogue with the Islamic World'. Accessed 13 May 2007: http://www.qantara.de/webcom/show_article.php/_c-307/_nr-28/_p-1/i.html?PHPSESSID=.

12
Modern interpretation of the Qur'an

METHODS OF INTERPRETATION OF THE Qur'an have continuously changed and developed over the course of Islamic history. Two of the many different trends are often referred to as the 'textualist' and 'contextualist' approaches. Today, the textualist approach remains the most widely adopted by Muslim interpreters of the Qur'an, particularly Sunni Muslims. In an attempt to understand the Qur'an's meanings, which are often assumed to be fixed and unchanging over time, proponents of this approach engage primarily in linguistic analyses of sources such as the Qur'an and hadith. In the modern era, an alternative, contextualist approach is beginning to gain more prominence. In their attempt to understand the Qur'an's meanings, of which the essence is assumed to be unchanging, proponents of this approach argue that textual study must be accompanied by knowledge of the social, cultural and political conditions of the time of revelation. In contrast to textualist scholars, contextualists engage not only in linguistic analysis, but also adopt approaches from alternative fields such as hermeneutics and literary theory. Thus, in keeping with the history of continuously evolving Qur'anic exegesis, many modern contextualists are seeking to develop new ways of approaching the Qur'an.

In this chapter we will discuss:

- The differences between textualist and contextualist scholarship;
- The predominant approach of most Qur'anic exegetes today;
- The approaches of five contemporary scholars of the Qur'an:

    - Fazlur Rahman,
    - Amina Wadud,
    - Muhammad Shahrour,
    - Mohammed Arkoun and
    - Khaled Abou El Fadl.

Differences between textualists and contextualists

Much of today's Qur'anic scholarship is based on a textualist methodology. This methodology also largely dominated exegesis in the pre-modern period. Textualist scholars rely on a referential theory of meaning to interpret the Qur'an, drawing mainly on linguistic rather than social or historical analysis. Scholars who adopt this approach believe that the language of the Qur'an has concrete, unchanging references, and therefore the meaning that a Qur'anic verse had upon its revelation still holds for the contemporary context. For most textualists, the meaning of the Qur'an is static: Muslims must adapt to this meaning. This approach is prominent in much of today's literature on the Qur'an and generally well understood.

In contrast, contextualist approaches are less well known and certainly much less understood than the more traditional approaches to exegesis. In general, the scholarship of contextualists is often associated with a form of Islamic reformism. In comparison to textualist approaches, it is arguable that contextualists have a more nuanced approach to finding 'meaning' in the Qur'anic texts, although the details of this approach will often vary between scholars. A common characteristic of contextualist scholars is that they argue that the meaning of a particular Qur'anic verse (or hadith) is, to a large degree, indeterminate. Meaning, in this sense, is said to evolve over time, and is dependent upon the socio-historical, cultural and linguistic contexts of the text. This approach to exegesis allows a scholar to consider any given word in the light of its context, and to arrive at an understanding which is believed to be more relevant to the circumstances of interpretation. Contextualists further argue that it is never possible to arrive at a truly objective meaning and that subjective factors will always intervene in our understandings. That is, the interpreter cannot approach the text without certain experiences, values, beliefs and presuppositions influencing their understanding.[1]

Modern contextualist scholars have sought in particular to engage with the ethico-legal teachings that can be derived from the Qur'an. From a contextualist perspective, the Qur'an is not considered to be a book of laws, but one which contains ideas, values and principles that can be applied through changing times and across different places. In order to arrive at these ideas, values and principles, a contextualist study of the Qur'an requires both broad and narrow contexts of the Qur'an to be understood. A broad contextual understanding allows a single verse to be compared to the overall intention and context of the Qur'anic text, which includes not only the Qur'an itself, but also the sunna of the Prophet. The narrow context must consider what appears directly before and after the verse in question and also the exact words of the verse itself.

Contextualist studies are also heavily influenced by modern hermeneutics, which represents a set of principles used in interpretation of texts, and can also be defined as a 'philosophical exploration of the character and necessary conditions for all understanding'.[2] Hermeneutics does not attempt to assign a fixed and stable meaning to a text, rather it presupposes that the meaning of a text is found in or assigned to it by the people who read it. Thus the role of the reader in the creation of meaning is emphasized.

Farid Esack, a South African Muslim scholar, discusses this in his work. He suggests that 'receiving a text and extracting meaning from it do not exist on their own' and so meaning is always partial.[3] In his work *Qur'an:*

Liberation and Pluralism, Esack states that 'hermeneutics' has not been associated with traditional Islamic scholarship. However, Esack speaks of developing a 'hermeneutic of liberation',[4] and also claims that the discipline of hermeneutics gradually began to influence Islamic scholarship of the twentieth century. As will be reflected in this chapter's profiles of modern Muslim scholars, 'hermeneutics' seems to be aligned with reformist and 'liberal' scholarship in contemporary Islamic thought. Such ideas directly confront the assertions of Muslim textualists, who do not assign any significant role to the reader in the identification of meaning.

This chapter will look at the thought and contributions of five contemporary scholars to the understanding of the Qur'an. Among them is Fazlur Rahman, who played a key role in developing notions associated with a hermeneutical approach within Islamic studies. Rahman is described as 'arguably the first modern reformist Muslim scholar to link the question of the origin of the Qur'an to both its context and interpretation.'[5] Following Rahman, there is an overview of the prominent American scholar Amina Wadud, a central figure in the formation of a 'hermeneutics of equality'.[6] Another pioneering figure of contemporary Islamic hermeneutics is Mohammed Arkoun, whose work was influenced by postmodern intellectuals such as Paul Ricoeur, Michel Foucault and Jacques Derrida. Similarly influenced by postmodernism, Muhammad Shahrour emphasizes the need to differentiate between the divine and human understandings of reality. Finally, we will end with an overview of the work of Khaled Abou El Fadl, a leading scholar of Islamic law and vocal opponent of literalist interpretations of the Qur'an.

Fazlur Rahman

Fazlur Rahman is best known for his major contribution to modern discussions of reform in Islamic thought. He wrote on a wide range of subjects, including Islamic education, interpretation of the Qur'an, hadith criticism, early development of Islamic intellectual traditions and reform of Islamic law and ethics.

Rahman was born in Pakistan in 1919, and spent most of his adult life studying and teaching in the UK, Canada, Pakistan and the USA. While living in England he wrote his dissertation at Oxford University on Ibn Sina, and subsequently taught Islamic philosophy for eight years at Durham University. He then moved to Canada, where he was appointed associate professor at the Institute of Islamic Studies at McGill University. He later returned to Pakistan to take up a position as visiting professor and then director of the Islamic Research Institute. From 1961 to 1968, while at the Institute, Rahman advised the then president, General Ayyub Khan, on how Pakistan could best steer a middle path between modernist and traditionalist Islam.

During his time in Pakistan, Rahman was criticized by those who wanted to maintain the dominant socio-religious practices of the time. When this criticism led to death threats, he sought safety in the United States. There, Rahman took up the position of Professor of Islamic Thought at the University of Chicago, a position he held until his death in 1988. One of Rahman's students at the University of Chicago was Nurcholish Madjid, a Muslim scholar who went on to become a leading Indonesian intellectual and played a major role in broadening Islamic studies and developing Islamic liberalism and democracy in Indonesia.

Rahman's methodology has also been applied by other scholars in areas such as women's rights, as is evident in the writing of the prominent American scholar Amina Wadud. Although Rahman spent a large part of his life in the West, he remained an avowedly Muslim scholar, committed to reaching and influencing a Muslim audience. Similarly, although he served as an advisor to General Ayyub Khan, Rahman was active mainly in the intellectual sphere of academia and did not seek popularity with a general audience or any direct influence over a political movement.

Rahman firmly believed that one of the primary purposes of the Qur'an was to create a society based on justice. He also saw the Prophet Muhammad as a social reformist, who sought to empower the poor, weak and vulnerable. Thus he viewed the Qur'an as a source from which ethical principles could be derived, rather than a book of laws. One of the aims of his scholarship was to help formulate a society devoid of exploitation of the weak. In his own words, Islam as a religion, and the teachings of the Qur'an in particular, could be seen as 'directed towards the creation of a meaningful and positive equality among human beings. As such the Islamic purpose cannot be realized until genuine freedom to human beings is restored and freedom from all forms of exploitation – social, spiritual, political and economic – assured.'[7] His position as a reformist was based on his belief that:

> [T]he implementation of the Qur'an cannot be carried out *literally* in the context of today because this may result in thwarting the very purposes of the Qur'an, and that, although the findings of the *fuqaha* [jurists] or the *ulama* [scholars] of Islam during the past thirteen centuries or so should be seriously studied and given due weight, it may well be found that in many cases their findings were either mistaken or sufficed for the needs of that society but not for today.[8]

For instance, Rahman argued that the practice of family law in Islamic history had not accorded females the equal rights to which they appear to be entitled, based on the Prophet's example and teachings of the Qur'an:

> The Qur'an insistently forbids the male [from] exploit[ing] the female on the strength of his stronger position in society, and Islam set[s] into motion the whole complex of measures – legal and moral – whereby sex exploitation would be completely eradicated. It forbade the recourse to polygamy under normal circumstances, allowed the woman to own and earn wealth, declared her to be an equal partner in the society: noting and allowing for the disadvantages she had in the society of that age. It laid down the basis of matrimonial life to be mutual love and affection, and that spouses were like garments unto each other. It strictly regulated the law of divorce.[9]

Rahman has been criticized for 'underestimating the complexity of the hermeneutical task and the intellectual pluralism intrinsic to it'.[10] However, it appears this issue was not central to Rahman's thought. His primary intention, it seems, was to address specific problems he believed needed attention from the perspective of Muslims who were aware of their own struggle to remain relevant in a constantly changing environment. His contribution to the argument for recognition of subjective elements in Qur'anic interpretation can be seen perhaps more accurately as a forerunner to the more recent scholarship of figures such as Amina Wadud and Khaled Abou El Fadl.

In summary, Rahman's primary contribution to the debate on Islam in the twentieth century was his assertion that in order to understand the Qur'an, Muslims must move away from reductionist and formulaic approaches which do not recognize the Qur'an's social, historical and linguistic context. His approach to the Qur'an can be seen as one of the most original and systematic of the second half of the twentieth century. Similarly, his emphasis on the context of revelation has had a far-reaching influence on contemporary Muslim debates on key issues such as human rights, women's rights and social justice. Rahman argued that without being aware of the social and political conditions of the society in which the Qur'an was revealed, one could not understand its message.[11] Despite some criticisms, Rahman's approach is increasingly being adopted by Muslims in their attempts to relate the Qur'an to contemporary needs, and it will likely continue to be influential among today's younger generation of Muslim intellectuals.

Amina Wadud

Amina Wadud is an African-American scholar of Qur'anic exegesis and gender. In 1992 she produced her first book, a Muslim feminist work of exegetical principles of the Qur'an entitled *Qur'an and Woman: Rereading the Sacred Text from a Woman's Perspective.*[12] The book was endorsed by a number of Arabic-speaking feminists,[13] and included controversial ideas such as the need to use more gender-neutral language in understanding the Qur'an.[14]

Amina Wadud was born into a Methodist family in 1952 in Maryland, USA. While growing up, Wadud felt like an outsider by virtue of both her ethnicity and gender. A fellow scholar of Islamic feminism, Asma Barlas, writes, 'If race is what defined her in the eyes of her White peers, gender is what seems to have defined her in the eyes of her Black ones.'[15] When she was studying at university, the 20-year-old Wadud decided to become Muslim. According to Barlas, Wadud's position as an African American, and thus 'Western', convert to Islam has enabled her to engage with Islam with a 'specific consciousness shaped by her identity'.[16] Wadud gained her PhD in Islamic studies from the University of Michigan in 1988 and at the time of writing is teaching at the Virginia Commonwealth University.

Wadud occupies a controversial position in contemporary Islamic thought. A strong advocate of gender equality, Wadud is considered to belong to the 'feminist' movement within Islam. She is perhaps most widely known for having delivered a Friday sermon in South Africa in 1994, and more recently for her controversial leading of a group of men and women in Friday prayers in 2005, acting as the *imam* or prayer leader. This event was commented on internationally and led to a number of *fatwas* insisting that leadership in prayer is reserved for Muslim men.[17]

Wadud also positions herself as a postmodernist. She has argued that postmodernism as a movement advocates 'rethinking' and 'reconfiguring' the past, a process which Wadud considers necessary in order to create a future which is more pluralistic and homogeneous.[18] This thinking aligns her with scholars such as Mohammed Arkoun and Muhammad Shahrour, who have both been influenced by postmodernist scholars. All three have sought to question the established methods of Islamic enquiry, arguing for awareness of the subjectivity of supposedly 'true' positions.

Wadud suggests that she is engaged in a 'gender jihad', a position reflected in her belief that the Qur'an both liberates and empowers women. She has criticized some common Muslim narratives as erroneous, such as the claim that woman was created from man and is thus a secondary creature. Wadud argues that there is no Qur'anic support for the belief, common among some Muslims, that woman was created after man. She cites verses such as Q.4:1, which speak of the first human being in gender-neutral terms, in support of her argument: 'People, be mindful of your Lord, who created you from a single soul, and from it created its mate, and from the pair of them spread countless men and women far and wide.'

Wadud emphasizes that the Qur'an does not 'assign responsibility for the expulsion of this pair [Adam and Eve] from Paradise to the woman'.[19] She also states that the Qur'an places men and women on the same ontological level, and she argues that the only basis for differentiation among human beings, both women and men, is their degree of 'God-consciousness' (*taqwa*). Wadud does not consider the verses which deal with polygamy to be evidence of the subordination of women to men. Instead, she considers the key teaching of the Qur'anic verse related to this issue[20] to be 'concerned with justice: dealing justly, managing funds justly, justice to the orphans, and justice to the wives'.[21]

Wadud's contribution to the study of the Qur'an has been summarized by Asma Barlas as follows:

> Wadud's critique of traditional *tafsir* is meant not only to reveal the flaws in patriarchal readings of the Qur'an, but also to get Muslims to realize what is at stake in rethinking their textual strategies, in devising new interpretative methods, and in including women in the processes of knowledge creation. She believes this will not only allow the women to develop a more authentic Muslim identity, but also will reflect 'new levels of understanding and human participation' in religious life.[22]

Muhammad Shahrour

Muhammad Shahrour was born in 1938 in Damascus, Syria. A civil engineer and self-taught scholar of Islam, Shahrour has written extensively on Islam and the Qur'an. As an outsider by profession, he argues that contemporary Muslims need to reconsider and question Islam's holy books, an idea which he expresses in his major work, a study of the Qur'an, *Al-Kitab wa al-Qur'an*.[23] Shahrour has been influenced by a wide range of intellectuals, from those as early as the Muslim philosopher al-Farabi (d.338/950), through to the philosopher of German idealism, Johann Gottlieb Fichte, and the English mathematician and philosopher, Alfred North Whitehead.[24]

Essential to Shahrour's thought is his differentiation between the divine and the human understanding of the divine reality. He also argues that, owing to developments in science, contemporary scholars are much better placed than those in the past to understand the 'divine will'.[25] As such, Shahrour seeks to create a new framework and methodology for understanding the Qur'an, and to this end has created his own categories for approaching the Qur'an.[26]

Shahrour, like Mohammed Arkoun, seeks to question the established patterns of reading the Qur'an. The method by which Shahrour proposes to do this is called 'defamiliarization', which involves 'the explicit wish to undermine the well-established canon of interpretations and to suggest alternative ways of reading a text. Andreas Christmann states that Shahrour wants his readers to understand the Qur'an 'as if the Prophet has just died and informed us of this book',[27] thus approaching the Qur'an as if reading it for the first time.[28]

Shahrour's books have attracted much criticism. The response to his work has been almost entirely negative: 'Even sympathetic scholars such as Nasr Hamid Abu Zayd, who himself advocates change and reform, criticize Shahrour's methodological naiveté.'[29] Others have also accused him of being an agent of Zionism and of attempting to spread disunity among Muslims. Shahrour has responded to these criticisms by claiming that such comments are an easy way of avoiding the discussion he is trying to initiate.

Despite these criticisms, at least one of the dominant ideas in Shahrour's thinking on Islam rings true with many contemporary reformist scholars of Islam. That is, that the Qur'an must be approached in a contemporary manner; studies or readings of the Qur'an should be considered in light of developments in other fields such as modern philosophy and linguistics. This 'contemporary' approach to the Qur'an appears to be evident in his application of theories of schools of thought ranging from 'process theology, evolutionism, liberalism, Marxism, Sufism, mathematics, statistics, quantum physics, psychoanalysis, linguistics and communication theory',[30] in his analysis of the Qur'an.

Mohammed Arkoun

Mohammed Arkoun was born in Algeria in 1928 and is culturally Berber, French and Arabic. After studying in Algeria, he gained a PhD from the Sorbonne in Paris. Arkoun is now widely known as a pioneering scholar of contemporary Islamic thought. He is credited with broadening the discipline of Islamic studies by borrowing and developing ideas from sources not generally associated with Islamic studies. One of his major works is *The Unthought in Contemporary Islamic Thought*.[31]

Arkoun went to the Sorbonne just before Algeria's independence, and there his intellectual development was enriched by the general changes that the humanities were experiencing during the 1950s and 1960s. During this time, 'the field of humanities . . . was characterized by a search for new perspectives and approaches, which led either to the creation of new intellectual movements or to the consolidation of existing theoretical and methodological approaches'.[32] Arkoun's thinking was also inspired by his research on the Persian intellectual and Islamic 'humanist' Miskawayh (d.421/1030) and his study of Arab humanism of the tenth century, which was also the subject of his PhD. He was 'impressed by the openness and receptiveness of Miskawayh and his contemporaries to other traditions like the Greek and the Persian [traditions]'.[33]

Arkoun is not generally respected by traditionalist Muslim scholars, due to his secularist approach to analysis of the Qur'an and the apparent influence on his work of intellectuals such as Derrida, Baudrillard and Foucault.[34] He is also criticized by some for his 'complex and elusive expressions, the abundant terminology [present within his writings] and the lack of systematization'.[35]

A key element of Arkoun's thinking is his questioning of Islamic ortho-doxy, and his view that orthodoxy is 'equivalent to an ideology' and is thus subject to a 'historical process'.[36] Orthodoxy involves a 'learned culture', which is steeped in 'writing' and which is expressed through 'the state'. This 'orthodoxy' is opposed by a 'heterodoxy', which facilitates a popular (and populist) culture, which makes use of (the freer, less stable) 'orality' and is present within (or creates) a segmented society.[37]

In summary, Ursula Günther argues that Arkoun's thinking displays the qualities of a rhizome, an idea closely associated with postmodernist thought. Günther states,

> [The rhizome] symbolises a shift of paradigm that has already occurred at different levels of modern life. It stands for integrity, wholeness and plurality in contrast to dualism, decomposition and particularism . . . In this respect Arkoun's approach bears features of postmodernism.[38]

Khaled Abou El Fadl

Khaled Abou El Fadl was born in Egypt in 1963. He is a leading scholar of Islamic law and a traditionally trained Muslim jurist. Abou El Fadl is a professor at the University of California. Although widely viewed as a respected scholar, his attacks on some movements within Islam, in particular the so-called Wahhabism, have led to his receiving numerous death threats. Among other things, he criticizes Wahhabism for the harsh restrictions it imposes on women. He argues that an 'ideology' such as Wahhabism, which obliges women to be 'blindly obedient' to men, effectively turns men into demigods.[39] He has also argued against the common position among traditionalist scholars regarding the compulsory wearing of the veil (*hijab*) for women, on the basis that women are not explicitly instructed to do so in the Qur'an. Abou El Fadl also speaks out strongly against all cultural practices that make women occupy subordinate positions in society. For him such practices are 'morally offensive' and strike at the core of what it means to be a Muslim.[40]

One of Abou El Fadl's major works is *Speaking in God's Name: Islamic Law, Authority and Women*.[41] This work seeks to address the role of the authoritative reader of religious texts, challenging the way in which self-proclaimed 'scholars' of the Qur'an, particularly in modern times, assume the role of spokespeople on behalf of God. He argues that in many cases, such 'scholars' displace God's authority, which he describes as 'an act of despotism'.[42] The introduction to Abou El Fadl's book draws on the work of Umberto Eco, among others, in asking questions about whether verses from the Qur'an call for an 'open' or 'closed' reading of the text.[43] Abou El Fadl highlights the importance of focusing on the interaction between the author of the Qur'an (God) and the reader, and the authoritative reader's responsibility, by virtue of this special position as interpreter of the text, to act as a faithful 'agent' for the 'principal' (God), and refrain from imposing their own subjective opinions unless they are clearly stated. In seeking to clarify the position of the reader in understanding the Qur'an, Abou El Fadl proposes questions such as:

> To what extent are my sensibilities and subjectivities determinative in constructing the text's meaning? May I or should I submit the text to my use, and permit my needs to be determinative in constructing a meaning for the text? If the peculiarities of the reader are determinative, what then happens to the intent of the author? Should the reader focus on the intent of the author and consider the author's intent determinative as to the meaning of the text? Isn't this more respectful towards the author, especially when the author is divine? But how can the intent of the author be ascertained if the author's motives are not accessible?[44]

The framing of a debate in this manner – which highlights the subjectivity of the reader's position – is clearly an attack on those who 'speak in God's name' by claiming the supposed authenticity and infallibility of 'literalist' or 'textualist' approaches.

In a similar vein to Arkoun and Wadud, Abou El Fadl also promotes the idea that there are many possible interpretations of the Qur'an, and opposes the views of conservative scholars who claim a monopoly on the interpretation of the Qur'an. However, Abou El Fadl argues that the idea of a 'European Islam' that is somehow different from Islam in general is superfluous, as the classical sources of Islam provide sufficient basis and also flexibility with which to engage with the issues of Muslims living in the West as minorities, without having to reformulate Islam entirely. He states, 'Islamic theology and Islamic law provide everything a Muslim needs to live in a secular, pluralist, and democratic society: tolerance, acceptance of pluralism, a rejection of coercion, participation in public life (as long as this is guided by moral principles), mercy, and love.'[45]

In debates on how the study of the Qur'an can be developed, Abou El Fadl has argued against the wholesale adoption of a literary or deconstructive approach. Instead, he suggests that Muslim scholars and interpreters of the Qur'an should use an approach that is rooted in the traditions of Islam and the Muslim experience. His recommendation is that Muslim scholars should start with the Muslim experience and consider how such discourses might be utilized in its service.[46]

Abou El Fadl sees the ideas and methodologies of postmodernism and post-structuralism as coming from the particular social context and historical experiences of the West, and thus as not being particularly relevant to contemporary Islamic thought. Although the questions these philosophies raise are 'fascinating', it is 'important not to superimpose an epistemology on Muslims that might not faithfully reflect the Muslim experience'.[47]

Although Abou El Fadl rejects the relevance of postmodernism to Islamic scholarship, his strong criticisms of those puritanical elements which impose a rigid orthodoxy on interpretations of the Qur'an link him with other movements which have developed in connection with postmodernism. However, unlike Arkoun and Shahrour, Abou El Fadl's criticism of conservative scholars is firmly grounded in Islamic jurisprudential methodology.

Summary

Some of the important points we have discussed in this chapter include:

- Textualist exegesis generally involves linguistic analysis of textual sources, and is based on the assumption that the meanings of the Qur'an are fixed over time.
- Contextualist exegesis involves a range of different techniques, and is based on the assumption that the meanings of the Qur'an are largely indeterminate.
- Textualist scholarship is still the most prevalent form of Qur'anic scholarship among Muslims today.
- Many modern Muslim scholars, including those outlined above, are beginning to pay greater attention to the importance of context in understanding the Qur'an.

Recommended reading

Mohammed Arkoun, 'Revelation', 'Exegesis', in *Rethinking Islam: Common Questions, Uncommon Answers*, translated and edited by Robert D. Lee, Boulder: Westview Press, 1994.

- In these two chapters in particular, Arkoun criticizes traditional approaches to the Qur'an and its interpretation. He argues for a rethinking of the exegetical tradition in light of the changing contexts of modern society. The topics of other chapters in this book range from 'Muhammad', 'Hadith', 'Women' and 'Sufism' to 'Authority', 'Mediterranean Culture', 'Secularism' and 'Human Rights'.

Farid Esack, *Qur'an, Liberalism and Pluralism*, Oxford: Oneworld, 1997.

- In this book Esack provides an alternative view of the Qur'an in relation to modern concepts of liberalism and pluralism. He argues that the Qur'an recognizes the ideas of freedom, tolerance and pluralism.

Fazlur Rahman, *Islam and Modernity: Transformation of an Intellectual Tradition*, Chicago: Chicago University Press, 1982; 'Modern Developments', 'Legacy and Prospects' and 'Epilogue', *Islam*, second edition, Chicago: University of Chicago Press, 2002, pages 212–265.

- In these books Rahman argues that there is a need to reinterpret the Qur'an. He critically re-evaluates the tradition of Islamic scholarship in light of socio-historical contexts and also argues that there is a need to recognize the difference between the Qur'an's reference to general principles and its specific responses to historical situations.

Suha Taji-Farouki (ed.), *Modern Muslim Intellectuals and the Qur'an*, Oxford: Oxford University Press, 2004.

- In this book Taji-Farouki presents a collection of academic articles on modern Muslim thinkers and their role in rethinking interpretation and application of the Qur'an. Together, the articles provide the reader with a broad overview of the major figures in this area and their ideas regarding modern approaches to the Qur'an.

Amina Wadud, *Qur'an and Women: Rereading the Sacred Text from a Woman's Perspective*, New York: Oxford University Press, 1999.

- In this book Wadud argues that there is a need for more feminist approaches to interpreting the Qur'anic text. In support of this argument, she highlights the fact that most traditional exegetical works have been written by male scholars within male-dominated socio-historical contexts. Given that the Qur'an is a book of guidance for both men and women, Wadud advocates the need for more scholars to read and interpret the Qur'an from a woman's perspective.

NOTES

1 Farid Esack, *Qur'an, Liberation and Pluralism*, Oxford: Oneworld, 1997, pp. 73–77.
2 Esack, *Qur'an, Liberation and Pluralism*, pp. 50–51.
3 Esack, *Qur'an, Liberation and Pluralism*, p. 75.
4 Esack, *Qur'an, Liberation and Pluralism*, p. 82.
5 Esack, *Qur'an, Liberation and Pluralism*, p. 65.
6 Suha Taji-Farouki (ed.), *Modern Muslim Intellectuals and the Qur'an*, Oxford: Oxford University Press, 2004, p. 106.
7 Fazlur Rahman, 'Some Reflections on the Reconstruction of Muslim Society in Pakistan', pp. 103–20, *Islamic Studies*, vol. 6, no. 9, 1967, p. 103.
8 Fazlur Rahman, 'The Impact of Modernity on Islam', p. 127, *Journal of Islamic Studies*, vol. 5, no. 2, June 1966, pp. 112–128.
9 Fazlur Rahman, 'The Impact of Modernity on Islam', p. 111.
10 Esack, *Qur'an, Liberation and Pluralism*, p. 67.
11 This approach has been rejected by a Turkish scholar, Huseyn Atay, who argues that the Qur'an needs to be 'liberated from historical and traditional culture'; see Taji-Farouki (ed.), *Modern Muslim Intellectuals*, p. 249.
12 New York: Oxford University Press, 1999.

13 Ruth Roded, 'Women and the Qur'an', in McAuliffe (ed.), *Encyclopaedia of the Qur'an*, vol. 5, p. 540.
14 Roded, 'Women and the Qur'an', p. 540.
15 Asma Barlas, 'Amina Wadud's Hermeneutics of the Qur'an: Women Rereading Sacred Texts', p. 99, in Taji-Farouki (ed.), *Modern Muslim Intellectuals*, pp. 97–123.
16 Barlas, 'Amina Wadud's Hermeneutics of the Qur'an', p. 97.
17 Nelly van Doorn-Harder, 'Teaching and Preaching the Qur'an', p. 227, in McAuliffe (ed.), *Encyclopaedia of the Qur'an*, vol. 5, 2006, pp. 205–231.
18 'Interview – Amina Wadud', *Frontline – Muslims*, March 2002. Accessed 25 February 2007: http://www.pbs.org/wgbh/pages/frontline/shows/muslims/interviews/wadud.html.
19 Barlas, 'Amina Wadud's Hermeneutics', p. 114.
20 Qur'an: 4:3 – 'If you fear you will not deal fairly with orphan girls, you may marry whichever [other] women seem good to you, two, three, or four. If you fear that you cannot be equitable [to them], then marry only one, or your slave(s): that is more likely to make you avoid bias.'
21 Barlas, 'Amina Wadud's Hermeneutics of the Qur'an', pp. 115–116.
22 Barlas, 'Amina Wadud's Hermeneutics of the Qur'an', p. 105.
23 *Al-Kitab wa al-Qur'an: Qira'a Mu'asira* (The Book and the Qur'an: A Contemporary Reading), Damascus: al-Ahli li al-Taba'a wa al-Nashr wa al-Tawzi', 1990.
24 Andreas Christmann, '"The Form is Permanent, but the Content Moves": The Qur'anic Text and its Interpretation(s) in Mohamad Shahrour's *al-Kitab wal-Qur'an*', in Taji-Farouki (ed.), *Modern Muslim Intellectuals*, p. 265.
25 Christmann, 'The Form is Permanent, but the Content Moves', p. 267.
26 Christmann, 'The Form is Permanent, but the Content Moves', p. 269.
27 Christmann, 'The Form is Permanent, but the Content Moves', p. 263.
28 Christmann, 'The Form is Permanent, but the Content Moves', p. 264.
29 Christmann, 'The Form is Permanent, but the Content Moves', p. 266.
30 Christmann, 'The Form is Permanent, but the Content Moves', p. 286.
31 London: Saqi, 2000.
32 Ursula Günther, 'Mohammed Arkoun: Towards a Radical Rethinking of Islamic Thought', in Taji-Farouki (ed.), *Modern Muslim Intellectuals and the Qur'an*, p. 128.
33 Günther, 'Mohammed Arkoun', p. 129.
34 Günther, 'Mohammed Arkoun', p. 137.
35 Günther, 'Mohammed Arkoun', p. 137.
36 Günther, 'Mohammed Arkoun', p. 141.
37 Günther, 'Mohammed Arkoun', p. 141.
38 Günther, 'Mohammed Arkoun', p. 153.
39 Monika Jung-Mounib, 'Khaled Abou El Fadl – God Does Not Have an Equal Partner', trans. Aingeal Flanagan, *Qantara.de – Dialogue with the Islamic World*, 2005. 11 January 2005, accessed 25 February 2007: http://www.qantara.de/webcom/show_article.php/_c-575/_nr-7/.html?PHPSESSID=5869.

40 Khaled Abou El Fadl, *Speaking in God's Name: Islamic Law, Authority and Women*, Oxford: Oneworld, 2001, p. xiii.
41 Oxford: Oneworld, 2001.
42 Abou El Fadl, *Speaking in God's Name*, p. 265.
43 The verse used as an example is 74:31, specifically the section which says: 'no one knows your Lord's forces except Him – this [description] is a warning to mortals.'
44 Abou El Fadl, *Speaking in God's Name*, p. 3.
45 Jung-Mounib, 'Khaled Abou El Fadl – God Does Not Have an Equal Partner'.
46 Taji-Farouki (ed.), *Modern Muslim Intellectuals*, p. 19.
47 Abou El Fadl, *Speaking in God's Name*, p. 100.

Glossary

Abbasid caliphate: the second major dynastic caliphate of Islam, which began in 132/750 with the caliph Abu al-Abbas al-Saffah.

abrogation: see *naskh*.

ahad hadith: a hadith which, at one or more points in its chain of transmission, has only one narrator. In Islamic jurisprudence, *ahad* hadith are seen as less authoritative than *mutawatir* hadith.

ahl al-kitab: see People of the Book.

ahl al-sunna wa al-jama'a: 'people of the sunna and the community'; Sunnis, 'orthodox' Muslims.

Allah: Arabic name for the One God; from *al-ilah* 'the God'.

al-lawh al-mahfuz: the 'Preserved Tablet'; Muslims believe God originally revealed the Qur'an to the Tablet before Gabriel transmitted it to the Prophet Muhammad.

arkan al-iman: essential beliefs; articles or pillars of faith, of which there are six (belief in God; His angels; His prophets; His holy scriptures; the Last Day; divine will).

arkan al-islam: essential practices; pillars of Islam, of which there are five (profession of faith in God and His Messenger, Muhammad; ritual prayer (*salat*); fasting in Ramadan (*sawm*); payment of alms (*zakat*); and the pilgrimage (*hajj*).

asbab al-nuzul: occasions of revelation; details of the immediate circumstances surrounding the revelation of a particular Qur'anic text.

Ash'ari school: one of the main early schools of Sunni theology; became the dominant school in most parts of the Muslim world; was opposed to the rationalistic Mu'tazila; holds that the Qur'an is uncreated.

aya (pl. ayat): literally meaning a 'sign'; also used to denote a unit of division of the Qur'anic text; often translated as 'verse'.

caliph: supreme leader of the Islamic political entity, caliphate.

caliphate: a system of governance that combines both religious and political rule.

Companion: a Muslim believed to have met, lived with or heard the Prophet during his lifetime. Many Companions are key figures in early Islamic history.

contextualist: a form of reason-based exegesis which emphasizes the socio-historical context of the Qur'an. Contextualist scholars conduct close textual study; however, they believe that the meaning of the text cannot be properly understood without knowledge of the social, cultural and political conditions surrounding its revelation. See also textualist.

fatwa (pl. fatawa): a legal opinion on a point of Islamic law, generally given by a jurist. *Fatwas* are generally considered non-binding.

fiqh: originally understanding, knowledge. It is usually understood as jurisprudence; the science of religious law in Islam; or human interpretation of religious law.

fuqaha' (sing. faqih): jurists in Islamic law; scholars of *fiqh*.

hadd (pl. hudud): 'limit, restriction'; has become the technical term for certain punishments under Islamic law that are explicitly mentioned in the Qur'an, for offences such as murder, adultery and theft.

hadith (pl. ahadith): a report or 'tradition' containing information about sayings and practices of the Prophet Muhammad. Hadith will often contain an account of when the Prophet commanded or prohibited something, or of his tacit approval of something said or done in his presence.

hadith qudsi: a hadith containing a report of a non-Qur'anic revelation from God expressed in the Prophet's own words (as opposed to the Qur'an, which is the 'direct' Word of God).

hafiz: a person who has memorized the Qur'an.

hajj: annual pilgrimage to Mecca. One of the five essential practices of Islam. Muslims are encouraged to undertake the *hajj* at least once in their lifetime if they are physically and financially able to do so.

halal: permissible. In Islamic law, whatever is not prohibited is generally permissible.

Hanafi school: a Sunni school of religious law (*madhhab*), named after the jurist Abu Hanifa (d.150/767) who lived in Iraq.

Hanbali school: a Sunni school of religious law, named after the jurist and scholar of hadith Ahmad ibn Hanbal (d.240/855).

haram: forbidden. In Islamic law, that which is prohibited.

hijab: a term used to denote any veil placed in front of a person or an object to conceal it from view or to isolate it. Commonly used to refer to the headscarf or veil that many Muslim women wear.

Hijaz: geographical area along the northwestern coast of the Arabian peninsula, containing the holy cities of Mecca and Medina.

hijra: the emigration of the Prophet Muhammad, with his Companions from Mecca to Medina in 622 CE. This event marks the end of the Meccan period of the Prophet's life and the beginning of the Medinan period; the year in which it took place is the first year of the Islamic calendar.

hukm: a rule or injunction.

ibada: in Islamic law, all acts performed as worship of God.

Iblis: the one who rejected God's command to bow down to Adam. In the Qur'an Iblis is referred to synonymously with the archetype of Satan.

i'jaz al-qur'an: 'the inimitability of the Qur'an'. A term used to describe the Qur'an's essentially unique or miraculous character; that quality of the Qur'an that is said to make it impossible for people to imitate it.

ijma': consensus on a point of belief or law.

ijtihad: exercise of individual judgement to arrive at a solution to a problem in Islamic law, usually performed by a jurist.

imam: leader of the congregational prayer; sometimes used to refer to the head of an Islamic state; for Shi'a, religious and political leader of the community.

iman: faith, belief.

inimitability of the Qur'an: see *i'jaz al-qur'an*.

Injil: the scripture revealed to Jesus; the Gospel.

isnad: chain of authorities who transmitted the text of a hadith, an essential part of verifying the authenticity of hadith.

isra'iliyyat: stories and traditions derived from Jewish or Christian sources; in early Muslim history *isra'iliyyat* stories were commonly referred to in *tafsir*, but much less so later.

Ja'fari school: a Shi'i school of religious law, named after one of the imams of Shi'a, Ja'far al-Sadiq. Ja'fari school of law is followed by Twelver Imam Shi'a, who constitute about 80 per cent of Shi'a.

jahiliyya: 'state of ignorance'; a term most often used to denote the circumstances in Arabia before the time of the Prophet Muhammad.

jinn: a spirit; an imperceptible being who, like humans, is capable of both good and evil. Said to be created from fire.

juz': one of 30 sections of the Qur'an, roughly equal in length.

Ka'ba: holiest shrine of Islam, located in Mecca; believed to be the first house of worship built for the worship of the One God, attributed to the Prophet Abraham. Muslims turn towards the Ka'ba for prayer.

kafir (pl. kafirun): a term used in the Qur'an to describe those who knowingly deny its message and refuse to submit themselves to God; an 'unbeliever'.

kahin (pl. kuhhan): pre-Islamic Arab soothsayer; occupied a role similar to that of a shaman as the spiritual guide of a tribe.

kalam: (literally, speech) the term was used by Muslim theologians and philosophers for scholastic theology developed under the influence of Greek philosophy and dialectic reasoning.

Kalam Allah: the Words of God; speech of God.

kalima (pl. kalimat): the spoken word, utterance, word.

khalq al-Qur'an: creation of the Qur'an; the famous debate over whether the Qur'an is created or not, which occurred during the Abbasid period.

Kharijis: an early puritanical group among Muslims. The Kharijis were initially supporters of Ali, but later condemned him for accepting arbitration with Mu'awiya.

kitab (pl. kutub): book, scripture.

kitab Allah: scripture of God; most often used to describe the Qur'an; the Torah of Moses (*Tawrat*) and Gospel of Jesus (*Injil*) are also described as scriptures of God by the Qur'an.

kufr: Arabic term whose literal meaning is 'concealing, covering'. Used by the Qur'an to describe the denial of its message. Often used in contradistinction to *iman*. See *kafir*.

madhhab (pl. madhahib): school of religious law. There are four Sunni *madhhabs* that still exist today: Hanafi, Hanbali, Maliki and Shafi'i. The Shi'a predominantly follow the Ja'fari *madhhab*. The *madhhabs* are schools of law rather than theology and are not sects as such.

Maliki: a Sunni school of religious law, named after Malik ibn Anas (d.179/795).

mansukh: an abrogated verse. See *naskh*.

maqasid al-shari'a: 'the aims or purposes of Islamic law'; a concept relating to fundamental values underpinning the rules or injunctions of Islamic law. Classical jurists usually named five *maqasid*: these were the protection or preservation of religion, life, intellect, honour or lineage, and property.

maslaha: 'public interest'; a principle of Islamic jurisprudence that allowed jurists to exercise discretion or juristic preference (*istihsan*) in matters that were not clearly covered by a textual source; public interest.

mathal (pl. amthal): popular saying; metaphor; parable.

mu'amalat: the branch of Islamic law dealing with all matters not covered by *ibadat* (worship). Includes laws relating to commercial transactions such as buying and selling.

mufassir: Arabic term meaning 'interpreter' or 'exegete'. Someone who writes *tafsir*; an interpreter or exegete of the Qur'an.

muhkam: a term denoting verses of the Qur'an which are thought to be 'clear' or unambiguous.

mujtahid: a person who engages in *ijtihad*.

mu'minun: believers; Muslims.

mushaf: the complete physical text of the Qur'an in written form; codex.

mushaf Uthmani: The codex of the Qur'an compiled during the caliphate of Uthman, the third caliph, and the version commonly accepted throughout the Muslim world today.

mutashabih: a term denoting verses of the Qur'an which are thought to be 'obscure' or ambiguous; not clearly intelligible to the human mind.

mutawatir hadith: a hadith which has multiple narrators at every stage in its chain of transmission.

Mu'tazili school: one of the main early schools of theology; it was for a time the dominant school. Mu'tazilis emphasized the absolute transcendence and Oneness of God and held that the Qur'an was created.

naskh: abrogation; a term used for a range of theories used in the fields of *tafsir*, hadith study and *fiqh* regarding the superseding or abrogation of a text of the Qur'an or hadith by another text.

occasions of revelation: see *asbab al-nuzul*.

People of the Book: people who received scriptures or revelations from God such as Jews and Christians.

pillars of faith: see *arkan al-iman*.

pillars of Islam: see *arkan al-islam*.

Preserved Tablet: see *al-lawh al-mahfuz*.

qira'at: recitation traditions; variant traditions for reciting the Qur'an, of which seven to ten are formally recognized. The variations between the *qira'at* are very minor and each is accepted as authentic.

qiyas: reasoning by analogy; in *fiqh*, a method for deriving law through analogical reasoning, one of the sources of Islamic law (after the Qur'an, the sunna and consensus).

Qur'an: Muslim holy scripture; literally means 'recitation'; the Word of God as received by the Prophet Muhammad. Often titled *al-Qur'an al-Karim*, 'the Noble Qur'an'.

Quraysh: a prominent Arab tribe that was dominant in Mecca during the time of the Prophet Muhammad. The Prophet belonged to one of its clans.

Ramadan: the ninth month of the Islamic lunar calendar; the month of fasting. The Qur'an is believed to have been first revealed to the Prophet Muhammad during the month of Ramadan.

Rashidun caliphs: the 'rightly guided caliphs'. For Sunni Muslims, the first four successors to the Prophet – Abu Bakr, Umar, Uthman and Ali – who are considered to have ruled in accordance with the Prophet's guidance. See also caliph.

rasm Uthmani: 'the Uthmanic orthography'; the way of writing the Qur'an adopted by the committee commissioned by Uthman to compile an authoritative codex of the Qur'an.

ra'y: opinion or individual judgement, reasoning.

riba: usury, interest or unlawful addition or gain; prohibited by the Qur'an.

salaf: 'pious ancestors'; for Sunnis, a term used generally to denote the first three generations of Muslims after the time of the Prophet as well as other leading figures of early Islam. Includes the Companions of the Prophet, the Successors and the Successors of the Successors.

Salafism: neo-orthodox movement of Sunni Islam; also an Islamic reformist movement originating in the late nineteenth century and centred on Egypt, aiming to regenerate Islam by a return to the tradition of the 'pious forefathers'. See also Wahhabism.

salat: the five daily obligatory prayers. One of the five essential practices of Islam.

Satan: in Arabic *shaytan* (pl. *shayatin*); the archetype of evil and rejection of God; in the Qur'an Satan or the 'satans' are described as enemies of humankind who attempt to lead them away from God. Also known by the proper name Iblis.

sawm: 'fasting'. Fasting during the month of Ramadan is one of the five essential practices of Muslims. A person performing *sawm* may not eat, drink, smoke or have sex from dawn to sunset.

Shafi'i: a Sunni school of religious law that developed from the teachings Muhammad ibn Idris al-Shafi'i (d.204/820).

shari'a: Islamic law; the rules and injunctions governing the lives of Muslims, derived from the Qur'an and hadith, and from secondary sources including *ijma'* (consensus) and *qiyas* (analogical reasoning).

Shi'a: a major religio-political group in Islam. The term is derived from 'Shi'at Ali' ('partisans of Ali'). Around 15–20 per cent of Muslims are Shi'a. The Shi'a believe that Ali and his direct descendants are the Prophet Muhammad's rightful successors, and they do not accept the first three Rashidun caliphs. The majority of Shi'a today are Twelver Imam Shi'a, who recognize a line of 12 Shi'i Imams, including Ali, who are believed to have divine guidance. See also imam, Sunni.

Successors: the generation of Muslims that followed the Companions; those Muslims who knew one or more of the Companions but not the Prophet himself.

Successors of the Successors: the generation of Muslims that followed the Successors; those Muslims who knew one or more Successor.

Sufi: one who practices *tasawwuf* or 'Sufism', the mystical dimension of Islam. Sufism is found in both Shi'i and Sunni Islam.

sunna: normative behaviour of the Prophet; his sayings, deeds and tacit approvals; sometimes used to refer to the hadith as a body of literature.

Sunni: a major religio-political group in Islam. The term is derived from 'people of the sunna and the community'. A majority (around 80 per cent) of Muslims are Sunni.

sura: term used to denote the 114 independent units of division of the Qur'anic text, often translated as 'chapter'.

tafsir: exegesis or interpretation, generally of the Qur'an. In many cases a work titled *tafsir* will follow the text of the Qur'an from beginning to end. Someone who engages in *tafsir* is a *mufassir*.

tafsir bi al-ma'thur: interpretation or exegesis primarily based on text/tradition; implies that the interpretation of the Qur'an should be guided by the Qur'an itself, the Prophet's instructions and his actual interpretations, or by his Companions and Successors.

tafsir bi al-ra'y: interpretation or exegesis primarily based on reason or considered opinion.

tahrif: 'distortion'; in *tafsir*, this refers to the idea, based on certain Qur'anic references, that the Jews and Christians had 'distorted' their scriptures.

ta'wil: allegorical interpretation or exegesis; originally more or less synonymous with *tafsir*; often used for mystical interpretation of the Qur'an; sometimes used for reason-based exegesis.

Tawrat: the scripture revealed to Prophet Moses, the Torah. One of the six essential beliefs of Islam (*arkan al-iman*) is belief in God's revealed scriptures, including the Torah.

textualist: a form of tradition-based *tafsir* which approaches interpretation from a strictly linguistic/text-based perspective; no importance is placed on the socio-historical context of the Qur'an. See also contextualist.

ulama (sing. alim): 'scholars', primarily of religion. In Sunni Islam, *ulama* are regarded as the transmitters and interpreters of religious knowledge; the term also embraces those who fulfill religious functions in the community that require a certain level of expertise in religious and judicial issues, such as judges and preachers, imams of mosques.

Umayyad caliphate: the first major dynastic caliphate of Islam, which began in 40/661 with the caliph Mu'awiya I.

umma: people, community; in the Qur'an *umma* usually refers to people sharing a common religion; in later history it usually refers to the Muslim community.

ummiy: a term used by the Qur'an to describe the Prophet Muhammad; commonly interpreted to mean 'unlettered', it can also mean 'gentile'.

usul al-fiqh: 'principles of jurisprudence'; the study of *usul al-fiqh* is concerned with the sources of the law (*fiqh*) and the methodology for extrapolating rules from these sources.

Wahhabism: puritanical neo-orthodox brand of Islamic reformism, originating in the late eighteenth century in the Najd region of the Arabian peninsula. Wahhabism has been criticized for its harsh, puritanical attitudes, particularly towards women and non-Muslims. See also Salafism.

wahy: 'inspiration'; a form of divine revelation in the form of communication without speech.

wudu': a form of ritual purification; the practice of washing parts of the body including the arms, face and feet with water prior to performing *salat*. Some Muslims also perform *wudu'* prior to touching or reading the Qur'an.

zakat: the 'purification' of wealth through the payment of a certain percentage in charity. One of the five essential practices of Islam (*arkan al-islam*).

Bibliography

Abbas, Ali (ed.), *A Shi'ite Encyclopedia*, accessed 20 February 2007, www.al-islam.org/encyclopedia/.

Abdel Haleem, Muhammad, *Understanding the Qur'an: Themes and Styles*, London: I.B. Tauris, 2001.

Abdel Haleem, Muhammad (trans.), *The Qur'an: A New Translation*, New York: Oxford University Press, 2004; recent edition, New York: Oxford University Press, 2005.

Abou El Fadl, Khaled, *Speaking in God's Name: Islamic Law, Authority and Women*, Oxford: Oneworld Publications, 2001.

Abrahamov, Binyamin, *Anthropomorphism and Interpretation of the Qur'an in the Theology of al-Qasim ibn Ibrahim: Kitab al-Mustarshid*, Leiden: E.J. Brill, 1996.

Abshar-Abdalla, Ulil, 'I Try to be like At-Tahtawi', *Liberal Islam Network*, 12 January 2004, accessed 20 February 2007, http://islamlib.com/en/page.php?page=article&id=599.

Abu Zayd, Nasr Hamid, *Falsafat al-ta'wil*, Dar al-Bayda': al-Markaz al-Thaqafi al-Arabi, 1998.

Abu Zayd, Nasr Hamid, *The Concept of the Text: A Study of the Qur'anic Sciences (Mafhum al-Nass: Dirasa fi Ulum al-Qur'an)*, Beirut and Cairo: General Egyptian Book Organisation (GEBO), 1990.

Abu Zayd, Nasr Hamid, *al-Nass wa al-sulta wa al-haqiqa*, Dar al-Bayda': al-Markaz al-Thaqafi al-Arabi, 2000.

Abul Quasem, Muhammad, *The Recitation and Interpretation of the Qur'an: Al-Ghazali's Theory*, London, Boston and Melbourne: Kegan Paul International, 1982.

Adang, Camilla, *Muslim Writers on Judaism and the Hebrew Bible: From Ibn Rabban to Ibn Hazm*, Leiden: Brill Academic Publishers, 1996.

Ali, Abdullah Yusuf, *The Holy Qur'an: Text, Translation and Commentary*,

Beirut: Dar Al Arabia, 1938, revised, New York: Tahrike Tarsile Qur'an 1995; repr. 1998, 2002, 2005.

Ali, Ahmad, *Al-Qur'an: A Contemporary Translation*, Karachi: Akrash Publishing, 1984; revised, New Jersey: Princeton University Press, 2001.

Ali, Kecia, 'Muslim Sexual Ethics: Understanding a Difficult Verse, Qur'an 4:34', *The Feminist Sexual Ethics Project*, 2007, accessed 13 September 2007, http://www.brandeis.edu/projects/fse/muslim/mus-essays/mus-ess-diffverse-transl.html.

Ali, Maulana Muhammad, *Introduction to the Study of the Holy Qur'an*, Columbus, OH: Ahmadiyya Anjuman Isha'at Islam Lahore Inc., 1992.

Ali, Muhammad, *The Holy Qur'an: Containing the Arabic Text with English Translation and Commentary*, Surrey, UK: The 'Islamic Review' Office, 1917; revised, *English Translation and Commentary of the Holy Qur'an*, Columbus: Ahmadiyya Anjuman Isha'at Islam Lahore, 1951; repr. 1991, 2002.

Ali, Sher, *The Holy Qur'an*, Rabwah, Pakistan: Oriental and Religious Publishing, 1979.

Ali, Syed V. Mir Ahmed, *The Holy Qur'an: Arabic Text with English Translation and Commentary*, New York: Tahrike Tarsile Qur'an, 1988.

Arberry, Arthur J., *The Koran Interpreted*, London: George Allen & Unwin, 1955; revised, *The Koran (Oxford World's Classics)*, Oxford: Oxford University Press, 1998.

Arkoun, Mohammed, *Rethinking Islam: Common Questions, Uncommon Answers*, trans. and ed. Robert D. Lee, Boulder: Westview Press, 1994.

Armstrong, Karen, *Muhammad: Prophet for Our Time*, London: HarperCollins, 2006.

Asad, Muhammad, *Islam at the Crossroads*, Gibraltar: Dar al-Andalus, 1987.

Asad, Muhammad, *The Message of the Qur'an*, Gibraltar: Dar al-Andalus, 1980; revised, Bristol: The Book Foundation, 2003.

Ashmawi, Muhammad Sa'id al-, 'Shar'ia: The Codification of Islamic Law', in Charles Kurzman (ed.), *Liberal Islam*, New York: Oxford University Press, 1998, pp. 49–56.

Asqalani, Ibn Hajar al-, *Fath al-Bari*, Beirut: Dar al-Fikr li al-Tiba'a wa al-Nashr wa al-Tawzi', 1990–1993.

Azad, Mawlana Abul Kalam, *The Opening Chapter of the Qur'an (Surat-ul-Fatiha)*, trans. Syed Abdul Latif, Kuala Lumpur: Islamic Book Trust, 1991.

Azami, Muhammad Mustafa al-, *The History of the Qur'anic Text from Revelation to Compilation*, Leicester: UK Islamic Academy, 2003.

Aziz, Zahid, 'Shakir Identified', *Lahore Ahmadiyya Movement*, 22 May 2007, accessed 30 August 2007, http://www.ahmadiyya.org/movement/shakir-2.htm.

Aziz, Zahid, 'Shakir's Quran Translation – Blatant Plagiarism of the First Edition of Maulana Muhammad Ali's translation', *Lahore Ahmadiyya Movement*, 22 May 2007, accessed 13 September 2007, http://www.ahmadiyya.org/movement/shakir.htm.

Badran, Margot, 'Feminism and the Qur'an', in Jane D. McAuliffe (ed.), *Encyclopaedia of the Qur'an*, Leiden: E.J. Brill, 2002, Vol.2, pp. 199–203.

Bakhtiar, Laleh, *The Sublime Qur'an*, Chicago: Kazi Productions, 2007, accessed 30 August 2007, http://www.sublimequran.org/index.php.

Baljon, J.M.S., *Modern Muslim Koran Interpretation (1880–1960)*, Leiden: E.J. Brill, 1961.

Bar-Asher, Meir M., *Scripture and Exegesis in Early Imami Shiism*, Leiden: E.J. Brill, 1999.

Bar-Asher, Meir, M., 'Shi'ism and the Qur'an', in Jane D. McAuliffe (ed.), *Encyclopaedia of the Qur'an*, Leiden: E.J. Brill, 2004, Vol.4, pp. 593–604.

Barlas, Asma, *'Believing Women' in Islam: Unreading Patriarchal Interpretations of the Qur'an*, Austin, TX: University of Texas Press, 2002.

Barlas, Asma, 'Amina Wadud's Hermeneutics of the Qur'an: Women Rereading Sacred Texts', in Suha Taji-Farouki (ed.), *Modern Muslim Intellectuals and the Qur'an*, Oxford: Oxford University Press, 2004, pp. 97–123.

Bearman, P., Bianquis, Th., Bosworth, C.E., Donzel, E. van, Heinrichs, W.P. (eds), *Encyclopaedia of Islam*, 2007, Brill Online, accessed 6 November 2007, http:/www.encislam.brill.nl/.

Bell, Richard, *The Qur'an Translated, with a Critical Rearrangement of the Surahs*, Edinburgh: T & T Clark, 1937–1939.

Bell, Richard, *Introduction to the Qur'an*, Edinburgh: Edinburgh University Press, 1953.

Benchrifa, Mohamed, 'Al-Andalus – Tolerance and Convergence', *UNESCO – The Routes of al-Andalus*, 7 June 2001, accessed 15 February 07, http://www.unesco.org/culture/al-andalus/html_eng/benchrifa.shtml.

Berg, Herbert, *The Development of Exegesis in Early Islam: The Authenticity of Muslim Literature from the Formative Period*, London: Curzon Press, 2000.

Bewley, Abdalhaqq and Bewley, Aisha, *The Noble Qur'an: A New Rendering of Its Meaning in English*, Norwich: Bookwork, 1999; revised, 2005.

Bobzin, Hartmut, 'Pre-1800 Preoccupations of Qur'anic Studies', in Jane D. McAuliffe (ed.), *Encyclopaedia of the Qur'an*, Leiden: E.J. Brill, 2004, Vol.4, pp. 235–253.

Bobzin, Hartmut, 'Translations of the Qur'an', in Jane D. McAuliffe (ed.), *Encyclopaedia of the Qur'an*, Leiden: E.J. Brill, 2006, Vol.5, pp. 340–358.

Bosworth, C.E., 'Al-Tabari, Abu Ja'far Muhammad b. Jarir b. Yazid', in P. Bearman, Th. Bianquis, C.E. Bosworth, E. van Donzel and W.P. Heinrichs (eds), *Encyclopaedia of Islam*, Leiden: Brill, 2000, Vol.10, pp. 12–16.

Boullatta, Issa J. (ed.), *Literary Structures of Religious Meaning in the Qur'an*, London: Curzon Press, 2000.

Böwering, Gerhard, *The Mystical Vision of Existence in Classical Islam: The Qur'anic Hermeneutics of the Sufi Sahl Al-Tustari (d.283/896)*, Berlin and New York: Walter de Gruyter, 1980.

Brown, Daniel W., *Rethinking Tradition in Modern Islamic Thought*, Cambridge and New York: Cambridge University Press, 1996.

Bucaille, Maurice, *The Bible, The Qur'an and Science*, Indianapolis, IN: American Trust Publications, 1979.

Bukhari, *Sahih al-Bukhari*, Beirut: Dar al-Kutub al-Ilmiya, 1975–1995.

Bukhari, *Sahih al-Bukhari*, trans. Muhammad Muhsin Khan, Riyadh: Dar-us-Salam Publications, 1996.

Burton, John, *The Collection of the Qur'an*, Cambridge and New York: Cambridge University Press, 1977.

Burton, John, *The Sources of Islamic Law: Islamic Theories of Abrogation*, Edinburgh: Edinburgh University Press, 1990.

Burton, John, 'The Collection of the Qur'an', in Jane D. McAuliffe (ed.), *Encyclopaedia of the Qur'an*, Leiden: E.J. Brill, 2001, Vol.1, pp. 351–361.

Calder, Norman, 'Review: Approaches to Islam in Religious Studies', *Bulletin of the School of Oriental and African Studies, University of London*, Vol.50, No.3, 1987, pp. 545–546.

Calder, Norman, 'Review: Approaches to the History of the Interpretation of the Qur'an', *Journal of Semitic Studies*, Vol.35, No.2, 1990, pp. 333–335.

Calder, Norman, '*Tafsir* from Tabari to Ibn Kathir: Problems in the Description of a Genre, Illustrated with References to the Story of Abraham', in G.R. Hawting and Abdul-Kader A. Shareef (eds), *Approaches to the Qur'an*, London: Routledge, 1993.

Calder, Norman, Mojaddedi, Jawid, and Rippin, Andrew (eds and trans.), *Classical Islam: A Sourcebook of Religious Literature*, London and New York: Routledge, 2003, pp. 101–140.

Cason, John, el-Fadl, Kamel and Walker, Fredrick (Fareed), *An Exhaustive Concordance of the Meaning of Qur'an*, Baltimore: Islamic Education and Community Development Foundation of Baltimore, 2000.

Chittick, William C., *The Self-Disclosure of God: Principles of Ibn al-Arabi's Cosmology*, Albany, NY: State University of New York Press, 1998.

Christmann, Andreas, 'Review: The Qur'an and Its Interpretative Tradition', *Journal of Semitic Studies*, Vol.47, No.2, 2002, pp. 374–375.

Christmann, Andreas, '"The Form is Permanent, but the Content Moves": the Qur'anic text and its interpretation(s) in Mohamad Shahrour's *al-Kitab wal-Qur'an*', in Suha Taji-Farouki (ed.), *Modern Muslim Intellectuals and the Qur'an*, Oxford: Oxford University Press, 2004, pp. 263–295.

Coggins, R.J. and Houlden, J.L. (eds), *A Dictionary of Biblical Interpretation*, London: SCM Press, 1990.

Cook, Michael, *Commanding Right and Forbidding Wrong in Islamic Thought*, Cambridge: Cambridge University Press, 2000.

Coulson, N.J., *History of Islamic Law*, Edinburgh: Edinburgh University Press, 1964.

Cragg, Kenneth, *The Mind of the Qur'an*, London: George Allen & Unwin, 1973.

Cragg, Kenneth, *Readings in the Qur'an*, London: HarperCollins, 1988.

Cragg, Kenneth (ed.), *Troubled by Truth*, Edinburgh: The Pentland Press, 1992.

Cragg, Kenneth, *A Certain Sympathy of Scriptures: Biblical and Quranic*, Brighton: Sussex Academic Press, 2004.

Crittenden, Stephen, 'John Wansbrough Remembered: Interview with Gerald Hawting', 26 June 2002, *ABC, Radio National – The Religion Report*, accessed 13 September 2007, http://www.abc.net.au/rn/talks/8.30/relrpt/stories/s591483.htm.

Crone, Patricia and Cook, Michael, *Hagarism: The Making of the Islamic World*, New York and Cambridge: Cambridge University Press, 1977.

Daniel, Norman, *Islam and the West: The Making of an Image*, Edinburgh: Edinburgh University Press, 1960.

Daryabadi, Abdul Majid, *The Glorious Quran: Text Translation and Commentary*, London: Islamic Foundation, 2001.

Dawood, Nessim J., *The Koran*, London: Penguin Books, 1956; revised, *The Koran (Penguin Classic)*, London: Penguin Classics, 2003.

Denffer, Ahmad von, *Ulum al-Qur'an: An Introduction to the Sciences of the Qur'an*, Leicester: The Islamic Foundation, 1985, reprint 1994.

Denffer, Ahmad von, 'Introduction to the Qur'an: A Rendition of the Original Work Titled – *Ulum al-Qur'an*', A.E. Souaiaia (ed.), *Studies in Islam and the Middle East (SIME) Journal*, SIME ePublishing (majalla.org), 2004, accessed 5 September 2007, http://www.majalla.org/books/2004/intro-to-quran/1-intoduction-to-the-quran.pdf.

Dhahabi, Muhammad Husayn al-, *al-Tafsir wa al-Mufassirun*, 3 vols, Cairo: Maktabat Wahba, 1995.

Doorn-Harder, Nelly van, 'Teaching and Preaching the Qur'an', in Jane D. McAuliffe (ed.), *Encyclopaedia of the Qur'an*, Leiden: E.J. Brill, 2006, Vol.5, pp. 205–231.

Draz, M.A., *Introduction to the Qur'an*, London: I.B. Tauris, 2000.

Dutton, Yasin, *The Origins of Islamic Law: The Qur'an, The Muwatta' and Madinan Amal*, Richmond, Surrey: Curzon, 1999.

Eliade, Mircea (ed.), *The Encyclopedia of Religion*, New York: MacMillan Publishing Company, 1987.

Engineer, Asghar Ali, *The Rights of Women in Islam*, London: C. Hurst & Co, 1992.

Esack, Farid, *Qur'an, Liberation and Pluralism*, Oxford: Oneworld Publications, 1997.

Esack, Farid, *The Qur'an: A Short Introduction*, Oxford: Oneworld Publications, 2001.

Esposito, John, *The Oxford Encyclopaedia of the Modern Islamic World*, 4 vols., New York: Oxford University Press, 1995.

Esposito, John, *Islam: The Straight Path*, New York and Oxford: Oxford University Press, 1998.

Fakhry, Majid, *An Interpretation of the Qur'an*, New York: New York University Press, 2002.

Falanga, Rosemarie E. and Silver, Cy H., 'Tzitzit and Early Reform Judaism', *Bluethread*, 29 November 1997, accessed 9 February 2007, http://www.bluethread.com/fringeref1.htm.

Francesca, Ersilia, 'Kharijis', in Jane D. McAuliffe (ed.), *Encyclopaedia of the Qur'an*, Leiden: E.J. Brill, 2003, Vol.3, pp. 84–90.

Gätje, Helmut, *The Qur'an and its Exegesis: Selected Texts with Classical and Modern Muslim Interpretations*, trans. Alford T. Welch, Oxford: Oneworld Publications, 1996.

Ghazali, Abu Hamid al-, *Ihya Ulum-id-Din*, trans. Fazul-ul-Karim, Lahore: Islamic Publications Bureau, n.d.

Ghazali, Muhammad al-, *A Thematic Commentary of the Qur'an, vol.1: Surahs 1–9*, trans. Ashur A. Shamis, Herndon, VA: International Institute of Islamic Thought, 1997.

Gibb, H.A.R. and Kramers, J.H. (eds), *Shorter Encyclopedia of Islam*, Leiden: E.J. Brill, 1961.

Gilliot, Claude, 'Exegesis of the Qur'an: Classical and Medieval', in Jane D. McAuliffe (ed.), *Encyclopaedia of the Qur'an*, Leiden: E.J. Brill, 2002, Vol.2, pp. 99–124.

Gilliot, Claude. 'Exegesis of the Qur'an: Early Modern and Contemporary', in Jane D. McAuliffe (ed.), *Encyclopaedia of the Qur'an*, Leiden: E.J. Brill, 2002, Vol.2, pp. 124–142.

Gilliot, Claude, 'Narratives', in Jane D. McAuliffe (ed.), *Encyclopaedia of the Qur'an*, Leiden: E.J. Brill, 2003, Vol.3, pp. 516–528.

Graham, William A., *Beyond the Written Word*, Cambridge: Cambridge University Press, 1993.

Günther, Ursula, 'Mohammed Arkoun: Towards a Radical Rethinking of Islamic Thought', in Suha Taji-Farouki (ed.), *Modern Muslim Intellectuals and the Qur'an*, Oxford: Oxford University Press, 2004, pp. 125–167.

Haddad, Yvonne Yazbeck and Stowasser, Barbara Freyer (eds), *Islamic Law and the Challenges of Modernity*, Lanham, MD: Rowman & Littlefield Publishers, 2004.

Hallaq, Wael B., *A History of Islamic Legal Theories: An Introduction to Sunni usul al-fiqh*, Cambridge: Cambridge University Press, 1997.

Hallaq, Wael B., *Authority, Continuity and Change in Islamic Law*, Cambridge: Cambridge University Press, 2001.

Hallaq, Wael B., 'Law and the Qur'an', in Jane D. McAuliffe (ed.), *Encyclopaedia of the Qur'an*, Leiden: E.J. Brill, 2003, Vol.3, pp. 149–172.

Hallaq, Wael B., *The Formation of Islamic Law*, Aldershot: Ashgate, 2004.

Hallaq, Wael B., *The Origins and Evolution of Islamic Law*, Cambridge: Cambridge University Press, 2005.

Hammerbeck, Dave, 'Voltaire's *Mahomet*, The Persistence of Cultural Memory and Pre-Modern Orientalism', *Agora: An Online Graduate Journal*, Vol.2, No.2, Spring 2003, accessed 27 May 2007, http://www.humanities.ualberta.ca/agora/Articles.cfm?ArticleNo=154.

Hasan, Ahmad, *Early Development of Islamic Jurisprudence*, Islamabad: Islamic Research Institute, 1970.

Hasani, Isma'il al-, *Nazariyyat al-Maqasid ind al-Imam Muhammad al-Tahir bin Ashur*, Virginia: International Institute of Islamic Thought, 1995.

Hawting, G.R. and Shareef, Abdul-Kader A. (eds), *Approaches to the Qur'an*, London: Routledge, 1993.

Hayes, Kevin J., 'How Thomas Jefferson Read the Qur'an', *iViews*, 27 January

2007, accessed 4 September 2007, http://www.iviews.com/Articles/articles. asp?ref=IV0701-3221.

Hilali, Taqiuddin al-, and Khan, Muhammad Muhsin, *The Noble Qur'an in the English Language*, Riyadh: Darussalam Publishers, 1994; repr. 1996, 2002.

Hodgson, Marshall G.S., *The Venture of Islam*, Chicago: University of Chicago Press, 1974.

Holloway, Richard, 'Obituary: William Montgomery Watt', The *Guardian*, 14 November 2006.

Humphreys, R. Stephen, *Islamic History: A Framework for Inquiry*, Princeton: Princeton University Press, 1991.

Ibn Abd Allah Kisai, Muhammad, *Tales of the Prophets (Qisas Al-Anbiya)*, trans. Wheeler Thackston, Chicago: Kazi Publications, 1997.

Ibn Kathir, Imad al-Din Abu al-Fida' Isma'il, *Tafsir al-Qur'an al-Azim*, Beirut: Dar al-Jil, n.d.

Ibn al-Muthanna, Abu Ubayda Ma'mar, *Majaz al-Qur'an*, ed. F. Sezgin, 2 vols, Cairo, 1954–1962.

Ibn Rushd, *The Distinguished Jurist's Primer,* trans. Imran Nyazee, Reading, UK: Garnet Publishing, 1994.

Ibn Rushd, *Fasl al-maqal*, Beirut: Markaz Dirasat al-Wihda al-Arabiya, 1999.

Ibn Taymiyya, Taqiyy al-Din, *al-Tafsir al-Kabir*, ed. Abd al-Rahman Umayra, Beirut: Dar al-Kutub al-Ilmiiya, n.d.

Ibn Warraq (ed.), *What the Koran Really Says*, New York: Prometheus Books, 2002.

Iqbal, Muhammad, *The Reconstruction of Religious Thought in Islam*, Lahore: Institute of Islamic Culture, 1986.

Irving, Thomas B. (Ta'lim Ali), *The Quran: The First American Version*, Vermont: Amana Books, 1985; revised, *The Noble Qur'an: The First American Translation and Commentary*, Vermont: Amana Books, 1992.

Izutsu, Toshihiko, *God and Man in the Koran*, Tokyo: The Keio Institute of Cultural and Linguistic Studies, 1964.

Izutsu, Toshihiko, *The Structure of Ethical Terms in the Qur'an*, Chicago: ABC International Group, 2000.

Izutsu, Toshihiko, *Ethico-Religious Concepts in the Qur'an*, Montreal: McGill-Queen's University Press, 2002.

Jeffery, A. and Mendelsohn, I., 'The Orthography of the Samarqand Codex', *Journal of the American Oriental Society*, Vol.63, New Haven: American Oriental Society, 1943, pp. 175–195.

Johns, A.H., 'Review: An Interpretation of the Qur'an', *Middle East Studies Association Bulletin*, Vol.38, No.1, June 2004, pp. 83–84.

Johns, Anthony H. and Saeed, Abdullah, 'Nurcholish Madjid and the Interpretation of the Qur'an: Religious Pluralism and Tolerance', in Suha Taji-Farouki (ed.), *Modern Muslim Intellectuals and the Qur'an*, Oxford: Oxford University Press, 2004, pp. 67–96.

Jones, Lindsey, *Encyclopedia of Religion*, Farmington: Thomson Gale, 2005.

Jung-Mounib, Monika, 'Khaled Abou El Fadl: God Does Not Have an Equal

Partner', trans. Aingeal Flanagan, *Qantara.de – Dialogue with the Islamic World*, 11 January 2005, accessed 25 February 2007, http://www.qantara.de/webcom/show_article.php/_c-575/_nr-7/i.html?PHPSESSID=5869.

Kamali, Mohammad Hashim, *Principles of Islamic Jurisprudence*, Selangor: Pelanduk Publications, 1995.

Khan, Abdullah Zafrullah, *The Quran: Arabic Text and English Translation*, London: Curzon Press, 1971; revised, New York: Interlink Publishing Group, 1997.

Khan, Liaquat Ali, 'Hagarism – The Story of a Book Written by Infidels for Infidels', *The Daily Star*, 28 April 2006, accessed 25 May 2007, http://www.thedailystar.net/2006/04/28/d60428020635.htm.

Khatib, Mohammad M., *The Bounteous Koran: A Translation of Meaning and Commentary*, London: MacMillan Press, 1986.

Kidwai, A.R., 'Translating the Untranslatable: A Survey of English Translations of the Qur'an', *The Muslim World Book Review*, Vol.7, No.4, Summer 1987.

Kidwai, A.R., 'English Translations of the Holy Qur'an – An Annotated Bibliography', *Anti-Ahmadiyya Movement in Islam*, October 2000, accessed 12 February 2007, http://alhafeez.org/rashid/qtranslate.html.

Kister, M.J., '*Haddithu an bani isra'ila wa-la haraja*. A Study of an early tradition', *Israel Oriental Studies*, Vol.2, 1972, pp. 215–239.

Kjeilen, Tore (ed.), 'Isma'ilism', *Encyclopaedia of the Orient*, LexicOrient 2007, accessed 11 May 2007, http://lexicorient.com/e.o/ismailis.htm.

Kurzman, Charles (ed.), *Liberal Islam: A Source Book*, New York: Oxford University Press, 1998.

Lane, Edward William, *Arabic-English Lexicon*, New York: Frederick Ungar Publishing, 1955–1956.

Lawson, Todd, 'Review: The Origins of the Koran: Classic Essays on Islam's Holy Book', *Journal of the American Oriental Society*, Vol.122, No.3, Jul–Sept 2002, p. 658.

Lester, Toby, 'What is the Koran?', *The Atlantic Monthly*, Vol.283, No.1, January 1999.

Lings, Martin, *Muhammad: His Life Based on the Earliest Sources*, London: George Allen & Unwin, 1983, 5th edition, Rochester, Vermont: Inner Traditions International, 2006.

Maan, Bashir and McIntosh, Alastair, 'Interview: William Montgomery Watt', *The Corale*, Vol.3, No.51, 2000, pp. 8–11 cited at *Alastair McIntosh*, accessed 13 May 2007, http://www.alastairmcintosh.com/articles/2000_watt.htm.

Madigan, Daniel A., 'Book', in Jane D. McAuliffe (ed.), *Encyclopaedia of the Qur'an*, Leiden: E.J. Brill, 2001, Vol.1, pp. 242–251.

Madigan, Daniel A., *The Qur'an's Self-Image: Writing and Authority in Islam's Scripture*, Princeton, NJ: Princeton University Press, 2001.

Madigan, Daniel A., 'Revelation and Inspiration', in Jane D. McAuliffe (ed.), *Encyclopaedia of the Qur'an*, Leiden: E.J. Brill, 2004, Vol.4, pp. 437–448.

Mahmassani, S., *Falsafat al-Tashri' Fi al-Islam: The Philosophy of Jurisprudence in Islam*, trans. Farhat J. Ziadeh, Leiden: E.J. Brill, 1961.

Martin, Richard C., 'Createdness of the Qur'an', in Jane D. McAuliffe (ed.), *Encyclopaedia of the Qur'an*, Leiden: E.J. Brill, 2001, Vol.1, pp. 467–472.

Mawdudi, Abul A'la, *The Meaning of the Qur'an*, trans. Zafar Ishaq Ansari, Lahore, 1967; revised, *Towards Understanding the Qur'an*, Leicester: The Islamic Foundation, 2006.

Mawdudi, Abul A'la, *Towards Understanding the Qur'an*, trans. Zafar Ishaq Ansari, Leicester: Islamic Foundation, 1995.

McAuliffe, Jane D., *Qur'anic Christians: An Analysis of Classical and Modern Exegesis*, New York: Cambridge University Press, 1991.

McAuliffe, Jane D. (ed.), *Encyclopaedia of the Qur'an*, Leiden: E.J. Brill, 5 vols, 2001–2006.

Mernissi, Fatima, *The Veil and the Male Elite: A Feminist Interpretation of Women's Rights in Islam*, trans. Mary Jo Lakeland, Cambridge, MA: Perseus, 1991.

Mernissi, Fatima, *Women and Islam: An Historical and Theological Enquiry*, trans. Mary Jo Lakeland, Oxford: Basil Blackwell, 1991.

Mir, Mustansir, 'Scientific Exegesis of the Qur'an – A Viable Project?', *Islam & Science*, Vol.2, No.1, Summer 2004, p. 33.

Mohammed, Khaleel, 'Assessing English Translations of the Qur'an', *Middle East Quarterly*, Vol.12, No.2, Spring 2005, pp. 59–71.

Mojaddedi, Jawid A., 'Taking Islam Seriously: The Legacy of John Wansbrough', *Journal of Semitic Studies*, Vol.45, No.1, Spring 2000, pp. 103–114.

Motzki, Harald, 'Mushaf', in Jane D. McAuliffe (ed.), *Encyclopaedia of the Qur'an*, Leiden: E.J. Brill, 2003, Vol.3, pp. 463–466.

Muslimi Ibn Hajjaj, *Sahih Muslim*, 9 vols, Beirut: Dar al-Kutub al-Ilmiyah, 1994.

Nasr, Seyyed Hossein, 'Islamic-Christian Dialogue – Problems and Obstacles to be Pondered and Overcome', *The Muslim World*, Vol.88, Nos.3–4, July–October, 1998, pp. 218–237.

Nasr, Seyyed Hossein, *The Heart of Islam: Enduring Values for Humanity*, New York: HarperCollins, 2004.

Nelson, Kristina L., *The Art of Reciting the Qur'an*, Austin: University of Texas Press, 1985.

Neuwirth, Angelika. 'Qur'an and History – A Disputed Relationship. Some Reflections on Qur'anic History and History in the Qur'an', *Journal of Qur'anic Studies*, Vol.5, No.1, 2003, pp. 1–18.

Nöldeke, Theodor, 'The Koran', in *Sketches from Eastern History*, trans. John Sutherland Black, Beirut: Khayats, 1963, pp. 21–59.

Novriantoni and El-Dardiry, Ramy, 'Interview with Asma Barlas: It is the Right for Every Muslim to Interpret the Quran for Themselves', *Liberal Islam Network*, 2005, cited at *Qantara.de – Dialogue with the Islamic World*, accessed 13 May 2007, http://www.qantara.de/webcom/show_article.php/_c-307/_nr-28/_p-1/i.html?PHPSESSID=.

Nwyia, Paul, *Exégèse coranique et langage mystique*, Beirut: Dar al-Machreq Editeurs, 1970.

Peters, Francis E., *Judaism, Christianity, and Islam: The Classical Texts and Their Interpretation*, Vols I–III, Princeton: Princeton University Press, 1990.

Peters, Francis E. (ed.), *A Reader on Classical Islam*, Princeton: Princeton University Press, 1994.

Peters, J.R.T.M., *God's Created Speech: A Study in the Speculative Theology of the Mu'tazili Qadi l-qudat Abul-Hasan Abd al-Jabbar ibn Ahmad al-Hamadani*, Leiden: E.J. Brill, 1976.

Pickthall, Marmaduke, *The Meaning of the Glorious Koran*, London: George Allen & Unwin, 1930.

Poonawala, Ismail K., 'Muhammad Darwaza's Principles of Modern Exegesis', in G.R. Hawting and Abdul-Kader A. Shareef (eds), *Approaches to the Qur'an*, London: Routledge, 1993, pp. 225–246.

Powers, David, *Studies in Qur'an and Hadith: The Formation of Islamic Law of Inheritance*, Berkeley: University of California Press, 1986.

Procter, Paul (ed.), *Longman Dictionary of Contemporary English*, Harlow: Longman, 1978.

Qadhi, Abu Ammaar Yasir, *An Introduction to the Sciences of the Qur'aan*, Birmingham: al-Hidayah Publishing and Distribution, 1999.

Qara'i, Ali Qull, 'Review: The Qur'an and Its Translators', *Al-Tawhid*, Vol.12, No.2, October–December 1994, accessed 6 February 2007, http://www.quran.org.uk/articles/ieb_quran_translators.htm#ETDL.

Qurtubi, Abu Abd Allah Muhammad ibn Ahmad al-Ansari al-, *Al-Jami' li Ahkam al-Qur'an*, Beirut: Dar al-Kutub al-Ilmiiya, 1993.

Qurtubi, Abu Abd Allah Muhammad ibn Ahmad al-Ansari al-, 'Etiquettes of Reading and Handling the Qur'an al-Kareem', trans. cited at *The As-Sunnah Foundation of America*, 27 August 2007, accessed 30 August 2007, www.sunnah.org/sources/ulumquran/conditions_of_handling_quran.htm.

Qutb, Sayyid, *Fi Zilal al-Qur'an*, Beirut: Dar al-Shuruq, 1996.

Qutb, Sayyid, *In the Shade of the Qur'an*, trans. Adil Salahi and Ashur Shamis, Leicester: The Islamic Foundation, 2000.

Radscheit, Matthias, 'Word of God', in Jane D. McAuliffe (ed.), *Encyclopaedia of the Qur'an*, Leiden: E.J. Brill, 2006, Vol.5, pp. 541–548.

Rahman, Fazlur, 'The Impact of Modernity on Islam', *Journal of Islamic Studies*, Vol.5, No.2, June 1966, pp. 112–128.

Rahman, Fazlur, 'Some Reflections on the Reconstruction of Muslim Society in Pakistan', *Islamic Studies*, Vol.6, No.9, 1967, pp. 103–120.

Rahman, Fazlur, *Islam*, Chicago: University of Chicago Press, 1979; second edition 2002.

Rahman, Fazlur, 'Towards Reformulating the Methodology of Islamic Law: Sheikh Yamani on Public Interest in Islamic Law', *New York University Journal of International Law and Politics*, Vol.12, 1979–1980, pp. 219–224.

Rahman, Fazlur, *Islam and Modernity: Transformation of an Intellectual Tradition*, Chicago: University of Chicago Press, 1994.

Rahman, Fazlur, *Major Themes of the Qur'an*, Minneapolis, MN: Bibliotheca Islamica, 1989.

Rahman, Fazlur, *Revival and Reform in Islam*, ed. Ebrahim Moosa, Oxford: Oneworld Publications, 2000.

Ramadan, Tariq, *In the Footsteps of the Prophet: Lessons from the Life of Muhammad*, New York: Oxford University Press, 2007.

Razi, Fakhr al-Din al-, *al-Tafsir al-Kabir*, third edition, Beirut: Dar Ihya' al-Turath al-Arabi, n.d.

Rida, Muhammad Rashid and Abduh, Muhammad, *Tafsir al-Qur'an al-Hakim al-Shahir bi-Tafsir al-Manar*, 12 Vols, Beirut: Dar al-Ma'rifa, n.d.

Rippin, Andrew (ed.), *Approaches to the History of the Interpretation of the Qur'an*, Oxford: Clarendon Press; New York: Oxford University Press, 1988.

Rippin, Andrew, 'Review: Reading the Qur'an with Richard Bell', *Journal of the American Oriental Society*, Vol.112, No.4, Oct–Dec 1992, pp. 639–647.

Rippin, Andrew (ed.), *The Qur'an: Formative Interpretation*, Aldershot: Ashgate/Variorum Publishing, 1999.

Rippin, Andrew (ed.), *The Qur'an and its Interpretative Tradition*, Aldershot: Variorum Publishing, 2001.

Rippin, Andrew, 'Occasions of Revelation', in Jane D. McAuliffe (ed.), *Encyclopaedia of the Qur'an*, Leiden: E.J. Brill, 2003, Vol.3, pp. 569–572.

Rippin, Andrew, *Muslims: Their Religious Beliefs and Practices*, London: Routledge, 2005.

Roded, Ruth, 'Women and the Qur'an', in Jane D. McAuliffe (ed.), *Encyclopaedia of the Qur'an*, Leiden: E.J. Brill, Vol.5, 2006, pp. 523–541.

Rubin, Uri, *Between Bible and Qur'an: The Children of Israel and the Islamic Self-Image*, Princeton: The Darwin Press, 1999.

Saeed, Abdullah, 'Rethinking "Revelation" as a Precondition for Reinterpreting the Qur'an: A Qur'anic Perspective', *Journal of Qur'anic Studies*, Vol.1, No.1, 1999, pp. 93–114.

Saeed, Abdullah, 'The Charge of Distortion of Jewish and Christian Scriptures', *The Muslim World*, Vol.92, No.3/4, Fall 2002, pp. 419–436.

Saeed, Abdullah, 'Fazlur Rahman: A Framework for Interpreting the Ethico-legal Content of the Qur'an', in Suha Taji-Farouki (ed.), *Modern Muslim Intellectuals and the Qur'an*, Oxford: Oxford University Press, 2004, pp. 37–66.

Saeed, Abdullah, 'Qur'an: Tradition of Scholarship and Interpretation', in Lindsey Jones (ed.), *Encyclopedia of Religion*, Farmington: Thomas Gale, 2005, Vol.11, pp. 7,561–7,570.

Saeed, Abdullah, *Interpreting the Qur'an: Towards a Contemporary Approach*, London and New York: Routledge, 2006.

Saeed, Abdullah, *Islamic Thought: An Introduction*, London and New York: Routledge, 2006.

Saeed, Abdullah and Saeed, Hassan, *Freedom of Religion, Apostasy and Islam*, Hampshire: Ashgate Publishing, 2004.

Said, Edward W., *Orientalism*, New York: Pantheon Books, 1978.

Said, Edward W., *Culture and Imperialism*, New York: Knopf, 1993.

Said, Edward W., *Reflections on Exile and Other Literary and Cultural Essays*, London: Granta, 2000, p. 199.

Sardar, Ziauddin, 'Lost in Translation: Most English-Language Editions of the Qur'an have Contained Numerous Errors, Omissions and Distortions', *Newstatesman*, 9 August 2004, accessed 13 September 2007, http://www.newstatesman.com/200408090035.

Schacht, Joseph, *The Origins of Muhammadan Jurisprudence*, Oxford: Clarendon Press, 1950.

Schick, Robert, 'Archaeology and the Qur'an', in Jane D. McAuliffe (ed.), *Encyclopaedia of the Qur'an*, Leiden: E.J. Brill, 2001, Vol.1, pp. 148–156.

Schmidtke, Sabine, 'Mu'tazila', in Jane D. McAuliffe (ed.), *Encyclopaedia of the Qur'an*, Leiden: E.J. Brill, 2003, Vol.3, pp. 466–471.

Sells, Michael A. (ed.), *Early Islamic Mysticism*, New Jersey: Paulist Press, 1996.

Sells, Michael A., *Approaching the Qur'an: The Early Revelations*, Ashland, OR: White Cloud Press, 1999.

Shakir, Mahomodali H., *Holy Qur'an*, New York: Tahrike Tarsile Qur'an, 1982; revised, *The Koran*, New Delhi: Goodword Books, 2000.

Shawkani, Muhammad ibn Ali al-, *Fath al-Qadir al-Jami' Bayna Fannay al-Riwaya wa al-Diraya fi Ilm al-Tafsir*, 5 vols, Cairo, 1930; repr, Beirut: Dar al-Ma'rifa, 1973.

Sherif, Faruq, *A Guide to the Contents of the Qur'an*, London, UK: Ithaca Press, 1985; revised, Reading, UK: Garnet Publishing, 1995.

Sivers, Peter von, 'The Islamic Origins Debate Goes Public', *History Compass*, Vol.1, November 2003, pp. 1–16.

Stearns, Peter N. (ed.), *The Encyclopedia of World History*, sixth edition, Boston: Houghton-Mifflin, 2001, cited in Ted Thornton, 'Umayyad Spain (*al-Andalus*)', *History of the Middle East Database*, August 2006, accessed 30 April 2007, http://www.nmhschool.org/tthornton/mehistorydatabase/umayyad_spain.php.

Stille, Alexander, 'Radical New Views of Islam and the Origins of the Koran', *New York Times*, 2 March 2002, accessed May 2007, http://www.rim.org/muslim/qurancrit.htm.

Stowasser, Barbara Freyer, *Women in the Qur'an, Traditions, and Interpretation*, New York: Oxford University Press, 1994.

Tabari, Abu Ja'far Muhammad b. Jarir al-, *Jami' al-Bayan an Ta'wil ay al-Qur'an*, Beirut: Dar al-Fikr, 1988.

Tabataba'i, Muhammad Husayn, *The Qur'an in Islam*, London: Zahra Publications, 1987.

Taji-Farouki, Suha (ed.), *Modern Muslim Intellectuals and the Qur'an*, Oxford: Oxford University Press, 2004.

Theil, Stefan, 'Challenging the Quran: Scholar's New Book, A Commentary on the Qur'an's Early Genesis', Newsweek, 28 July 2003, cited in Nerina Rustomji, 'American Visions of the *Houri*', *The Muslim World*, Vol.97, No.1, January 2007, pp. 79–92.

Todorov, Tzvetan, *Symbolism and Interpretation*, Ithaca: Cornell University Press, 1982.

Toomer, G.J., *Eastern Wisedome and Learning: The Study of Arabic in Seventeenth-century England*, New York: Oxford University Press, 1996.

Troll, Christian, *Sayyid Ahmad Khan: A Reinterpretation of Muslim Theology*, New Delhi: Vikas Publishing House, 1978.

Versteegh, C.H.M., *Arabic Grammar and Qur'anic Exegesis in Early Islam*, Leiden: E.J. Brill, 1993.

Waardenburg, Jacques (ed.), *Muslim Perceptions of Other Religions*, New York and Oxford: Oxford University Press, 1999.

Waardenburg, J.D.J., 'Mustashrikun', in P. Bearman et al. (eds,) *Encyclopaedia of Islam*, Brill Online, 2007, accessed 27 August 2007, http://www.encislam. brill.nl.ezproxy.lib.unimelb.edu.au/subscriber/entry?entry=islam_COM-0818.

Wadud-Muhsin, Amina, 'Qur'an and Woman', in Charles Kurzman (ed.), *Liberal Islam*, New York: Oxford University Press, 1998, pp. 127–138.

Wadud-Muhsin, Amina, *Qur'an and Women: Rereading the Sacred Text from a Woman's Perspective*, New York: Oxford University Press, 1999.

Walzer, R., 'Al Farabi, Abu Nasr Muhammad ibn Muhammad ibn Tarkhan ibn Awzalagh', in P. Bearman et al. (eds), *Encyclopaedia of Islam*, Leiden: Brill, 1965, Vol.2, pp. 778–781.

Wansbrough, John, 'Review: Hagarism: The Making of the Islamic World', *Bulletin of the School of Oriental and African Studies, University of London*, Vol.41, No.1, 1978, pp. 155–156

Wansbrough, John, *Quranic Studies: Sources and Methods of Scriptural Interpretation*, Oxford: Oxford University Press, 1977; repr. Amherst, NY: Prometheus Books, 2004.

Watt, W. Montgomery, *Muhammad at Mecca*, Oxford: Oxford University Press, 1953.

Watt, W. Montgomery, *Muhammad at Medina*, Karachi: Oxford University Press, 1981.

Watt, W. Montgomery and Bell, Richard, *Introduction to the Qur'an*, Edinburgh: Edinburgh University Press, 1970; repr. 1995, 2001.

Wensinck, A.J., *The Muslim Creed*, Cambridge: Cambridge University Press, 1932.

Whelan, Estelle, 'Forgotten Witness: Evidence for the Early Codification of the Qur'an', *Journal of the American Oriental Society*, Vol.118, No.1, January–March 1998, pp. 1–14.

Wigoder, Geoffrey (ed.), 'Revelation', *Encyclopedia of Judaism*, New York: MacMillan Publishing Company, 1989, pp. 599–601.

Wild, Stefan (ed.), *The Qur'an as Text*, Leiden: E.J. Brill, 1996.

Yuksel, Edip, *www.19.org*, cited in Thomas, Dave, 'Code 19 in the Quran?', *New Mexicans for Science and Reason*, 15 June 2004, accessed 18 February 2007, http://www.nmsr.org/code19.htm.

Yuksel, Edip, 'Beating Women, or Beating Around the Bush, or . . .', *The Islamic Reformer*, 3 June 2005, accessed 2 February 2007, http://www.yuksel.org/e/religion/unorthodox.htm.

Zamakhshari, *al-Kashshaf*, in Gätje, Helmut, *The Qur'an and its Exegesis*, trans. and ed. Alford T. Welch, Oxford: Oneworld Publications, 1997.

Zemach, Eddy M., *The Reality of Meaning and the Meaning of Reality*, Hanover, NH: University Press of New England for Brown University Press, 1992.

Index

Related titles from Routledge

Interpreting the Qur'an
Towards a contemporary approach

Abdullah Saeed

'Debates among Muslims over the conception of the authority of the Qur'an underlie much of what is read about Islam in the popular media these days. This book by Abdullah Saeed will add a new voice to those debates and, as its impact is felt, broaden the popular conception of what Islam is all about today.' – *Andrew Rippin, University of Victoria, Canada*

How is the Qur'an – central to all Muslims societies – to be understood today in order to meet the needs of these societies? Abdullah Saeed, a distinguished Muslim scholar, explores the interpretation of the ethico-legal content of the Qur'an, whilst taking into consideration the changing nature of the modern world.

Saeed explores the current debates surrounding the interpretation of the Qur'an, and their impact on contemporary understanding of this sacred text. Discussing the text's relevance to modern issues without compromising the overall framework of the Qur'an and its core beliefs and practices, he proposes a fresh approach, which takes into account the historical and contemporary contexts of interpretation.

Inspiring healthy debate, this book is essential reading for students and scholars seeking a contemporary approach to the interpretation of the Qur'anic text.

ISBN10: 0–415–36537–6 (hbk)
ISBN10: 0–415–36538–4 (pbk)

ISBN13: 978–0–145–36537–6 (hbk)
ISBN13: 978–0–145–36538–3 (pbk)

Available at all good bookshops
For ordering and further information please visit:
www.routledge.com

Related titles from Routledge

The Qu'ran: The Basics

Massimo Campanini
and
Oliver Leaman

This highly topical new introduction to the holy book of Islam includes essential reference resources such as a chronology of the revelation, weblinks and extensive guides to further reading.

Exploring the Qur'an's reception through history, its key teachings and its place in contemporary thought and belief, the book analyzes:

- the Qur'an as the word of God
- its reception and communication by the Prophet Muhammad
- the structure and language of the text
- conceptions of God, the holy law and jihad
- Islamic commentaries on Qur'anic teachings through the ages.

The Qur'an: The Basics is a concise and easy-to-read introduction to the text that provides the foundations of Muslim faith, right-living and daily worship.

ISBN13: 978–0–415–41162–2 (hbk)
ISBN13: 978–0–415–41163–9 (pbk)

Available at all good bookshops
For ordering and further information please visit:
www.routledge.com